PLANNING AND POLLUTION

PLANNING
AND
POLLUTION

An examination of the
role of land use planning
in the protection of
environmental quality

CHRISTOPHER MILLER
AND
CHRISTOPHER WOOD

CLARENDON PRESS · OXFORD
1983

Oxford University Press, Walton Street, Oxford OX2 6DP

London Glasgow New York Toronto
Delhi Bombay Calcutta Madras Karachi
Kuala Lumpur Singapore Hong Kong Tokyo
Nairobi Dar es Salaam Cape Town
Melbourne Auckland
and associates in
Beirut Berlin Ibadan Mexico City Nicosia

Oxford is a trade mark of Oxford University Press

Published in the United States by
Oxford University Press, New York

British Library Cataloguing in Publication Data

Miller, Christopher
Planning and pollution.
1. Pollution
I. Title   II. Wood, Christopher, 1944-
628.5   TD174
ISBN 0-19-823245-4

Library of Congress Cataloging in Publication Data
Miller, Christopher, 1948-
Planning and pollution.
Bibliography: p.
Includes index.
1. Land use—Great Britain—Planning.   2. Environ-
mental protection—Great Britain—Planning.   3. Land
use—Law and legislation—Great Britain.   4. Environ-
mental law—Great Britain. I. Wood, C. M. (Christopher
Maxwell) II. Title.
HD596.M54 1983   363.7'3'0941   82-22502
ISBN 0-19-823245-4 (U.S.)

Set by DMB (Typesetting), Oxford
and printed and bound
in Great Britain by
Biddles Ltd, Guildford and King's Lynn

PREFACE

This book examines the role of land use planning in the control of environmental pollution. It is concerned primarily with the practices of local planning authorities in using their legal powers to minimize the discharge of pollutants and to limit their effects upon the environment. The nature of these legal powers (the utilization of which varies substantially according to the type of pollution involved: air, water, land, and noise) is explained. In addition, the book explores the relationships which have developed between the planning authorities and other bodies which have statutory powers to control pollution.

The book is a distillation of a four-volume report of a research programme, financed by the Social Science Research Council and carried out between 1977 and 1980, on land use planning and the control of pollution, at the Pollution Research Unit of the University of Manchester. As well as presenting a number of detailed investigations of instances of planning intervention to control pollution, the book draws upon a large number of interviews with practitioners in planning and pollution control authorities and upon studies of the legal framework of town and country planning and of the structures of planning authorities and other agencies of pollution control at the central, regional, and local levels of government. The preliminary results of the research were tested at three seminars at which practitioners in the field were invited to comment and present their own views.

In devising and implementing the study, it was never the intention to produce another account of nationally known major planning issues—whether celebrated planning decisions or environmental disasters. The aim was more modest: to examine the extent to which local planning authorities can reasonably use their powers to minimize pollution associated with developments which, although not trivial, are of local rather than national significance and can be treated within the conventional procedures of planning control. For all but a handful of environmental pollutants, ambient concentrations and the damage they cause can be attributed primarily, not to occasional accidental releases of the scale of the Seveso incident, but to routine discharges which are either accepted by the regulatory bodies or escape effective control.

Although this eschewal of the 'major issues' was deliberate, it is significant that the majority of the case studies presented relate to instances in which planning authorities have either failed or been unable to intervene decisively in the regulation or eradication of a source of pollution, with the result that local inhabitants were subjected to considerable and, sometimes, avoidable pollution and a perceptible decline in the quality of their environment. Moreover, these case studies contain few instances in which there is no dispute between planning and pollution control authorities over the level of environ-, mental safeguards which should be imposed.

The use of the case study approach perhaps requires explanation. The complexity of the factors involved in determining the outcome of a local planning authority's decision on whether or not to allow a development likely to give rise to pollution problems was apparent at the outset. It was therefore decided that the only satisfactory method of analysis would be to investigate a number of such instances in great detail, and then to validate the conclusions by questionnaire surveys, by interviews with other practitioners, and by discussions at specially convened seminars. The case studies were selected, as far as possible, to represent interesting examples of the planning control of air pollution, water pollution, land pollution, and noise pollution in different local authorities. In fact, the case studies were seldom confined to a single pollution medium.

The preponderance of examples of the *failure* of planning intervention in pollution control is not entirely unintentional. It is necessary to recognize what is perhaps an inherent bias in studies of this kind: where, for instance, a planner strives to ensure that a proposed kindergarten is not sited in the shadow of a lead smelter, his intervention will be forgotten with the passing of time; but should he fail to separate such manifestly incompatible uses, his 'error' will be as visible and as durable as bricks and mortar. The invisibility of the successful and calculated application of planning control must not be allowed to bestow undue significance upon the failures. Nevertheless, it is from a disinterested analysis of the less successful instances that existing shortcomings and recommendations to improve procedures to identify and to mitigate potential threats to the environment will emerge.

Chapter 1 provides a general review of the role of land use planning in the control of environmental pollution. Chapter 2 relates specifically to the control of air pollution by local planning authorities and Chapters 3 and 4 present case studies principally concerned with planning and air pollution control. Chapter 5 discusses the roles of the local planning authority and the regional water authority in controlling water pollution and Chapter 6 describes an instance where water pollution control was an important factor in a planning decision. Chapters 7 and 8 deal with land pollution and Chapters 9 and 10 with noise pollution, though the case histories presented are by no means confined solely to these types of pollution.

The final chapter summarizes the failures of the statutory powers and the practices of both the planning authorities and the pollution control agencies, as exemplified in the case studies, not only to minimize pollution but also to ensure a just distribution of the disbenefits

which it entailed. Comparison is made with the legislation which
governs the control of radioactive wastes, and suggestions are offered
on possible changes in legislation and official attitudes which might
assist in removing shortcomings in the anticipatory regulation of
pollution.

The separate legal systems in Scotland and Northern Ireland mean
that detailed discussion is confined to planning and pollution in
England and Wales. However, it is believed that the more general conclusions are of much wider relevance, and will be of interest wherever
land use controls are employed to attempt to control pollution problems.

The authors are grateful to the Controller of Her Majesty's Station-
ery Office for permission to reproduce extracts from a number of their
publications and from inspectors' reports of, and ministers' decision
letters regarding, local inquiries. The maps are also reproduced with
the consent of the Controller of HMSO. We acknowledge the kindness
of Cheshire County Council, Greater Manchester County Council,
and Merseyside in granting permission to quote from their structure
plans.

During the research programme and in the writing of this book,
invaluable assistance—by way of advice, discussions, and permission
to quote from unpublished documents—was received from a large
number of industrial concerns and from central and local government
departments. Whilst not undervaluing the help of others, the generous
co-operation of the following is especially acknowledged: the Department of the Environment, HM Alkali and Clean Air Inspectorate, the
North West Water Authority, Cheshire County Council, Ellesmere
Port and Neston Borough Council, St Helens Metropolitan Borough
Council, Kirklees Metropolitan Borough Council, Warrington
Borough Council, Bolton Metropolitan Borough Council, and
Chloride Ltd.

An immeasurable debt of gratitude is owed to colleagues at the
University of Manchester: to James McLoughlin (Reader in Law) who
(with Christopher Wood) was co-supervisor of the original research
programme and who has continued to be an unfailing source of advice
on the legal aspects of planning and pollution; to Norman Lee (Senior
Lecturer in Economics) whose informed and constructive criticisms of
the final draft have been of inestimable value; to Jackie Jolley and
Margaret Barrow for their patience and skill in the typing of numerous
drafts; and to Geoff Wheeler for his excellent photographs. Notwithstanding the depth of their indebtedness to others, responsibility for
errors of fact or of interpretation remains with the authors alone.

CHRISTOPHER MILLER
Manchester 1982   CHRISTOPHER WOOD

PLATE 1. Ince Marshes. View from Helsby Hill. The village of Elton lies between Stanlow oil refinery (stacks visible in the distance) and Ince power station. The UKF fertilizer works can be seen to the right of the photograph, with the Mersey estuary beyond.

CONTENTS

PLATES

FIGURES

TABLES

1
INTRODUCTION

Pollution has been described elsewhere as 'the introduction by man of waste matter or surplus energy into the environment directly or indirectly causing damage to persons other than himself, his household, those in his employment or those with whom he has a direct trading relationship.'[1] By including 'surplus energy' as well as 'waste matter' this definition embraces noise, vibration, radioactivity, and microwave radiation. The exclusion of damage to those with whom a contractual relationship exists distinguishes pollution from the concerns of occupational hygiene and consumer protection.

'Damage' occasioned by pollution can take many forms: noise from aircraft may reduce property values; emissions of smoke and sulphur dioxide from coal-fired power stations may impair public health; effluent from sewage treatment plants may adversely affect a river's fish population and diminish its potential as a recreational resource. The geographical range of the damage may be global, as with the pollution of the atmosphere or the oceans; or, as with noise, it may be no more than local in effect. The detrimental effects of a pollutant may, as with noise or a malodorous discharge, be immediately apparent to the senses or, as is the case with low-level radiation, they may go undetected for years.

Pollution may arise at any stage in the economic system: in the extraction of raw materials; in the generation of energy; in the production, distribution, or consumption of goods. Pollution may be regulated either directly, by limiting the amounts of harmful wastes arising, or indirectly, by minimizing the exposure of third parties to the hazards posed by the presence of those wastes in the environment. Reducing the discharges to one waste-receiving medium may entail adding to the burden of another. Often, the interrelationships can be complex, e.g. the disposal of toxic materials by incineration, rather than by landfill, increases discharges to the atmosphere, whilst the 'scrubbing' of gaseous incinerator emissions can ultimately add to the pollution of watercourses.

Historically, an individual's ability to obtain redress when subjected to pollution or nuisance was largely governed by the rights attached to property in his possession. For instance, a riparian owner has a right to receive unpolluted water. Again, action in private nuisance is open to anyone whose enjoyment of land (of which he has a right of occupation) is interfered with by gaseous discharges, noises, water pollution, or solid wastes originating elsewhere. Where pollution damage stems from many sources control cannot readily be achieved by the actions of individuals. From the latter half of the last century, the regulation of activities which pollute 'common property resources' such as the atmosphere, the oceans, and the main rivers has increasingly been seen as the role of public authorities.

There are now few forms of pollution which fall outside the powers of the appropriate regulatory bodies: the Alkali Inspectorate; the regional water authority; the environmental health authority; the waste disposal authority, etc. In addition to these specific controls over certain polluters, land use planning can afford, at any stage in the economic system, a means not only of preventing or minimizing additional waste discharges but also of limiting the amount of harm suffered from new sources of pollution. By preventing the juxtaposition of polluting and pollution-sensitive land uses or by establishing 'buffer zones' around sources of waste discharge, planning affords a means of indirect, but nevertheless effective, control.[2] Further, by permitting a change of land use subject to limits on the amount of waste to be discharged, or the degree of pollution to be sustained, a direct form of pollution control is available.

Such powers of control, which can mainly be utilized when some new development is contemplated and are thus essentially anticipatory rather than retrospective (below), are conferred upon local planning authorities and the Secretary of State by the Town and Country Planning Act 1971. Regulation of development with pollution implications can, in general, be achieved by withholding planning permission[3] or by the imposition of conditions[4] to any consent. Alternatively, pollution control clauses can be incorporated in voluntary planning agreements between the developer and the planning authority.[5] In addition, planning authorities may include within development plans strategic policies on pollution and the environment to serve as a framework for decisions on individual projects.[6]

The primary and unique role of land use planning lies in *preventing* pollution by the spatial separation of incompatible land uses, most notably, residential or similarly sensitive development, and industrial plants from which the discharge of polluting matter or noise is inevitable. Where prevention by separation is impracticable, a planning authority may, as a secondary measure, impose some limits on the volume of waste emitted by the polluting development and it is here that most conflicts with other control bodies arise. It is necessary, however, to recognize that a converse effect can sometimes apply: the use of land can be restricted as a result of the application of pollution control powers. For instance, irrespective of any decision by a planning authority, an area of land cannot be used for the disposal of waste unless a site licence is granted by the waste disposal authority under the Control of Pollution Act, 1974. This quasi-planning effect of pollution controls may be more general; another provision of the 1974 Act empowers the Secretary of State to designate an area wherein activities likely to cause water pollution, may be prohibited or restricted.[7] Similarly, the designation of a noise abatement zone can deny the area concerned to heavy industry or other uses from which high noise emissions are inevitable.[8]

The factors which influence the role of land use planning in the control of pollution are many and varied. However, there are three principal themes which appear to be central to an understanding of the events described in the case studies presented in later chapters. These are:

(a) uncertainty concerning the legitimacy of the use of planning powers to control pollution, especially in so far as it encroaches upon the jurisdiction of the pollution control authorities;
(b) the political character of planning decisions which involve pollution; and
(c) the social distribution of the costs of both pollution control and pollution damage.

The role of the local planning authority

The 1971 Town and Country Planning Act requires that the 'written statement' of a structure plan 'shall' include 'measures for the improvement of the physical environment'.[6] In the case of local plans, such measures may be included at the discretion of the local planning authority. The most recent circular offering advice on the preparation of development plans explains that:

The term 'physical environment' should be interpreted as including not only policies to protect an environment already regarded as being of high quality and policies for improving a poor environment (e.g. derelict land reclamation schemes), but also land use policies designed to minimize non-visual intrusions such as noise, smell and dirt. The authority should show in the reasoned justification:
(a) how environmental considerations had been taken into account in the formulation of their policies; and
(b) the relationship of the policy and general proposals to other measures for reducing water and air pollution and noise.[9]

Whilst an earlier circular[10] had revealed a rather greater enthusiasm by the Department of the Environment for the inclusion of pollution policies in development plans, the above quotation is nevertheless an indication that the control of environmental pollution is accepted by central government as a legitimate objective of land use planning.

In the great majority of cases, structure plans have been prepared by county planning authorities and local plans by the districts. The

Local Government Act, 1972, outlines the division of responsibilities between the two tiers of local government in deciding individual planning issues.[11] While a few counties have included important policies on pollution in their structure plans, it is in the regulation of development that planning control of pollution has been most evident. In this connection, it must be remembered that the term 'development' has a distinct meaning in planning law and can include the change of use of land or buildings as well as 'the carrying out of building, engineering, mining'.[12] However, the power of intervention by local planning authorities is far from universal.

'Permitted development' is the term applied to a wide range of constructions and changes of land use which may be undertaken without the need to secure planning permission.[13] A local planning authority may withdraw the right of permitted development but this procedure usually requires the consent of the Secretary of State and is rarely used as an instrument of pollution control. Permitted development can have implications for pollution levels: for example, the installation, within an existing building, of additional plant or machinery, although adding significantly to the wastes generated, may be undertaken without planning approval. In most cases, the tipping of colliery waste by the National Coal Board constitutes 'permitted development' and no planning controls can be applied even though spoil tips are notorious sources of air and water pollution. The 1971 Act excludes much of the potentially polluting development by statutory undertakers (e.g. the Central Electricity Generating Board) from the jurisdiction of local planning authorities,[14] though 'deemed' permissions under other legislation have to be obtained.

In order to constitute 'development' a change of use of land or of a building must be not only a 'material change' but a change from one use class, as defined in the Use Classes Order, to another.[15] Development does not necessarily occur even when, and despite a greatly increased threat of pollution, the use of a 'general industrial building' (see Chapter 6) changes from an environmentally innocuous process to one involving toxic chemicals.

However, the most important observation to be made on the development control powers of local planning authorities is that they are most effective when applied to proposed, as distinct from existing, development. While the Act does confer powers which could be used to regulate pollution from established land uses, these powers almost invariably entail the payment of compensation to those with an interest in the land or building in question. The case described in Chapter 4 is a very rare example of an attempt (in this instance, unsuccessful) to use a planning power to secure the closure of a large industrial works considered to be the source of unacceptable pollution.

Whilst a few of the larger county planning departments have recruited environmental scientists, it is generally true that most officers of planning authorities lack the formal scientific training which an appraisal of the environmental implications of complex technological developments can demand. Technical advice can be sought from various sources: universities and polytechnics, professional consultants, and the pollution control authorities. Within the last-named must be included the environmental health authorities; in the great majority of cases, liaison between planning and environmental health officers amounts to inter-departmental collaboration within one district council.

The environmental health departments (formerly known as public health departments) can trace their origin back to the sanitary reform movement of the last century. Town and country planning emerged from the same tradition, and the links between them remain intimate. From the exercise of functions in respect of air pollution and noise, environmental health officers should be able to advise their colleagues in the planning department of those areas where pollution levels indicate that sensitive development, notably housing, should be avoided. There is evidence to suggest that consultation between environmental health and planning departments is now routine in the majority of district authorities.[16] Apart from consulting on planning applications, some county planning authorities have invited environmental health officers from the districts to assist in preparing the environmental input to their structure plans. In addition, it is not uncommon for environmental health officers to assist in the enforcement of planning conditions (e.g. the measuring of noise levels and of atmospheric pollutant concentrations).

It is rare for pollution to be cited as the sole or even the principal reason for the refusal of planning consent. Even in periods of comparatively high employment, the benefits of increased rate revenue to be gained from industrial development will often be deemed, by the members of the planning committee, to outweigh the notional costs to the community occasioned by any loss of amenity in surrounding areas. Far more common are attempts to secure some compromise: planning consent is granted but with conditions (or, with increasing frequency, clauses within a planning agreement) designed to ensure that atmospheric emissions or noise levels at the factory boundary are kept below a value adjudged to be environmentally acceptable. In periods of recession, a greater desire to replace lost jobs will have the effect of making local authorities' environmental standards less demanding in order to attract to their areas any opportunity of raising local employment. Indeed, the original philosophy underlying the 'free enterprise zone' concept was that all planning controls, whether for pollution or other purposes, should be abandoned in those urban areas where the need for industrial regeneration is the overriding social and economic priority.[17] However, when the enterprise zones were actually introduced, most planning controls remained.[18]

The planning control of pollution must be seen as one part of the exercise of political power within the democratic framework of local government. In theory, the members of a district or county council are no less answerable to their electorates for any deterioration in the quality of the local environment than they are for any impediment to industrial expansion. But unless it can be demonstrated that those who will suffer the noise and air pollution emitted by a proposed factory will derive some commensurate benefit from the increased rate revenues or secure some of the jobs created, it is possible that equity considerations may justify planning refusal even in the most depressed areas. No planning issue is value-free: a decision which favours industrial growth at the expense of the environment is no less political in essence than one which chooses between conflicting economic policies. But, as the Royal Commission on Environmental Pollution has observed: 'Our concern is not that pollution is not given top priority; it is that it is often dealt with inadequately and sometimes forgotten altogether in the planning process.'[19]

The role of the Secretary of State

The preparation of a structure plan and the inclusion of measures for the improvement of the physical environment are mandatory requirements of the 1971 Act. In the planning control of pollution, the majority of relevant powers are permissive in character: the manner in which they are applied lies at the discretion of the local authority. Associated with this formidable array of discretionary powers is the right of appeal to the Secretary of State[20] by an applicant aggrieved by any decision of the local planning authority. He also exercises the power of an approval of all structure plans and certain local plans; the power to assume the duties of any local planning authority held to be in default; and the power to confirm or reject orders and directions issued by the local authority. In addition, the 1971 Act confers upon the Secretary of State the power to require any planning application to be referred to him for a decision. This 'call in' procedure tends to be invoked in the case of developments which entail a substantial departure from an approved development plan and those which have implications which are of more than local significance.[21]

When the Secretary of State decides an appeal against planning refusal, or when a planning application is called in, his decision is usually preceded by a local inquiry. An inspector is appointed to hear evidence from the applicant, the local planning authority involved and from any interested parties—a term which may include conservation groups and local amenity societies as well as individuals affected by the development in question.[22] In the case of applications with unusual technical or environmental implications, one or more assessors may be appointed to offer specialist advice to the inspector. Nevertheless, the writing of the report of the inquiry and of the recommendations to the Secretary of State remains the responsibility of the inspector alone.

Planning inquiries are quasi-judicial in character, with the rules of procedure being laid down by statutory instrument.[23] However, the inquiry inspector enjoys wide discretion in deciding what shall constitute permissible evidence. In the case of called-in applications, the Secretary of State informs all parties to the inquiry of his reasons for the call-in and 'of any points which seem to him to be likely to be relevant to his consideration of the facts of the case as set down in the inspector's report'.[23]

Since these inquiries are set up under planning legislation, it can be argued that discussion should be confined to the land use planning implications of the proposed development. However, this begs the question of what constitutes a legitimate planning matter. Noise levels in the vicinity of an airport and aerial emissions from a chemical plant could have serious repercussions for the use of adjacent land and these should therefore constitute relevant considerations, even though this has not always been recognized. Over recent years, planning authorities and inquiry inspectors have gradually shown a greater readiness to cite particular forms of pollution (e.g. noise, odour, gaseous emissions) rather than rely upon vague phrases such as 'prejudicial to amenity' in order to defend refusals of consent for environmentally unacceptable development (see, for example, Chapter 3).

While pollution is now accepted as a material consideration, doubt persists over the question of 'need'. It may be a legitimate objection to a plan to tip toxic waste that watercourses will be seriously polluted; but the argument that a new tip should not be permitted because others have surplus capacity could be dismissed as invalid since it is not 'reasonably related' (see below) to the use of the land in question. However, it must be reiterated that considerable discretion is now granted to inspectors in deciding what shall constitute relevant evidence. Nowhere was this more apparent than at the Windscale inquiry of 1977 which, although an inquiry into a called-in application, embraced such diverse issues as nuclear proliferation, civil liberties, and the economics of nuclear fuel reprocessing as well as generally affording a public forum for the discussion of energy futures.[24]

Examining ministerial decisions in appeals and referred applications which involve the environment gives some indication of central government's attitude to the planning control of pollution. Further insight into departmental thinking can only be inferred from the circulars issued by the Department of the Environment. However, with the notable exception of a circular devoted to planning and noise (see Chapter 9), only incidental reference to planning control of pollution is to be found in these documents.

Reference has already been made to a circular which contained a guarded acceptance of the inclusion of pollution control policies in structure plans.[9] With the onset of the current economic recession, a subsequent circular urged local authorities to do all in their power to assist manufacturing industry.[25] Where the interests of the economy and the environment conflict, the circular stated, the exigencies of the national economic decline justified a shift in the balance in favour of industrial expansion. Nevertheless:

The need to take all possible steps to assist industry in no way obviates the need for vigilance where there may be health and safety hazards or pollution problems. It is important that in such cases planning authorities should work in close liaison with those responsible for pollution control and the disposal of waste.[25]

The need for planning authorities to liaise closely with those bodies with direct responsibilities for pollution control has been emphasized on numerous occasions by central government. On a closely related issue, it remains departmental policy[26] that planning conditions should not seek to duplicate controls available under other legislation:

Planning authorities are reminded however that they should exercise care in considering the use of conditional planning permission. ... planning conditions should not be imposed in an attempt to deal with problems which are the subject of controls under separate environmental legislation, whether the controlling authority belongs to central or local government.[25]

Although this advice was intended to be of general application, it has been most quoted in connection with attempts by planning authorities to acquire powers of control over atmospheric pollution, through the use of planning conditions, which would overlap those granted under the Alkali, etc., Works Regulation Act, 1906.

To summarize, the Department of the Environment sees the planning process primarily as offering an opportunity to anticipate and hence forestall the juxtaposition of unacceptably conflicting land uses. Further intervention, for instance, the imposition of planning conditions directly to limit the quantity of waste matter (but not noise), has generally, but not categorically, been viewed with disfavour. Moreover, the Department considers the optimum balance between amenity, agriculture, industry, etc. to be, normally, a local issue to be decided by local councillors. However, intervention by the central authority is necessary whenever there exists the possibility of the wider national interest being ignored.

It must be remembered that most of the events described in the following chapters precede the change in administration which occurred in May 1979, and the deepening of the economic recession in 1980. The most recent central government circular to touch upon planning and pollution stresses the need for planning authorities to recognize the 'vital role of small-scale enterprises in promoting future economic growth' and the need for expedition in determining planning consent for such developments whilst not neglecting 'health and safety standards, noise, smell or other pollution problems'. Of more interest are this circular's comments on planning conditions:

when small-scale commercial or industrial activities are proposed particularly in existing buildings, in areas which are primarily residential or rural, permission should be granted unless there are specific and convincing objections such as intrusion into open countryside, noise, smell, safety, health or excessive traffic generation. Where there are planning objections it will often be possible to meet them to a sufficient degree by attaching conditions to the permission or by the use of agreements under section 52 of the Town and Country Planning Act, 1971, rather than refusing the application. Such opportunities should be taken.[27]

In the extract quoted planning conditions appear to be presented, not as a means of applying effective controls over pollution sources, but as anodyne expedients by which objections to offensive developments can be assuaged. Whether this is a true interpretation of current central government attitudes can be judged only the outcome of inquiries which may arise in connection with the enforcement of such conditions.

The role of the High Court

Historically, common law actions in trespass, negligence, public or private nuisance have been used to secure compensation or an injunction to prevent the recurrence of many activities which today would be labelled 'polluting'.[28] These remedies, together with action in statutory nuisance (under the Public Health Act, 1936), remain available. However, they are little used in comparison with the legal (and extra-legal) powers of regulatory bodies such as the regional water authorities and the environmental health authorities.

The discretionary powers of the pollution control authorities, the local planning authorities, and the Secretary of State must be exercised in a reasonable manner and in keeping with the principles of natural justice. The High Court can to some extent control the exer-

cise of these powers by means of the prerogative orders of *certiorari,*
mandamus, and *prohibition.* Of more immediate relevance is the right of
individuals to question the validity of certain planning decisions of
the Secretary of State in the High Court.[29] A ministerial decision may
be challenged only on a point of law, not on points of fact. Nevertheless, the ownership and the use of land were traditionally governed by
common law and the judiciary has not been reluctant to remind the
executive of the limits of statutory powers over land use. Many of
these cases, especially those which have entailed judicial interpreta-
tions of the validity of planning conditions, have important implications for the use of planning controls over sources of pollution.

An application from the Pyx Granite Company for planning permission to extend their area of granite quarrying in the Malvern Hills
was 'called in' for determination by the Minister of Housing and
Local Government. The Minister elected to grant planning consent,
but with conditions requiring certain measures to minimize nuisance
from noise and dust generated by a stone-crushing plant which had
been the subject of an earlier planning approval. The applicants
sought to have these condition rescinded as *ultra vires* in that they
related to a use of land not the subject of the planning consent to
which they had been appended. In the High Court, Pyx Granite's
argument was accepted. However, that decision was reversed in the
Court of Appeal where Lord Denning stated that, while conditions
may not be imposed in pursuance of an ulterior motive, provided
they 'fairly and reasonably relate to the permitted development' they
may refer to the use of any land under the developer's control.[30]

This ruling was of central importance in a more recent case where,
again, the planning conditions at issue related to quarrying in an area
of natural beauty.[31] However, in this instance, the plaintiff (the Peak
Park Planning Board) sought the quashing of a ministerial decision
that planning conditions, relating among other things to the rate of
limestone extraction from another quarry not the subject of the application in question, were *ultra vires.* Although the two quarries were
separated by over a kilometre, distance was held to be irrelevant in
deciding whether the conditions were 'reasonably' related.[32] However, the fact that limestone from the approved development was to
be processed by plant situated at the other quarry was influential in
Sir Douglas Frank's judgment. The Secretary of State's decision was
quashed and the Minister was invited to reconsider the planning conditions originally proposed by the Peak Park Planning Board. Much
the same result obtained in the Penwith plastics factory case (Chapter 9).

It is legitimate, therefore, for a planning condition to require
improved pollution abatement, or the installation of pollution moni-

toring equipment, at a site under the applicant's control but not the subject of the planning application. Provided the condition is not only reasonable in itself[33] but also reasonably related to the development, a measure of control over existing pollution is possible: for example, planning consent for a chemical works involving atmospheric discharges could conceivably be made conditional upon the emissions from another plant, under the applicant's control and located in the same airshed, being reduced until the total discharge was acceptable.

Anticipatory and retrospective powers

Given the powers of environmental health authorities and of the other pollution control bodies, it might be thought that regulation by planning is inevitably duplicative. In practice, there are certain forms of pollution for which 'anticipatory' control can be secured only by the use of planning powers; in particular, planning conditions or planning agreements. An anticipatory or prospective control is one which specifies measures to be taken to prevent pollution or to reduce the risk of a polluting incident. If such measures are not taken, or if they fail to meet with the approval of the controlling authority, then the defaulting individual is liable to enforcement action (even though the pollution may not have occurred). In contrast, a 'retrospective' control is more penal or admonitory in character: it specifies a form of pollution or nuisance which may not be allowed to arise. By definition enforcement of a retrospective control is possible only after the occurrence of the specified polluting incident.

This distinction is of more than merely legalistic interest. A planning authority may well be forced by local opinion to be able to demonstrate that, for instance, a new chemical plant will be allowed to operate only when the most sophisticated pollution arrestment equipment has been installed and tested to the authority's satisfaction. Such a control is to be compared with one which simply imposes a fine upon the operators on conviction of causing nuisance by allowing a pollution discharge from the works.

While planning powers can readily enable anticipatory control, their procedures for enforcing retrospective control are generally considered to be inferior to those of pollution legislation, which entail the serving of an abatement notice and action in a magistrate's court should this notice be ignored. In the event of development without planning consent or the breach of a planning condition, an enforcement notice is served; but there remains the right of appeal to the Secretary of State who will decide the matter following a local inquiry. During this period, which may be lengthy, any pollution resulting from the activity or development at issue may continue, unless a 'stop-notice' is served.[34]

Where a stop-notice has been served and an appeal against the enforcement notice succeeds, then compensation is payable. One of the effects of this, and other weaknesses of the enforcement powers of planning authorities, has been to encourage the use of planning agreements (and similar agreements under provisions to be found in local acts) which are enforceable by action in the High Court.

In summary proceedings in statutory nuisance, it is a defence for the occupiers of industrial or trade premises to demonstrate that the 'best practicable means' had been used to prevent or to minimize nuisance arising from emissions to the air and from deposits of waste. This concept of 'best practicable means' has been central to British legislation on air pollution, public health and, more recently, the control of noise. The term encapsulates the traditional, pragmatic approach by which a source of nuisance is controlled to a degree which reflects not only the effects of the nuisance on the population and the environment but also the cost of measures to minimize and prevent waste discharge. The phrase 'best practicable means' has not been the subject of judicial *dicta*, but in the closely allied field of industrial safety, it has been authoritatively argued that the related term 'reasonably practicable':

is a narrower term than 'physically possible', and implies that a computation must be made in which the quantum of risk is placed on one scale and the sacrifice involved in the measures necessary for averting the risk (whether in money, time, or trouble) is placed in the other, and that, if it be shown that there is a *gross disproportion* between them—the risk being insignificant in relation to the sacrifice—the defendants discharge the onus upon them. Moreover this computation falls to be made by the owner at a point anterior to the accident.[35]

In economic terms, practicability implies an optimal point at which the marginal cost of pollution control is equal to the marginal costs (in so far as they can be computed in monetary terms) of pollution damage to public health, personal property, the environment, etc. Any planning authority is free to use its statutory powers to control pollution in this time-honoured manner. Indeed, the environmental policies of a number of structure plans include a commitment to observe a criterion of reasonable practicability in the use of planning powers over pollution sources and to judge each development on its individual merits and on its effect on neighbouring land uses. On the other hand, a planning authority could, at least in theory, exercise its powers so as to impose within its area an inflexible system of numerical limits on the emission of wastes to the atmosphere, land, or rivers. Such emission limits could be rigidly enforced notwithstanding the capacity of the medium to absorb such amounts and regardless of the economic consequences to the industries concerned.

Whether any planning authority could pursue the latter course in the face of the inevitable and active opposition of the Secretary of State and other regulatory bodies is very doubtful. Nevertheless, there are arguments in favour of emission standards when enforced over a sufficiently wide area: with no geographic variation in control, operators of polluting industries in one location are not placed at a commercial disadvantage relative to their competitors operating elsewhere. Equally, there is some justification, in terms of social equity, for the alternative system of 'environmental quality objectives' in which a target is set for concentrations of pollutants in each receiving medium. By encouraging uniformity in ambient concentrations, this approach reduces the risk of undue burdens of pollution damage being borne by the inhabitants of those areas which contain a number of discharges and where natural dispersion is poor: an inhabitant of Bermondsey has no less a right to enjoy clean air than a resident of Berkeley Square.[36] However, opinion among the founder member states of the European Economic Community has tended to favour the use of uniform emission standards; it could be that the UK will find it difficult to maintain its traditional approach to pollution control in which a balanced consideration is paid to pollutant concentrations, their effects and the economic implications of reducing them.

The 'polluter-pays' principle

Another consequence of membership of the Common Market has been a commitment to implement the 'polluter-pays' principle.[37] This principle requires that the costs of pollution, whether incurred in preventing wastes or in repairing pollution damage, should be 'internalized'; in other words, the costs should be met, in the first instance, by whoever causes the pollution.[38] There are circumstances in which planning controls may violate this principle. Planning powers (such as the discontinuance order) which apply to existing land uses restrict the right of those with an interest in the land to enjoy it as they would wish. It has become accepted in planning law that compensation should be paid in such instances and the statutes have been drafted accordingly.[39] If a planning authority chooses to use a discontinuance order to close an established pollution source, then compensation consists of payment from the polluted (in effect, the local ratepayers) to the polluter. Compensation is, however, not usually payable when closure is brought about by proceedings under other legislation (for example, under the Public Health Act, 1936).[40]

A landowner has no 'right' of development and, in general, compensation is not payable when an application for planning consent is refused. Thus where the prospect of unacceptable levels of pollution motivates a planning authority to exercise its power of refusal, the 'polluter-pays' principle is not infringed; any financial loss (e.g. the loss of development value) incurred in eradicating the pollution threat is borne by the would-be polluter alone. But, as the following chapters will reveal, this is only one of several reasons why the prevention of pollution is to be preferred to its cure.

REFERENCES AND NOTES

¹ N. Lee and J. A. Luker, 'An Introduction to the Economics of Pollution', *Economics*, Summer 1971, 19-32.
² C. Wood, *Town Planning and Pollution Control*, Manchester University Press, Manchester, 1976.
³ Town and Country Planning Act, 1971, s. 29.
⁴ Ibid., s. 30.
⁵ Ibid., s. 52.
⁶ Ibid., ss. 7-11.
⁷ Control of Pollution Act, 1974, s. 31(5) (yet to be implemented).
⁸ Ibid., s. 63.
⁹ 'Memorandum on Structure and Local Plans', Dept. of the Environment, Circular 4/79, HMSO, London, 1979.
¹⁰ 'Town and Country Planning Act, 1968—Part I of the Town and Country Planning (Structure and Local Plans) Regulations, 1971: and Memorandum', Dept. of the Environment, Circular 44/71, HMSO, London, 1971. (Superseded by Circular 4/79, above.)
¹¹ Local Government Act, 1972, para. 32, Schedule 16, as amended by the Local Government, Planning and Land Act, 1980.
¹² Town and Country Planning Act, 1971, s. 22, as interpreted by various judicial *dicta*.
¹³ Town and Country Planning (General Development) Order, 1977 (SI 1977, No. 289).
¹⁴ See Town and Country Planning Act, 1971, ss. 40, 222-41 and 270-2
¹⁵ Town and Country Planning (Use Classes) Order, 1972 (SI 1972, No. 1385).
¹⁶ C. E. Miller, C. Wood, and J. McLoughlin, 'Land Use Planning and Pollution Control', Report to the Social Science Research Council, Pollution Research Unit, University of Manchester, 1980, vols. I and IV.
¹⁷ P. Hall, 'Green Fields and Grey Areas', *Proceedings Royal Town Planning Institute Annual Conference*, RTPI, London, 1977.
¹⁸ Local Government, Planning and Land Act, 1980, Schedule 32.
¹⁹ Royal Commission on Environmental Pollution, *Fifth Report. Air Pollution Control: an Integrated Approach*, Cmnd. 6371, HMSO, London, 1976.
²⁰ Unless otherwise stated, this term will be used to denote the Secretary of State for the Environment in referring to planning matters in England, and to the Secretary of State for Wales in referring to planning matters in Wales.
²¹ Town and Country Planning Act, 1971, s. 35.
²² Ibid., s. 29.
²³ Town and Country Planning (Inquiries Procedure) Rules, 1974 (SI 1974, No. 419).
²⁴ *The Windscale Inquiry: Report by the Hon. Mr Justice Parker*, Dept. of the Environment, HMSO, London, 1978.

[25] 'Local Government and the Industrial Strategy', Dept. of the Environment, Circular 71/77, HMSO, London, 1977. (Cancelled by Circular 22/80, below.)

[26] 'The Use of Conditions in Planning Permissions', Ministry of Housing and Local Government, Circular 5/68, HMSO, London, 1968.

[27] 'Development Control—Policy and Practice', Dept. of the Environment, Circular 22/80, HMSO, London, 1980.

[28] For an account of the relationship between common law actions in nuisance, trespass and negligence, and the control of pollution, see J. McLoughlin, *The Law and Practice Relating to Pollution Control in the United Kingdom*, Graham & Trotman, London, 1976.

[29] Town and Country Planning Act, 1971, ss. 242-6.

[30] Pyx Granite Company v. Minister of Housing and Local Government [1958] 1 QB, 554; [1959] 3 All ER1.

[31] 'Peak Park Joint Planning Board v. Secretary of State for the Environment and Imperial Chemical Industries Ltd', *Journal of Environmental and Planning Law* (1980), 114-19.

[32] In the Pyx Granite case, the crushing plant was on the site of the quarry.

[33] Mixnam's Properties v. Chertsey UDC' [1974] 1 QB 214; [1975] AC 735.

[34] Town and Country Planning Act, 1971, s. 90, as amended.

[35] I. Fife and E. Machin, *Redgrave's Health and Safety in Factories*, Butterworth, London, 1976.

[36] Lord Justice Thesiger, in Sturgess v. Bridgman (1879) *11 Ch D* 856.

[37] 'Community Action Programme on the Environment', Commission of the European Communities, Brussels, 1973. (Adopted by the Council of Ministers in July 1973.)

[38] The principle does not imply that the costs of pollution control should not be passed on to the consumer by, for example, higher prices: it requires only that the costs are borne initially by the polluter. See *The 'Polluter-Pays' Principle : Definition, Analysis, Implementation*, Organization for Economic Co-operation and Development, Paris, 1975.

[39] See, for instance, the dictum of Lord Justice Willmer in Hall & Co. Ltd v. Shoreham-by-Sea UDC [1964] 1 WLR 240, who said: 'I can certainly find no clear and unambiguous words in the Town and Country Planning Act 1947, authorising the defendants in effect to sway the plaintiffs' rights of property without compensation by the imposition of conditions such as those sought to be imposed.' For a judgment of more general application, see that of Lord Warrington of Clyffe in Colonial Sugar Refining C. Ltd v. Melbourne Harbour Trust Commissioners [1927] AC 343, PC.

[40] Public Health Act, 1936, s. 100.

2

PLANNING AND AIR POLLUTION

The Clean Air Acts of 1956 and 1968 and changes in domestic heating methods have been instrumental in bringing about the marked improvement in the overall quality of the atmosphere observed in the UK during the last twenty years (Figs. 2.1 and 2.2). There remain, of course, isolated urban pockets of high concentrations of smoke and sulphur dioxide, but attention in recent years has tended to be focused on the health effects of specific air pollutants (notably lead) and on the global consequences of the burning of fossil fuels (for example, the so-called 'greenhouse effect'). A concern with the effects of lead in motor exhaust fumes has prompted the introduction of regulations under the Control of Pollution Act, 1974, limiting the amount of this metal in petrol. While these latest powers are exercised by central government, in keeping with directives promulgated by the Commission of the European Communities, local government has nevertheless retained an active interest in maintaining and improving atmospheric quality.

This local interest has been most apparent in the creation of about 5,500 smoke control orders covering over 8,000,000 premises.[1] In addition, the replacement of obsolete housing stock in the inner cities by modern residential development with smokeless forms of space heating leads automatically to *de facto* smokeless zones. Large-scale urban renewal also affords an opportunity to remove long-standing 'bad neighbours' such as animal treatment works, dye works, tanneries, etc. from residential areas. While public health and the smoke control programmes are among the principal responsibilities of the environmental health departments of local authorities, planning departments have also shown a readiness to use statutory powers, both in the control of development and in the preparation of development plans, to prevent atmospheric pollution or to mitigate its effects upon the population.

Development control powers have been found, with air pollution as with other types of pollution (Chapter 1), to be most effective when applied to new (as distinct from established) development when they can prevent the juxtaposition of polluter and polluted. Few planners possess any detailed knowledge of pollution control technology and it is generally accepted that planning powers should be used to ameliorate air pollution problems only after consultation with the pollution control authorities: the environmental health departments and the Alkali Inspectorate. In the former case, consultation usually consists

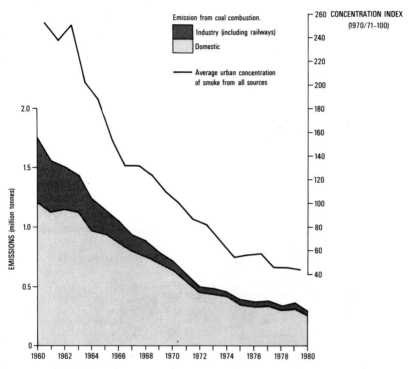

Fig. 2.1 Trends in emissions and average urban concentrations of smoke, UK, 1960-80. *Source*: Reference 1.

of discussions between officers of a single district council. In the case of liaison between planning departments and the Alkali Inspectorate, relations have occasionally been strained by antagonisms and conflicts of interest when stem from fundamental differences, in both attitudes and responsibilities, between the local and the central bodies. The role of the Alkali Inspectorate, and its relationship with local planning authorities, must be examined in more detail.

HM Alkali and Clean Air Inspectorate

Created by an Act of Parliament in 1863, the body now styled Her Majesty's Alkali and Clean Air Inspectorate has come under the jurisdiction of various central government departments; but since 1975 it has formed one constituent of the Health and Safety Executive, under the authority of the Health and Safety Commission. The principal function of the Alkali Inspectorate is the enforcement of the Alkali, etc., Works Regulation Act, 1906, as amended by successive

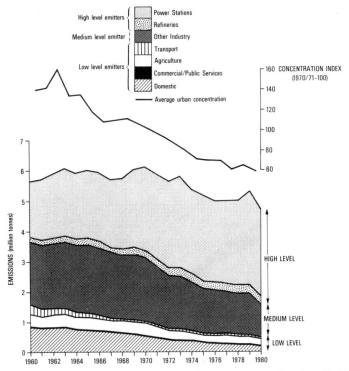

FIG. 2.2   Trends in emissions and average urban concentrations of sulphur dioxide, UK, 1960-80. *Source*: Reference 1

orders and regulations.[2] The purpose of this recondite body of legislation has been the control of certain noxious atmospheric emissions from a number of specified chemical, metallurgical, and other industrial processes. The processes which have been added to the Inspectorate's jurisdiction are those which, by virtue of their complexity in terms of air pollution control, are considered to require a greater degree of technical expertise than can generally be expected to be possessed by local authority environmental health departments.

The Act of 1863 and the Inspectorate take their respective titles from the early 'alkali' (Leblanc) process for the manufacture of sodium carbonate, the first stage of which involved treating rocksalt (and hence the concentration of alkali works in and around Cheshire) with sulphuric acid. The first Alkali Act required that only 5 per cent of the hydrogen chloride gas generated during this process be allowed to reach the atmosphere. An Act of 1874 imposed another statutory limit on hydrogen chloride emissions from alkali works and introduced what is now the crucial concept of 'best practicable means', namely measures which operators of alkali works must take to prevent the discharge of certain specified noxious gases.

The consolidating Act of 1906, albeit with many provisions repealed by recent legislation, remains in force today. For fifty-nine of the sixty-one processes listed in a much amended schedule to the 1906 Act, no statutory limit on emissions is involved and control is effected solely by requiring the operators of such 'scheduled processes' to use:

the best practicable means for preventing the escape of noxious or offensive gases by the exit flue of any apparatus used in the work, and for preventing the discharge, whether directly or indirectly, of such gases into the atmosphere, and for rendering such gases where discharged harmless and inoffensive.[3]

Once a particular process is, by order of the Secretary of State for the Environment and following a public inquiry, added to the schedule, the Chief Alkali Inspector, after consulting representatives of the industry concerned, prepares a set of guidelines on the requirements of the 'best practicable means' to be observed in the operation of that process. Subsequently, these guidelines are published as 'Notes on Best Practicable Means'.[4] These notes may refer to the type of pollution-arrestment equipment which must be installed, or they may refer to maintenance and operating procedures which must be adopted. They may, in addition, specify a (non-statutory) 'presumptive standard' of emission which, if exceeded, would indicate a *prima facie* breach of the 'best practicable means'. Almost without exception, such published notes have been prefaced by the qualification:

These notes are not claimed to be comprehensive, but they do provide a basis for negotiation between works' management and the Inspectorate. Flexibility is left to meet special local circumstances by consultation. There are likely to be matters revealed during routine inspections which will need attention to meet the Alkali Act.[5]

In practice, the District Alkali Inspector,[6] acting on the Chief Inspector's behalf and following discussions with the works' management, specifies exactly what 'best practicable means' for that works shall entail. The finally agreed requirements may be equivalent to, or stricter than, those published in the 'Notes on Best Practicable Means' for that process. In determining the particular requirements for a works, local circumstances such as topography, micro-meteorology, prevailing winds, the proximity of housing or similarly vulnerable land uses may be considered. Moreover, the existing levels of air pollution in the area might also be included in the calculations. In this context, a Chief Inspector has written: 'The Chief Inspector, with the help of his deputies, lays down broad national policies and provided 'they keep within these broad lines, inspectors in the field have plenty of flexibility to take into account local circumstances and make suitable decisions.'[5]

It is an offence to operate a works in default of the agreed 'best practicable means'. However, it has become the tradition of the Inspectorate to prosecute only in the event of the most flagrant and persistent abuses. Usually the Inspectorate considers it sufficient to issue an admonition in the form of an 'infraction letter' indicating the nature of the violation and the measures necessary to secure adherence to the 'best practicable means'.

The policy of reliance on the extra-legal methods of persuasion and informed advice, rather than penal sanctions, is apparent from the observation that, in 1976, sixty-six infractions were recorded, leading to eight prosecutions (four of which were held over for hearing in 1977).[7] Yet even these low figures represent something of a recent shift in policy; for, between 1920 and 1966, a total of only two prosecutions was brought by the Inspectorate.[8] The relatively more numerous prosecutions of recent years have been directed, in the main, against small-scale operations, e.g. metal recovery—cable-burning and the melting of lead batteries in the open air.[9,10]

Neither the Alkali Act, nor any subsidiary instrument, gives a definition of the term 'best practicable means'. However, the Clean Air Act, 1956, does offer an elaboration of the closely allied term 'reasonably practicable': 'reasonably practicable having regard, amongst other things to local conditions and circumstances, to the financial implications and to the current state of technical knowledge.'[11] It must be assumed that this interpretation is accepted by the Inspectorate for the Chief Inspector has stated that 'it would be unreasonable to interpret the Alkali Act differently'.[5]

Thus, 'best practicable means' as enforced by the Alkali Inspectorate, amounts to a pragmatic system of pollution control with account taken of three broad sets of factors: technological, environmental, and economic. On the last of these factors, it has been stated that: 'The expression "best practicable means" takes into account economics in all its financial implications, and we interpret this not just in the narrow sense of the works dipping into its own pockets, but including the wider effect on the community.'[12] No further information has been given on the relative weighting of the various factors which are included in the determination of 'best practical means' for a particular works.

It will be apparent that the determination of 'best practicable means' lies at the discretion of the Chief Inspector. Moreover, it has traditionally been the view of the Inspectorate that the superiority of the 'best practicable means' approach over other systems of pollution control (for example, air quality or emission standards, pollution licences or charges) lies in its discretionary character and its flexibility both in formulation and in implementation. It might be argued that the Inspectorate has gradually assumed a degree of discretion in the exercise of its duties and, in particular, the determination of 'best practicable means', in excess of that originally intended by Parliament. This assertion, of course, could be tested only in the courts. However, it seems unlikely, in view of the extent of consultation with the relevant industry which precedes the determination of the 'best practicable means' for the process involved, that such a test case will ever arise.

Planning controls and registered works

In the exercise of its primary function, the implementation and enforcement of 'best practicable means', the Alkali Inspectorate is involved in a continuing dialogue with the operators of scheduled processes: there is only incidental involvement of other parties. However, the Inspectorate has come to acquire an additional role as a source of technical advice on air pollution to local authorities.

Indeed, many local authorities seek the Inspectorate's opinion on planning applications for registrable works as a matter of course. In some cases, the advice received would appear to be perfunctory, consisting of a simple reiteration of the operator's obligation to comply with the 'best practicable means' without specifying what they will consist of, or more pertinently, what the consequences of the permitted discharges might subsequently be.[13]

The consultative role of the Inspectorate is not confined to offering advice on the location of what might be termed 'sources' of atmospheric pollution. It is willing, indeed often eager, to comment on the wisdom of permitting sensitive development, notably housing, in the vicinity of existing registered works:

The Royal Commission on Environmental Pollution recommended there should be a mandatory obligation on planning authorities to consult the Inspectorate on all applications to build or alter registrable works. The Health and Safety Commission support this recommendation and consider that the obligation should extend to consulting about other developments near to existing registered works.[7]

In practice, it is usually the environmental health officers, rather than the planning officers, of a local authority who liaise with the Alkali Inspectorate, as they possess more technical knowledge and share a common vocabulary. Moreover, relations between the Inspectorate and planning departments have occasionally been impaired by the former's antipathy to the application of planning powers which encroach upon those conferred by the 1906 Act.

The draft of a circular on planning and clean air was distributed for comment among local authorities and other bodies with an interest in air pollution control in 1972.[14] It emphasized the need for local planning authorities to take account of air pollution in the exercise of their functions and it stressed the need to seek the advice of their environmental health departments and of the Inspectorate. Generally, this draft circular considered planning conditions limiting emissions from registered works to be inappropriate; however, it did concede that 'in exceptional cases' planning conditions restricting, for example, the sulphur content of fuel oils consumed in registered works and the hours of operation of scheduled processes might be justified.

Apart from this qualified concession in a draft circular (which has remained unpublished),[15] the Department of the Environment has consistently supported the Alkali Inspectorate in its contention that planning legislation, and planning conditions in particular, should not seek to regulate atmospheric discharges from registered works. This view was endorsed by the Royal Commission on Environmental Pollution:

> In deciding applications for industrial development and especially for registered works local planning authorities sometimes impose planning conditions designed to control air pollution from the plant, even though separate legislation exists for that purpose. This practice is misguided. The Alkali Inspectorate are legally responsible for controlling emissions from registered works and it is wrong in principle that local authorities should attempt to assume this authority by use of the planning laws. It is also confusing and potentially counter-productive in practice: conditions identical to those imposed by the pollution control authority serve no useful purpose in the short term but, because planning conditions cannot be updated, could in the long term undermine the pollution control authority's work in seeking progressive improvements in control. Planning conditions which conflict with the Inspectorate's or the local authority's own pollution control requirements can only create confusion. If the planning conditions are less stringent than the pollution control requirements then the developer is given an argument against those requirements. The pollution control requirements are likely to be set close to the best the plant can physically achieve: it is therefore unlikely that any more stringent requirements imposed as planning conditions could be regularly met. If the planning authority, using air quality guidelines, consider that an unacceptable amount of pollution is likely to be emitted from a proposed plant when the Alkali Inspector's requirements have been met their sanction should be the refusal of planning permission not the imposition of planning conditions designed to control emissions. ... We note here that the Secretary of State and the Courts take a strict view of the proper scope of planning conditions and are likely to quash conditions which purport to cover matters already covered by other legislation.[9]

It must be emphasized that the majority of local planning authorities accept the general principles outlined by the Royal Commission.

Many, of course, have no registered works within their areas. The importance of the actions of the minority stems, not from their numbers, but from the significance of the issues which provoke the dissension.[13] In addition, many of these instances of dissent relate to large-scale chemical and allied concerns whose business is of a national rather than merely a local importance and which are members of politically influential trade associations such as the Chemical Industries Association. Conflicts between the Inspectorate and planning authorities thus tend to become celebrated.

In the case of the UKF ammonia plant at Ince (Chapter 3) the crucial issue was concerned with information about discharges of air pollutants. When an application was submitted for permission to expand the plant, the local planning authorities sought a condition requiring the developer to monitor atmospheric discharges from the works. This the applicant would not accept, and the Secretary of State for the Environment, when determining the application under the 'call-in' procedure, excluded the requirement from the conditions which he finally imposed, against his Inspector's advice.

Monitoring of emissions cannot strictly be considered as a form of control. The local planning authorities, and Cheshire County Council in particular, were not seeking to supplement the controls of the Inspectorate, but rather to require the developer to supply information on the additional contribution, albeit small, to the ambient air pollution of the area. Cheshire would contend that this not unreasonable requirement should be seen in the context of a local planning authority's general responsibility for the quality of the local environment, including the atmosphere, as a whole.

In his decision letter in this case, the Secretary of State pointed out that a local authority's right to seek information on emissions from registered works is limited to such information as might be supplied to the Alkali Inspector in the exercise of his duties.[16] On the question of the specificity of the Inspectorate's role in comparison with the generality of the responsibility of a local planning authority, a senior member of the Inspectorate has argued that this body does pay heed to the general quality of the atmosphere in the locality of a registered works.[17] Air quality, it is maintained, is one of a number of local circumstances which are included in the deliberations which precede the determination of the form of 'best practicable means' for a particular registered works.

Cheshire's concern with the general quality of the atmosphere is somewhat unusual; more often disputes between local authorities and the Inspectorate have centred upon localized nuisance from specific sources of emission. In a number of instances local planning authorities have sought to impose planning conditions on consent for a proposed registered works since past experience had shown that the Inspectorate's requirements, although sufficient to safeguard the health of the local community, did not offer an adequate defence against the risk of nuisance: 'notwithstanding an industry may adopt "the best practicable means" to minimize pollution from a scheduled process [it is clear] that an environmental nuisance can still be caused'.[13]

The Alkali Inspectorate is not statutorily obliged to ensure that 'nuisance' is never occasioned to the public as a result of emissions from a scheduled process; it is required only to ensure that the 'best practicable means' are used to prevent emissions or to render them harmless and inoffensive. The Inspectorate insists that attention is nevertheless paid to the threat of nuisance which emissions from scheduled processes may occasion. This consideration is subordinate to the primary responsibility to safeguard health, but it is included together with other 'local circumstances' in determining the requirements to be observed at any particular works.

The Inspectorate's devotion to the 'best practicable means' concept is such that it only rarely admits publicly to any instance in which they fail to offer adequate environmental safeguards. However, given the cautious tone customarily adopted by the Chief Inspector in his published pronouncements, the severity of the pollution involved in one instance can be gauged from the observation that:

It seems very doubtful to the Inspectorate that the Disticoke process [for the manufacture of smokeless fuel from coal] can be made environmentally acceptable without virutally complete redesign and rebuild, particularly in view of the topographical situation of its present location. The Inspectorate are pressing for firm indication of how [the operators] propose to deal with the situation but no clear picture had emerged at the year end. This work will continue in 1979 to be the Inspectorate's most difficult registration in its class and demanding much necessary attention.[18]

Ironically, such plants are an essential concomitant of the smoke control programmes in urban areas. However, this particular plant, run by a subsidiary of the National Coal Board, is situated in a locality (a populated valley in South Wales) which is totally unsuited to such a process: even with tall stacks, the surrounding hills prevent the dispersion of the voluminous discharges of sulphur dioxide, smoke, and aerosols of tar and other organic compounds. There is some evidence to suggest that the Inspectorate sought to use extra-legal persuasion to secure the cessation of the worst parts of the operation.[19] But 900 men worked at the plant and many more were employed in nearby collieries in mining the 9,000,000 tonnes of coal processed each year. The National Coal Board failed to secure a central government loan to carry out the required rebuilding of the plant and the efforts of the Inspectorate proved unavailing.

If the 'polluter-pays' principle were to be rigorously applied in this case, then the cost of plant improvements and more sophisticated pollution-arrestment equipment should be borne by the operator in the first instance. These costs would then be recouped by increasing the price of the smokeless fuel produced; however, increasing the cost of smokeless fuel relative to untreated coal is tantamount to a tax on pollution prevention. Such economic considerations would not have arisen had planning permission for the plant to be sited in a sensitive area not been granted.[20]

The more usual situation, perhaps, is that in which local authority desires the closure of a registered works. Few authorities, however, would contemplate the compensation that would have been involved had St Helens been successful in closing a sulphuric acid plant which had occasioned nuisance to nearby residents since its commissioning (Chapter 4). The Inspectorate's contention that 'best practicable means' had been observed was one of the more significant statements made at a local inquiry which preceded the Secretary of State's decision not to confirm the discontinuance order. In this case, planning powers proved ineffective in removing a source of pollution. In contrast, Shoreham-by-Sea Urban District Council found proceedings under the Public Health Act, 1936, to be successful in securing the closure of an animal-rendering works which, on account of its offensive odour, had been a long-standing source of nuisance. In 1971 the local authority began proceedings in statutory nuisance against a firm engaged in recovering protein from chicken feathers. An injunction was served on the company requiring it to prevent further odour. When it failed to do so, and following further legal proceedings, the company was ordered to cease operation, despite evidence from the Alkali Inspector that the 'best practicable means' had been observed.[21, 22]

Many of the most odoriferous industrial processes are scheduled: where, as with the treatment of chicken feathers or hogs' hair, significant amounts of hydrogen sulphide are generated, then the premises must be registered and the 'best practicable means' for 'sulphide works' is applied. However, odours are notoriously difficult to control; the most minute concentrations of mercaptans (sulphur-containing organic gases), for example, can be offensive and the Inspectorate has actively encouraged research into better abatement techniques. This approach is preferred to the prosecution or closure of works which incur the opposition of local inhabitants:

Local reaction to these animal waste treatment works is mounting despite the use of best practicable means and the obvious improvements that have been made. Zero odour is being demanded and in some cases nothing will satisfy local residents except closure. Injunctions have been taken against several works or renewal of licences under the offensive trades provisions of the

Public Health Act 1936 to operate has been refused. I view with some apprehension the effect of closure of animal waste treatment works if local authorities continue to pursue this policy.[23]

These views conflict somewhat with those contained in a central government circular devoted to the problem of the control of odours from animal treatment works.[24] This circular recognizes that, in the worst cases, only closure of offending works can obviate nuisance to neighbouring residents but advises that, should processing recommence at new premises in a less sensitive location, the 'best practicable means' should be used from the outset to minimize emissions.

There is a rarely used provision in the Alkali Act by which a local authority may make representations to the Secretary of State over any complaint of nuisance alleged to arise from the failure of the operator of a registered works to observe 'best practicable means'.[25] Few examples of the use of this procedure are apparent, presumably because action under other legislation is generally thought more likely to secure redress. However, in 1971 Northfleet Urban District Council alleged that 'best practicable means' were not being used to prevent emissions of dust from a large cement production works. An inquiry was held under the chairmanship of a civil servant at the Department of the Environment, who subsequently submitted a report on his findings to the Secretary of State. The Minister concluded that 'best practicable means' had, in fact, been observed. Nevertheless, the local authority initiated proceedings, under the Public Health Act, 1936, in the High Court: the result is still awaited at the time of writing.

It might be argued that this inquiry procedure could provide a forum for the resolution of disputes between the owner of an existing registered works and the local authority without the need for lengthy and expensive resort to the courts. However, such a forum appears to be provided by informal liaison groups, often set up at the instigation of the Alkali Inspectorate. The Inspectorate is now represented on some fifty such committees where pollution problems can be discussed in a relatively informal setting with representatives of the local authority and of the residents of areas subject to nuisance from scheduled processes.[7]

It should not be assumed that the 'best practicable means' approach is seen by those authorities at odds with the Inspectorate to be an inherently inferior system of air pollution regulation or one which inevitably conflicts with land use planning. Often it is not the stringency or the form of the controls which provokes dispute, but rather it is an issue of exactly who shall have the power to enforce them. With a development which generates significant local hostility, it may be politically imperative to withhold planning consent unless the planning authority can demonstrate that its own officers possess sufficient readily enforceable powers to safeguard the environment. Planning conditions and planning agreements (which, being voluntary, entail no right of appeal to the Secretary of State) have been seen as offering such safeguards.[13]

It is not suggested that Alkali Inspectors are totally insensitive to public opinion; their membership of numerous local liaison committees bears witness to a willingness to hear the views of those living in the vicinity of registered works. Nevertheless, the Inspectorate's accountability (via the Health and Safety Commission, and the Secretary of State for the Environment, to Parliament) is far removed from that of the members of a district council's planning committee who face elections every three years. For the latter, the balance between the conflicting demands of the local economy and environment is, primarily and overtly, a political decision—selecting from among a number of policy options that which promises to serve the best interests of the majority of the population. In contrast, Alkali Inspectors are scientists or engineers; their training and experience are focused almost exclusively on the technological dimension of air pollution control, as indeed is the Alkali Act.

The 'best practicable means' concept recognizes that total elimination of pollution, even if technically feasible, is economically prohibitive. However, the Inspectorate never reveals exactly how it determines what shall constitute a 'practicable' level of control for a particular works, nor does it ever offer an explicit cost-benefit case against demanding additional regulation. Public suspicion of the Inspectorate's procedures has not been assuaged by its repeated insistence on its obligation to preserve trade secrets.

The Inspectorate wishes to be seen by industry as a source of technical advice and not simply as an agency enforcing emission limits. A persuasive but reasonable approach, it argues, is more effective than a policy of prosecution for the most minor infraction. Whether or not it is true that the Inspectorate is therefore 'industry's ally'[26] there seems little doubt that an industrialist's anguished prophecy of insolvency if further pollution arrestment is demanded receives a more sympathetic hearing than the protests of those who suffer the effects of emissions from registered works.

Planning controls and non-registered works

While the scheduled processes pose the more technically intractable problems of control, it must be remembered that the 2,100 registered works are greatly outnumbered by the 30,000-50,000 industrial premises not covered by the Alkali Act and from which significant quantities of pollutants are emitted to the atmosphere.[9] There are two such types of operation: those involving combustion processes and those employing non-combustion processes.

Where sources of pollution are not registered but involve combustion (i.e. industrial boilers and furnaces) the Clean Air Acts grant local authorities certain anticipatory powers to forestall pollution as well as the right to prosecute emitters of dark smoke. In addition to the right to approve the height of any chimney, there is, in some cases, a power of prior approval of equipment to regulate the emission of grit and dust.[27] Despite the existence of these powers under the Clean Air Acts, it would appear that it is quite common for local planning authorities to employ planning powers to control such pollution sources.[13, 17]

It must be remembered, however, that controls over discharges from combustion processes under the Clean Air Acts are not as comprehensive as those over scheduled processes under the Alkali Act, and thus a desire to intervene with additional planning controls is not unexpected. In particular, a local authority has no power specifically to restrict emissions of sulphur dioxide. Past attempts to achieve this end by applying a planning condition limiting the sulphur content of fuel oils have generally met with the opposition of central government,[28] though not without exception.[14, 29] With the coming into force of regulations made by the Secretary of State for the Environment, under the Control of Pollution Act, 1974, to impose limits on the sulphur content of fuel oil used in engines and furnaces, there is some justification for the contention that additional control in the form of planning conditions would be superfluous. However, while the Secretary of State may make different provisions for different areas and for different circumstances, it is very doubtful whether his discretion extends to the making of specific provisions for individual works.[30]

Where a process giving rise to atmospheric discharges is neither scheduled nor involves combustion, then (save for the rights to approve the height of any chimney installed and to approve the establishment of 'offensive trades' designated in the Public Health Act, 1936) the local environmental health authority has no power of prior approval of measures to reduce or render harmless any discharge to the atmosphere. There are numerous such stationary sources of atmospheric pollution which lie outside the scope of both of the Alkali Act and the Clean Air Acts. There is, of course, the sanction of taking action under the Public Health Act, 1936, once a nuisance or a danger to public health has arisen. However, this retrospective power is generally seen as inferior to the right to intervene at an earlier stage and to require the installation of equipment, and the observance of operating procedures, which ensure that the risk of such nuisance is reduced to a minimum. In consequence, many local planning authorities have used planning conditions and planning agreements to secure some form of anticipatory control over these types of premises. Although the manufacture of 'carbon-black' is a scheduled process, its use, notably in the production of motor tyres, does not entail registration; hence prior approval of measures to reduce the risk of discharge of this particularly offensive material is possible only during the determination of a planning consent. Thus, the Borough Council of Newcastle under Lyme imposed several planning conditions, at the request of the Director of Health and Housing, to reduce the pollution risk from a newly installed plant at a works where discharge of carbon-black had previously been a cause of complaints:

2. Loading, unloading and all handling of carbon-black shall be carried out within the buildings.
3. Filtration equipment shall be installed ... with the addition of the electro static filter ... so that 99.9% filtration is achieved.
4. No air passed through the filtration system shall be discharged to the external air.[31]

Included within this category of air pollution sources are those agricultural developments, particularly intensive livestock units, from which malodorous emissions may be released. The Royal Commission on Environmental Pollution has recommended that such units should no longer constitute 'permitted development' and thereby escape the control of the local planning authority.[32] However, the Commission argues against the use of planning conditions to limit odour nuisance, preferring instead to see such controls being enforced by environmental health departments with the assistance of a new specialist body within the Ministry of Agriculture, Fisheries and Food. These controls, the Commission recommends, should be contained in revised legislation on statutory nuisance and would, for the first time, confer on local authorities powers of prior approval (following the 'best practicable means' approach) over non-scheduled, non-combustion sources of air pollution.[17]

If the new controls are not introduced then planning conditions will play a continuing role in anticipatory controls over odour pollution[32] (see also Chapter 5). The Royal Commission seeks to clarify misinterpretations of the section of the Fifth Report quoted above,[9] which attempt to extend the strictures against the use of planning conditions to non-registered, as well as to registered works:

The Commission's views on this point must, however, be seen against its recommendations as a whole. The Commission did not argue that conditions relating to pollution control should not be imposed on new developments but

that these conditions should be determined under pollution control legislation rather than rigidly embodied in planning consents. Powers to set such
conditions are available under existing legislation for registered works where
responsibility for control rests with the Alkali Inspectorate but not generally
for non-registered works where local authorities can take action under the
public health legislation only after a nuisance has occurred. The Commission
envisaged that new, comprehensive legislation should be introduced, providing the same basis for control for all industrial discharges to air.[32]

The Commission then directed its general comments about planning conditions to intensive livestock units in particular (see also
Chapter 5):

the views expressed in the Commission's Fifth Report imply no acceptance of
the proposition that it would be wrong to set constraints on intensive livestock
developments from the pollution viewpoint, or even that it would be wrong in
principle to do so through planning conditions when no alternative means
exists under pollution control legislation.[32]

Development plans and air quality objectives

The powers conferred upon the Secretary of State by the Control
of Pollution Act[30] are aimed, not at the mitigation of localized
nuisances, but at the amelioration of respiratory disorders and other
benefits consequent upon a reduction in average ambient concentrations of sulphur dioxide. The regulations do not apply to coal-fired
furnaces, and oil-fired power stations are specifically exempted.
While the tall stack policy of the Central Electricity Generating Board
(encouraged by the Alkali Inspectorate) reduces concentrations at the
local and regional levels only a co-ordinated policy of emission controls can solve the various global and transfrontier problems, such as
the notorious 'acid rain' in Scandinavia caused by the emissions from
the more industrialized parts of Europe.

Even with controls over the sulphur content of oil, Central London
is still prone to pockets of excessive concentrations of sulphur dioxide
in areas where dense, high buildings both emit large quantities of this
pollutant from space-heating furnace emissions and hinder its dispersion. The Greater London Council has therefore found it necessary
to adopt the long-term targets for atmospheric quality recommended
by the World Health Organization.[33] Recognition of the state of
London's atmosphere caused the planning authority in Islington to
include within a draft local plan a policy reserving the least polluted
areas for housing: 'Preference will be given to residential development in areas where air pollution levels are below the GLC guideline
concentration.'[13] Other district councils with a worse legacy of air
pollution, such as Barnsley and Rossendale, have made reference to

air quality standards in their development plans, and to their intentions to meet these targets principally by means of their domestic smoke control programmes.[13]

Cheshire County Council went much further: it sought to include, within its structure plan, policies on air quality which could have had a significant effect on the expansion of the County's principal industrial base (Chapter 3). The most radical of those policies proposed that, in those areas where the World Health Organization target concentrations for smoke and sulphur dioxide were not exceeded, any new development (industrial or otherwise), the emissions from which might cause these levels to be exceeded, would not normally be permitted.[34] On the south bank of the River Mersey there are areas of land ideally suited to the expansion of the established petrochemical industries. The stringent application of the proposed policies could well jeopardize such expansion. Obviously, the industries concerned were hostile to Cheshire's proposals; during the Examination in Public of the structure plan, they were supported in their opposition by the Department of Industry and by the Alkali Inspectorate, who stressed the technical problems and uncertainties in calculating the effect of individual discharges on ambient concentrations.

In the Secretary of State's modifications to Cheshire's plan, those policies which originally made reference to the World Health Organization targets were either deleted or revised so as to remove the quantitative standards (Chapter 3). Cheshire was seeking to apply the powers of land use regulation to a part of the physical environment, the atmosphere, where controls and enforcement have traditionally been less than rigorous: such a departure from the accepted norms, and especially on an *ad hoc*, purely local basis, was obviously not acceptable to central government.

The interest shown by planning authorities in standards of atmospheric quality stems from their immediate concern with the effects of a polluted atmosphere upon a local population. A control authority such as the Alkali Inspectorate is more concerned with formulating and enforcing the statutory requirements on pollution arrestment to be observed by a relatively small number of industrialists. The 'best practicable means' approach (with emission standards embodied in the non-statutory presumptive limits) can be readily translated into a series of working practices and instructions which can be understood by management. Assessing the effect on ambient concentrations of a given discharge from a factory chimney requires the application of a model of atmospheric dispersion. Even in ideal conditions, the predictions of such models are accurate to no more than factors of two or three; near buildings or other topographical features concentrations may diverge widely from the calculated levels. Moreover, in areas containing a number of sources of emission, it would be almost impossible to attribute any violation of the air quality standard to the discharge from a particular stack. These intractable problems of enforcement are cited by both industry and the Alkali Inspectorate as one of the principal objections to air quality standards as a system of pollution control.

Nevertheless, the Royal Commission on Environmental Pollution has expressed itself to be, in very general terms, in favour of the use of air quality 'guidelines'.[9] These would not be fixed, statutory limits, but would form 'a framework for the rational consideration of air quality, and especially to assist in regional planning and in the formulation of long-term aims for pollution reduction.' By proposing 'target bands' rather than a simple limit; by suggesting separate bands for rural and for industrial areas; by advocating existing methods (such as 'best practicable means' and smoke control areas) for the achievement of the proposed objective, the scheme formulated by the Royal Commission arguably possesses a sufficient degree of flexibility and pragmatism to be compatible with the traditional UK approach to pollution control.

Although the Department of the Environment has not, at the time of writing, formally responded to the Royal Commission's Fifth Report, the advice it contained is acknowledged in the most recent circular concerned with clean air.[35] In addition to some minor amendments to the Clean Air Acts,[36] this circular is concerned with possible changes in the practice of air pollution control as a result of a Commission of the European Communities' directive[37] on air quality guidelines (very similar to those recommended independently by the Royal Commission).[34] Other member states of the European Economic Community do not share the UK's long-standing aversion to quantitative standards in pollution control and the directive sets limits on the permissible concentrations of sulphur dioxide and suspended particulates.

Local authorities containing areas where limits are currently exceeded are urged, in this circular, to 'take into account the need to attain the limit values within a reasonable time when preparing or reviewing structure plans or local plans.'[35] Nevertheless, policies as stringent as the ones sought by Cheshire are still rejected, for the circular explicitly states that adherence to the directive does not imply a prohibition on the siting of air pollution sources in areas where existing concentrations fall below the limit values. The circular makes no concessions on the role of planning conditions: they must not be used to secure controls which are available under specific pollution legislation. Moreover, the sanction of planning refusal should be used only when the development 'would result in a significant deterioration of local air quality even after the use of specific powers to control pollution.'[25]

It is perhaps a telling reflection on the effectiveness of those 'specific powers' that, despite their application, a 'significant deterioration' remains a possibility. While such occurrences remain conceivable it seems likely that few planning authorities will voluntarily deny themselves the use of their own statutory powers to prevent additional pollution of the local atmosphere.

REFERENCES AND NOTES

[1] *Digest of Environmental Pollution and Water Statistics*, 4, Dept. of the Environment, HMSO, London, 1982.

[2] The Health and Safety at Work Act, 1974, and the Control of Pollution Act, 1974, repealed the majority of the lesser provisions of the Alkali Act. The Inspectorate currently operates under the authority of the remaining (but substantial) sections of the 1906 Act and the relevant sections of the Health and Safety at Work Act. It is proposed to repeal the Alkali Act *in toto* and to confer similar powers of control (i.e. the 'best practicable means' approach) by orders under the 1974 Act.

[3] Alkali, etc., Works Regulation Act, 1906, s. 7(1).

[4] Obtainable singly but also published as appendices to the Inspectorate's annual reports.

[5] *110th Annual Report on Alkali, etc., Works 1973*, Department of the Environment, HMSO, London, 1974.

[6] For operational purposes England and Wales are divided into fifteen districts, in each of which the duties are exercised, in the name of the Chief Inspector, by a District Alkali Inspector assisted by one, or in some cases, two Alkali Inspectors. The Chief Inspector, his three deputies and four technical assistants, are based at the London headquarters.

[7] *Industrial Air Pollution 1976*, Health and Safety Executive, HMSO, London, 1978.

[8] *104th Annual Report on Alkali, etc., Works 1967*, Ministry of Housing and Local Government, HMSO, London, 1968.

[9] Royal Commission on Environmental Pollution, *Fifth Report. Air Pollution Control: an Integrated Approach*, Cmnd. 6371, HMSO, London, 1976.

[10] The Commission reports, it should be noted, that the local authorities prosecute a smaller percentage of offenders against the Clean Air Acts than does the Inspectorate under the Alkali Act.

[11] Clean Air Act, 1956, s. 34(1).

[12] *103rd Annual Report on Alkali, etc., Works 1966*, Ministry of Housing and Local Government, HMSO, London, 1967.

[13] Questionnaire returns, quoted in C. E. Miller, C. Wood, and J. McLoughlin, 'Land Use Planning and Pollution Control', *Report to the Social Science Research Council*, Pollution Research Unit, University of Manchester, 1980, vol. I.

[14] 'Planning and Clean Air', Draft circular (unpublished), Department of the Environment, London, 1972.

[15] Publication was deferred pending the *Fifth Report* of the Royal Commission on Environmental Pollution to which the Government had not responded in early 1982.

[16] Control of Pollution Act, 1974, ss. 79 and 80.

[17] C. E. Miller *et al.*, op.cit., vol. IV.

[18] *Industrial Air Pollution 1978*, Health and Safety Executive, HMSO, London, 1980.

[19] F. Pearce, 'Fear of the Dole Keeps Britain's Dirtiest Factory Open', *New Scientist*, 90 (1981), 745.

[20] Or, it must be added, if a tax was levied on smoke-producing fuels.

[21] Local Government Reports (71 *LGR* 261).

[22] The observance of 'best practicable means' is a sufficient defence in summary proceedings under the Public Health Act, 1936, s. 94, but not for action in the High Court under s. 100.

[23] *109th Annual Report on Alkali, etc., Works 1972*, Department of the Environment, HMSO, London, 1973.

[24] 'Control of Smells from the Animal Waste Processing Industry', Department of the Environment, Circular 43/76, HMSO, London, 1976.

[25] Alkali, etc. Works Regulation Act, 1906, s. 22.

[26] See, for instance, J. Bugler, *Polluting Britain*, Penguin, Harmondsworth, 1972 or 'The Alkali Inspectorate', Social Audit, London, 1974.

[27] Clean Air Act, 1956, s. 10. This right of approval applies to any chimney emitting 'gases' and not merely gaseous products of combustion.

[28] C. Wood, *Town Planning and Pollution Control*, Manchester University Press, Manchester, 1976.

[29] In 1976 the Secretary of State for Scotland, following a lengthy public inquiry, imposed some seventy conditions on an outline planning consent for the construction of an oil refinery at Nigg Point in Ross and Cromarty. Among the many pollution-related conditions was one which required that 'the sulphur content of any fuel burnt in the refinery shall not exceed 2.5% by weight'.

[30] Control of Pollution Act, 1974, ss. 76(3)(d) and 104 (1)(a) and the Oil Fuel (Sulphur Content of Gas Oil) Regulations, 1976 (SI 1976, No. 1988).

[31] 'Planning Files', Application N.4090, Newcastle under Lyme Borough Council, Newcastle under Lyme, 1977.

[32] Royal Commission on Environmental Pollution, *Seventh Report: Agriculture and Pollution*, Cmnd. 7644, HMSO, London, 1979.

[33] In 1975, the Greater London Council published its 'guidelines' on the ambient concentrations of five atmospheric pollutants; sulphur dioxide, smoke, carbon monoxide, ozone, and lead ('Joint Report of the Planning Committee and Public Services Committee', Council Minutes, Greater London Council, London, 1975). For the first three pollutants listed above, the guidelines correspond to the World Health Organization standards.

[34] *Air Quality Criteria and Guides for Urban Air Pollutants*, World Health Organization, Geneva, 1972.

[35] 'Clean Air', Dept. of the Environment, Circular 11/81, HMSO, London, 1981.

[36] Included in the Local Government, Planning and Land Act, 1980, schedule 2.

[37] 'Council Directive on Air Quality Limit Values and Guide Values for Sulphur Dioxide and Suspended Particulates', 80/779/EEC, *Official Journal of the European Communities*, 23, L 229/30, 30 Aug. 1980.

3
AIR POLLUTION IN CHESHIRE

The 1970s witnessed a remarkable change in public expectations of the quality of their surroundings. Yet demands for an improved environment were often accompanied by equally urgent calls for industrial growth, for more housing, for ever greater agricultural output, and for more areas of 'green open space'. A recognition of the incompatibility of these aims was not always achieved painlessly. Cheshire may be described as the birthplace of the chemical industry; and there occurred within one small area of this county a number of developments which well illustrated the role of land use planning in arbitrating between these conflicting aspirations (Plate 1).

To the east, the area of interest is bounded by the River Weaver and, to the west, by the M531 motorway and the line of its proposed extension. Running north-east, the M56 and its proposed extension form another natural barrier; while to the north lies the Mersey Estuary, with an expanse of mud flats and sandbanks extending from Ellesmere Port to the mouth of the Weaver at Runcorn. South of the sandbanks lies the Manchester Ship Canal which, together with a railway line and the motorways, provides this part of Cheshire with unusually good communication links (Fig. 3.1).

This area is quite flat, and only a little above sea-level, although to the south-east, Helsby Hill (141 m) and Overton Hill (146 m) are striking features in an otherwise unimpressive landscape. These two escarpments, capped with Keuper sandstone, form the northern edge of the Mid-Cheshire Ridge and offer superb views of the estuary to the north and the Cheshire Plain to the south and west. Lying in the lee of the Clywd Hills, the area is somewhat sheltered from the moist south-westerly winds and its rainfall is a little less than the national average; it is, however, prone to fog.

Dominating the area, the petrochemical complex at Stanlow covers some 800 ha and is the largest site of its kind in Britain. With the Shell and the smaller Burmah oil refineries, together with their various subsidiary chemical plants, it stands in stark contrast to the natural grandeur of Helsby Hill. 'Visually intrusive' it certainly is, but by its very magnitude and the vast confusion of pipes, retorts, heat exchangers, and storage tanks, it makes a powerful impression on the observer. The Stanlow complex dates from 1923; construction of the fertilizer works at nearby Ince began in the late 1960s. Two oil-fired power stations, Ince 'A' and Ince 'B', complete the industrial land uses in the area. The remainder of the land is currently in agricultural

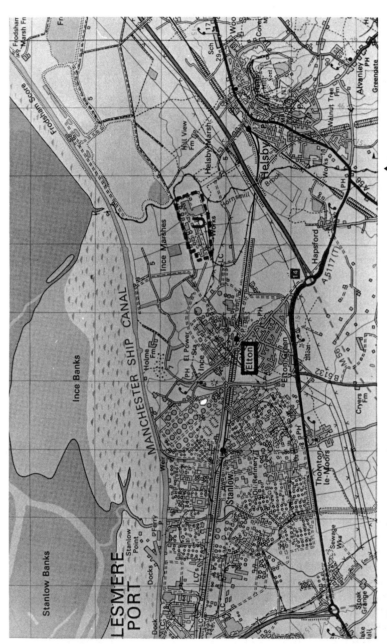

Fig. 3.1   Ince Marshes, Cheshire: UKF Fertilizer works and Elton village U: UKF,   1 : 50,000 ◀ N.   Crown copyright reserved

(dairying) use, Helsby and Frodsham Marshes having been drained during the 1939-45 War. Parts of these marshes have been used as tipping sites for silt deposits dredged from the Ship Canal but these were reclaimed for agricultural use immediately afterwards. The peat subsoil of the marshes has enabled a number of colonies of rare plants to become established; the marshes are also famous for wildfowl, especially teal and pintail, and they have been designated a 'Site of Special Scientific Interest' by the Nature Conservancy Council.

The expansion of the village of Elton (with a current population of approximately 2,000) began in the late 1960s and was a response to the demand for housing generated by the establishment of the Vauxhall car factory at Ellesmere Port and the continued growth of the petrochemical and chemical industries at Stanlow and Runcorn respectively. Elton, together with the two small towns of Helsby (population 4,500) and Frodsham (10,500), which lie to the south of the M56 and beneath the escarpments, comprise the principal areas of residential settlement in the area of interest.

The first planning applications

The Shellstar Company, a joint venture between Shell Chemicals and the American chemical concern Armour, was formed in 1963. In September 1965, Shellstar applied to Ellesmere Port Municipal Borough Council for planning permission for the construction of an ammonia plant and a fertilizer plant on a site of some 70 ha (then subject to an option by Shell Chemicals) on Ince Marshes. Since this represented a sizeable industrial development in an area designated as 'white land'[1] in the Cheshire County Development Plan of 1958, the application was eventually 'called in' for determination by the Minister of Housing and Local Government.

A local inquiry was held in connection with this application in May 1966; the Inspector was assisted by the Chief Alkali Inspector sitting as the Technical Assessor.[2] One extract from the Inspector's report of this inquiry stated that 'ammonia would be completely contained and leaks could not be tolerated for safety reasons'.[3] This statement by the applicants was neither challenged in cross-examination nor questioned in the Assessor's report. In his concluding remarks, the Inspector opined that 'the proper future of the option land' was the most important consideration before the inquiry.[3]

Planning permission was granted for the development. The decision letter of June 1966 quoted extracts from the Inspector's report, including the observation that 'it is reasonable on the information available to plan on the assumption that this area, with its particular locational advantages for petrochemical industries may all be required eventually for industrial expansion.'[3] The development was to proceed in two phases: Phase I, using, as feedstock, naphtha from the Stanlow refinery, was intended to have an annual output of 586,000 tonnes of fertilizer; Phase II was designed to raise the output to 840,000 tonnes.

During the period preceding this planning decision, a development company had acquired a large amount of land in and around Elton, a village with a population, at that time, of no more than 300. Informal contacts between developers and the local authorities, Chester Rural District Council (RDC), and Cheshire County Council, were held during which the developers were advised that their proposed target population of 5,000-6,000 was unacceptably high. However, the expansion of Elton had been anticipated in 1961 when proposals for a West Cheshire Green Belt were drawn up.

In October 1966, the planners intimated that a development catering for a population of about 2,500 would be regarded with more favour. This figure was considered to be more compatible with the capacity of a new sewage disposal works, which Chester RDC was proposing to construct in the vicinity. Consultations with the Mersey and Weaver River Authority (now part of the North West Water Authority) and the Ministry of Agriculture produced no objections to the proposals. Outline planning permission was then sought for the development of 37 ha of the 58 ha believed to be owned by the developers. Twenty-three hectares (of the 37 ha) lay in the submitted Green Belt; to the west, the proposed development reached to within 400 m of the perimeter of the Stanlow complex; while, a comparable distance to the north, lay the Ince 'A' power station. The site of the proposed Shellstar works was about one mile to the north-east. Chester RDC had made no observations during the local inquiry which preceded the Shellstar decision, even though they were then aware of the proposals for Elton's expansion.

The Rural District desired the expansion of Elton; the County planners, however, were somewhat concerned at the prospect of residential developments so close to industry. The application was advertised and submitted to the Minister as a significant departure from the County Development Plan. The Minister subsequently informed the County that he would not intervene and that they were to decide the matter as they saw fit. In July 1967, the Development Subcommittee of Cheshire County Council granted outline planning permission for the scheme, subject to conditions relating to the layout, design, and phasing of the development.

Early in 1968, after informal approaches from the developers, the local planning authority agreed that an increased target population for the expanded Elton could be considered, subject to the satisfactory provision of sewage disposal facilities. The developers then consulted the sewage disposal authority (Chester RDC) and were informed that the capacity of the works, due to be completed in 1969, could cater for an additional population of the order of 4,350. By increasing the area of land for housing to 49 ha (by decreasing the proportion allocated for 'amenity' and tree belts) and by raising the average density to thirty houses per hectare, a total of approximately 1,400 dwellings could be built, housing a population of the order of 4,500.

In mid-1968, a revised master plan was submitted to Chester RDC, who held delegated powers of development control from the County Council under the Town and Country Planning Act, 1962, and planning permission was granted, subject to a few modifications, in February 1969. The main points of the finally agreed proposals related to the development of a site of around 40 ha (part of which was rather closer to the refinery than the original plan), a target population of 4,500, a tree belt and a peripheral road system to surround and limit the village. Building was to be carried out in six phases, beginning in 1969 and to be completed in 1977. In October 1969, the first residents moved in and began to complain (in most cases, directly to Shell) about the pollution to which they were subjected, especially odours emanating from the refinery complex. Meanwhile, the recently completed Shellstar plant was also experiencing problems.

Two attempts to 'start up' the ammonia plant were unsuccessful and, with the advent of abundant supplies of natural gas from the North Sea, naphtha was replaced as the basic feedstock. In 1969, Armour left the venture and Shellstar became a wholly-owned subsidiary of Shell. A serious fire in 1971 further delayed production, and in 1973 Shell sold Shellstar to a Dutch company, UKF (Unie van Kunstmestfabrieken) who, unlike Shell, had considerable experience of this type of plant. A major programme of work was begun to improve the performance of the plant. By 1975, the annual output of fertilizer had reached 430,000 tonnes (77 per cent of the Phase I target figure). It is now conceded by the company that promises on noise, nuisance, and air pollution given at the 1966 inquiry were, although made in good faith, somewhat over-optimistic. In their defence, they now maintain that expensive modifications led to eventual improvements; that the earlier faults could be attributed to design inadequacies often associated with construction under a 'fixed price contract'; and that the manufacture of fertilizers lay outside the main stream of Shell's activities. Nevertheless, by 1974, Shellstar had acquired a poor reputation among the residents of nearby communities, especially Helsby, who repeatedly complained about smell, noise, and gaseous emissions from the plant. In consequence, when UKF sought permission to extend the plant in 1974 they were to meet with an organized, informed, and determined local opposition: unlike 1966, bland assurances on pollution would not go unchallenged.

Subsequent applications

Before considering the planning application for the third phase of the fertilizer works, it is necessary to note a number of further attempts to gain consent for residential development in Elton. Successive decisions reveal a gradual change in the attitudes of the local and central authorities to sensitive development in an area which, with consent given in December 1970 for a second oil-fired power station, Ince 'B', was soon to be encircled by major industrial installations, all of which were registered under the Alkali Act and were sources of atmospheric pollution.

A few landowners in the area attempted to take advantage of the booming market in land at that time. In one particular application, relating to 4 ha of land to the south-west of the village centre and bounded to the south by the A5117 trunk road, pollution was ingenuously cited as the justification for the change of use from agriculture to housing. A letter accompanying the application read:

The land around the holding is mostly developed for industrial or residential use. The holding is not large enough to be worked so as to provide a living and the factory effluence in the air does not encourage good grass to grow. In consequence, we feel that residential development is the only logical [*sic*] use to which this land can be put.[4]

Cheshire County Council consulted the river authority, who raised no objection to this application; however, as with the master plan, neither the local public health authorities nor the Alkali Inspector was consulted. In refusing permission, the County Council's stated reasons referred, not to pollution, but to Green Belt conservation and to the need to contain Elton's expansion within the limits of the peripheral road detailed in the master plan.

The applicant then appealed against this refusal to the Secretary of State and a local inquiry was held. In his report, the Inspector at this inquiry commented 'housing development should be kept well away from the large industrial complex … but the appeal site is just sufficiently far from the industrial area so as not to be unduly affected by it.'[5] The Secretary of State accepted his Inspector's recommendation and in June 1972 allowed the appeal, subject to conditions which included the planting of trees on the southern boundary of the site. Precisely what led the Inspector to conclude that the site was 'just sufficiently far' from the Stanlow complex to be not 'unduly affected' is not made clear. However, in another ministerial decision, given only a year later, a hardening of official attitudes is apparent.

The original developers, now under the aegis of Bovis Homes, sought to increase the extent of their Phase 3, to the west of the village. This involved another encroachment on the Green Belt and a further advance towards the Stanlow refinery. The County Council, however, had gradually grown concerned at the environmental implications of the Elton expansion. So much so that they informed Chester Rural District of the need to retain an adequate buffer zone between the new housing and both the trunk road and the refinery. However, once again it was on grounds of Green Belt conservation, not pollution, that Chester RDC, acting on the recommendation of the County Planning Officer, refused planning permission.

The County then consulted Shell, who declared their opposition to housing close to the boundary of their complex, and stated that 'large areas of land to the east of the refinery have attendant noise and air-borne effluent problems'. Shell then proceeded to buy up large areas of land to the west of Elton to preclude the possibility of further housing (and complaints). When the County belatedly consulted the Alkali Inspectorate, this body was similarly opposed to housing so close to major petrochemical industry.

When a second application for permission to develop on this site was refused, Bovis appealed to the Secretary of State. This appeal was dealt with by written representations. Statements were received from Shell (UK) Ltd, the Alkali Inspectorate, and the Department of Trade and Industry. Shell contended that:

On general grounds it would appear to be good planning to leave open a green belt between the residential area and the boundary of such a large industrial complex and furthermore whereas the original scheme for development showed playing fields on the westerly side, the latest proposals are for houses to be built on this land and on the land under appeal. All these areas lie downwind of the refinery for 40% of the time ... While the Company makes continuous efforts to minimise any detrimental effects on the environment as a result of industrial activities, it doubts whether new residents in this area will in practice find the quality of life they may have expected. We see already a strong upward tendency in the number of their complaints against alleged nuisance.[4]

The statement from the Alkali Inspectorate echoed these views and declared that the land in question could be subject to odours. However, in their submission, Bovis did not forgo the opportunity of reminding the Secretary of State that, only a year earlier, he had seen fit to grant permission for residential development on a site equally close to the refinery.

Cheshire's refusal to give permission in this and earlier applications had been confined to Green Belt considerations because they were not convinced that pollution alone constituted legitimate (i.e.

land use planning) reasons for denying consent. These doubts were to be dispelled when the decision letter of October 1973 rejecting the Bovis appeal explained 'the evidence which has been given on the risk of air pollution on this site is in itself a conclusive reason why this land should not be released for housing.'[6]

The UKF application

In November 1974, the Planning Department of Ellesmere Port and Neston Borough Council received an application for planning permission for an extension (Phase III) of the UKF works. Permission was sought for development on a 10 ha site adjacent to the north of the existing works, for 'the construction of plant and machinery and for the manufacture of ammonia, and associated plant and buildings for use in connection with the manufacture of chemical fertilisers'. The application was considered to be a 'county matter', involving as it did a departure from the 1958 County Development Plan which designated Ince Marshes as 'white land'.

The County planners were aware of the proposed additional ammonia plant and had made some preliminary preparations prior to the formal submission of the application. In so far as the application involved no new chemical processes, only the duplication of existing plant, it was fairly straightforward. However, the principal concern of the local planning authority was that this proposal, if permitted, would represent yet another encroachment on Ince Marshes. Granting permission in this instance might prejudice their case, should they choose to oppose similar developments in the future. The gradual expansion of industry in this locality could lead to a situation in which eventually the whole of Ince Marshes, and conceivably Helsby and Frodsham Marshes as well, would be given over to industry, thereby completing a continuous belt of development along the estuary of the Mersey from New Brighton to Runcorn.

Cheshire asked Cremer and Warner, a firm of chemical consultants who had recently been commissioned to carry out a county-wide study of the chemical industry,[7] to examine the possible hazard and pollution potential which might be associated with the proposals. However, these preparations were brought to an abortive conclusion when, in March 1975 and to the surprise of the Cheshire officers, the Secretary of State announced his intention to decide the application himself 'in view of the need to consider the environmental implications of further petrochemical plants in this area, and the questions which the application raised about safety and the risks of pollution and noise disturbance.'

Once the Minister had decided to invoke the 'call in' procedure, of course, responsibility for determining the UKF application passed from local to central government. Nevertheless, the County and the various district councils were not content to leave the matter there. With the 1966 inquiry very much in their minds, they were resolved to prepare a cogent case to present at any inquiry into this application. They were especially anxious to secure real safeguards on pollution and hazard from the proposed extension to what had been an unsatisfactory plant. Both neighbouring authorities, Chester District Council (who were now concerned about the effect on Elton) and Vale Royal District Council, resolved to oppose the development.

Earlier, the County had received the Cremer and Warner report on the proposals: after a thorough investigation, with the willing co-operation of the UKF management, the consultants concluded that they knew of no technical reason for opposing the development. Nevertheless, they listed a series of suggestions for measures to assist in controlling atmospheric emissions and noise levels and in reducing hazard potential, which could be proposed as planning conditions should the Minister ultimately approve the application.

These recommendations from Cremer and Warner, a study of the implications of further development on Ince Marshes, and the letters of objection received from local organizations, were incorporated in a joint report prepared by the planning departments of Cheshire County and Ellesmere Port Borough. This document, together with a report by the Borough Chief Environmental Health Officer, were before the members of the Ellesmere Port Planning Committee, when, in June 1975, the district officers recommended that no objection to the application be raised, subject to the imposition of satisfactory conditions, should the Minister finally give his approval. The officers were aware of the 'controls which will be enforced under legislation other than the Planning Acts'[8] and confined their conditions to noise, drainage requirements, landscaping, and access. They did, however further recommend that the Borough Planning Officer and the Chief Environmental Health Officer be empowered to seek an agreement with UKF, under the Cheshire County Council Act[9] and planning legislation, to secure maximum improvement of the existing plant and compliance with the Health Officer's recommendations, namely that UKF give assurances on the control of noise and gaseous and particulate emissions from the new plant.

The elected members of the Committee, however, were not disposed to accept their officers' advice. Instead, they resolved to inform the County that they were 'seriously concerned at the implications of the application and on the basis of the evidence so far adduced were opposed to it'. They went on to list stringent conditions to be imposed if permission were to be given, including a provision under which UKF should forgo their rights to carry out 'permitted development'.[10]

By including this clause on permitted development the members were presumably seeking to prevent the possibility of the applicants subsequently increasing the capacity of (and hence the pollution from) the works by making a series of minor, and therefore permitted, additions and improvements to the plant. Whether the members realized the consequences of this measure is open to question since, in practice, it would have meant that the Borough Planning Department would be deluged by a flood of planning applications for trivial additions and alterations to the plant.

This resolution was before the members of the County Planning Subcommittee when they met shortly afterwards. They too received a copy of the joint report and their officers similarly recommended that no objection be raised to the application, while urging the Secretary of State to impose conditions should he finally elect to grant planning permission. Again, the officers' advice was rejected and overwhelming opposition to the proposal was declared on the grounds that inadequate safeguards on health, safety, and environment had been given. The Committee passed a resolution, a composite of those from Vale Royal[11] and Ellesmere Port, stating their objections and listing their required conditions, including the clause precluding permitted development.

HM Alkali and Clean Air Inspectorate had been involved with this application from the outset. The developers had discussed their proposals informally with the District Alkali Inspector before seeking planning approval. When the application had become a county matter, Cheshire's planning department also sought the views of the Inspectorate. In January 1975, the Alkali Inspector, together with representatives of the Factory Inspectorate, the planning departments of Cheshire and Ellesmere Port, and their consultants, Cremer and Warner, attended a meeting at County Hall during which the air pollution and hazard implications of the UKF proposals were discussed. After reading the Cremer and Warner report, the Alkali Inspector wrote to the County Planner in April 1975 and informed him that there was little in the document with which he disagreed. He went on to state that the Alkali Inspectorate was the statutory air pollution control authority and he gave an assurance that the points raised by the consultants would be included in his 'best practicable means' requirements for the proposed ammonia plant.

However, this assurance from the Alkali Inspector was not sufficient to satisfy the members of the local authorities. In seeking further controls in the form of stringent planning conditions and formal agreements with the developers, the councillors were taking account of the considerable local feeling against the existing works and hostility towards its expansion. Not surprisingly, the UKF management resented the stance adopted by the local authorities over atmospheric discharges: they felt they were being asked to serve two masters, the Alkali Inspector and the planner. Moreover, they particularly resented the attitude of the Ellesmere Port Council who had constantly stated their wish to encourage expansion of the petrochemical industry and the industrial development of Ince Marshes: why, then, had they chosen to oppose this, the first major industrial application since local government reorganization in April 1974?

It can be assumed that considerable informal negotiation occurred between Cheshire, Ellesmere Port, and the UKF management, for at a full council meeting in November 1975, the Chairman of Ellesmere Port Planning Committee made a public statement seeking to make the Council's position perfectly clear and to explain the apparent contradiction in its attitude. While it remained, he declared, the policy of Ellesmere Port to do all in its power to encourage expansion of existing industries and to allow the development of Ince Marshes, in this particular case, they were concerned at the environmental implications of the UKF proposals. Nevertheless, if UKF were prepared to offer adequate safeguards to protect 'amenities, environment and health', their opposition would be overcome. A similar statement was made a few weeks later at a meeting of the Cheshire County Planning Subcommittee.

With the views of their members made clearer, the planners of Cheshire, Ellesmere Port, and Vale Royal prepared a joint case for presentation at the forthcoming local inquiry. In addition, they embarked upon a series of meetings with UKF in order to arrive at a list of mutually agreed measures satisfying the requirements of the various councils and to be suggested as planning conditions in the event of the Secretary of State finally granting his consent to the development.

UKF were happy to accept standard conditions relating to such matters as the submission of detailed plans, time-limits on the planning permission, access arrangements, and landscaping. They accepted conditions relating to noise, not only noise during construction but noise generated on first commissioning the plant; they also agreed to undertake to monitor and restrict noise levels during normal operation. On atmospheric pollution, they undertook to co-operate with the Alkali Inspector and to incorporate in the design measures to minimize emissions of ammonia and other gaseous products. However, on the single question of the monitoring of gaseous and particulate emissions, they maintained, and were to maintain, an emphatic and unequivocal refusal to accept the following condition:

Equipment to be agreed by the Local Planning Authority to monitor ammonia and particulate emissions and other matters shall be provided, operated and maintained by the Applicant at points and frequencies to be agreed with the

Local Planning Authority. Access to these monitors and records shall be given at all times to persons duly authorised by the County and District Councils. The full monitoring programme will be reviewed at least annually by the Local Planning Authority in association with the Applicant and amended as necessary.[4]

Unlike the other local authorities, the City of Chester Council[12] àdhered to an attitude of total opposition to the UKF expansion scheme. If the 10 ha addition to the UKF site were merely a prelude to the industrial development of all the land on Ince Marshes in Shell Chemicals' ownership, Elton (and Ince) would eventually be bounded on three sides by polluting industries. This was clearly unacceptable to the local authority and, in their first indication that the decision to allow the Elton expansion might perhaps have been less than prudent, the Chester City Planning Committee decided, in May 1975, to ask the Secretary of State to consider whether the village of Elton should be permitted to expand to its target size, in the event of Ince Marshes being given over totally to petrochemical industry.

Exactly what the Secretary of State was expected to do is not clear. Presumably, the Chester City councillors were mooting the possibility of revoking planning permission for the later phases of development yet to be built, and the possibility that the resulting compensation to Bovis might be paid from central funds. Chester City argued that if they were to use revocation to abort the now regretted scheme, the inevitable and enormous compensation could not be met by one single district, but should come from the national or perhaps county revenues, especially since it was Cheshire County, albeit with the active encouragement of Chester RDC, who originally approved the whole development.[13] However, at one stage it appeared possible to curtail the expansion of Elton without expense to the public purse.

In 1975, doubts arose among the county planners on the status of the outstanding planning permission for the later phases (3, 5, and 6) of the expansion scheme. Accordingly, Cheshire sought the advice of counsel and were informed that, since not *all* details of the scheme had been submitted within the statutory time-limit,[14] the original outline permission of 1967 for the as yet unbuilt phases had lapsed. Presumably, Bovis were similarly aware of this anomalous position, which put the development value of their land in jeopardy, for, in August 1975, they submitted an application for detailed planning permission for Phase 5.

No decision was given either by the County or by Chester City, and Bovis lodged an appeal against non-determination[15] with the Secretary of State. However, this appeal was withdrawn after Bovis, early in 1976, re-submitted an application for full planning permission for Phase 5—an act which could be interpreted as an admission that planning consent, under the 1967 permission, had lapsed by default. If, as it was believed, planning permission on the later phases had lapsed by virtue of a technicality, then hypothetical questions about revocation (and hence compensation) did not arise. By refusing consent for the re-submitted applications, Chester City could, without expense to ratepayers, have terminated the scheme and halted the growth of Elton's population at well below the envisaged 4,500.

In the event, Chester City Council chose not to take such a course. In July 1976, they granted full planning consent for Phase 5. In justifying this decision, a Chester City planner has argued that, while the local planning authority might have a responsibility to deter prospective Elton residents, they are no less responsible to the occupants of the houses already built (Phases 1, 2, and 4). Any action by the local authority which publicly indicated that the environment of Elton was less than satisfactory could result in the latter being left with virtually unsaleable properties—a novel form of planning blight.[13]

The local inquiry

At the local inquiry into the UKF application, held between 13 and 27 January 1976, UKF began their case by outlining the economic rationale of the proposed expansion. The United Kingdom imported 15 per cent of its ammonia, principally from countries which could no longer be considered reliable sources following the oil crisis of 1974. The rival plant under construction at Billingham would lead to UK self-sufficiency in ammonia; but increasing demand, both for fertilizer and industrial uses, would lead to a 350,000 tonnes shortfall by 1980-81. It was precisely to meet this deficit that a second ammonia plant was required at Ince. This plant would cost £40,000,000-£50,000,000, half of which would be in the form of much-needed foreign (Dutch) investment, and it would create 120 permanent jobs in an area of high unemployment. The principal advantage in building at Ince lay in the opportunity to exploit the technical skill and management expertise which had been acquired by the staff of the existing works. In addition, the site was already well served by rail, sea, and road communications. The proposed and existing sites were 'white land' under the County Development Plan of 1958 and, as recently as 1975, Ellesmere Port Borough and Cheshire County Councils had expressed the view that Ince Marshes should be given over to industrial development.'

Having argued the need for the ammonia plant, having given their reasons for wishing to build it at Ince, and having stated their presumed right to do so, the developers then turned to the question of visual amenity, health, safety, and pollution in anticipation of the objections to come. The new plant, the applicants claimed, would be hidden from view from Elton and Ince by the power stations, and 'this was presumably the reason for the lack of any objections from residents of these two communities.' Similarly, when viewed from Helsby, the new plant would merge with the existing works. Technical experts were called and the safety record of UKF was extolled. These experts concluded that the risks of explosion in the plant were minimal and acceptable; even in the worst imaginable combination of circumstances Helsby would suffer no more than a few broken windows. In a similar expression of confidence, it was maintained that there would be little addition to noise levels attributable to the new plant.

On the subject of atmospheric pollution, three eminent authorities gave evidence in support of UKF's claim that the design and operation of the proposed plant would be such as to limit gaseous emissions—even in the event of major system failure—to levels which posed no conceivable health risk to nearby residents.[16] Nevertheless, UKF were not prepared to monitor gaseous and particulate emissions and make the data available, as required by the local planning authorities in the list of suggested conditions. The new plant would involve a scheduled process and thus control of atmospheric emissions came under the jurisdiction of the Alkali Inspectorate: duplication of control by means of a planning condition was not acceptable to the UKF management. However, they continued:

If ever a relatively simple and proven accurate method of monitoring was devised then the company undertook to discuss immediately with the planning authorities the uses of such equipment; but with existing sophisticated methods requiring the time of skilled operators, they were reluctant to enter into a full monitoring programme.[17]

The District Alkali Inspector gave evidence to the effect that the measures proposed by the company to minimize discharges to the atmosphere from the new plant were adequate in so far as they met the 'best practicable means' criteria. At start-up or during breakdowns, passing the waste gases through a flare before discharge would prevent the escape of gases like hydrogen, carbon monoxide, and methane. Should unfavourable meteorological conditions coincide with accidental discharges of large amounts of pollutants, then Helsby residents might be aware of them; however, such occurrences would pose no risk to public health. The Alkali Inspector finally declared that 'the Health and Safety Executive neither opposed nor supported the application.'[17]

The representative of the Transport and General Workers' Union, on the other hand, was only too ready to voice his union's support for the development. UKF has proved to be a good employer and any addition to the number of established, secure jobs in this area of high unemployment was to be welcomed.

The desire of the local authorities to secure assurances on noise and atmospheric pollution was felt to be, to some extent, compromised by their frequently stated aim of encouraging industrial expansion and thus alleviating unemployment. The degree to which their case might influence the final decision of the Secretary of State was imponderable. However, a searching and thorough cross-examination by an experienced counsel might evince from the applicants clear and explicit statements on pollution limitation, which might be used to exert moral, if not exactly legal, pressure in any future dispute. Conscious of the poor record of the Shellstar plant and the largely unquestioned acceptance of the evidence given at the 1966 inquiry, the local planning authorities were determined to pursue a more vigorous examination on this occasion.

Prior to the inquiry, Cheshire County and the Districts of Vale Royal and Ellesmere Port had been in close collaboration over the application. Cheshire and Vale Royal briefed counsel to present their views, while Ellesmere Port, whose case was almost identical, were represented by their Deputy Borough Secretary, a solicitor. Chester City Council remained adamant in their opposition to the development.

The representative of the County Planning Department began by describing the extent of the public feeling aroused by the pollution, mostly in the form of smell, noise, and fumes, which had resulted from the malfunctioning of the existing plant, and the consequent fears that the conditions could only be aggravated by the addition of another ammonia plant. These fears were apparent not only from forty-two letters received opposing the application but also from comments forcefully expressed during recent public participation exercises in connection with the preparation of the draft Structure Plan. Aware of the depth of public concern, the County Council were determined to ensure that any new development in the area should impose no further burden on the amenity, environment, and health of the local communities.

Evidence by the County's Chief Environmental Health Officer[18] on the pollution, safety, and noise implications of the new plant was not substantially different from that given by the developer's witnesses. Nevertheless, the County wished to urge the Secretary of State to grant permission only with the imposition of stringent safeguards along the lines of the agreed conditions together with the disputed condition on monitoring. In justification of this demand, this officer declared[17] that a planning condition requiring an applicant to undertake to monitor gaseous emissions could not be seen as contravening the Town and Country Planning Act, 1971, nor the government's advisory document on the use of planning conditions.[19] In his opinion, the members of the Royal Commission on Environmental Pollution were mistaken when, in their Fifth Report,[20] they had opposed the use of planning conditions to control discharges from scheduled works: in reality there was no duplication of powers, since the Alkali Inspector was concerned only with emissions from specific works, whereas the planning authority was responsible for air quality in general, i.e. for the accumulation of emissions to the atmosphere from all sources—domestic and both scheduled and non-scheduled industrial processes.

The most determined opposition to the proposed development came, not surprisingly, from the local parish councils and amenity societies. The parish councils of Alvanley, Elton, Frodsham, and Helsby together with the Helsby Environmental Protection Association, the Frodsham Society, and Elton Ratepayers' Association combined as a united opposition to UKF's proposals. The desire for a rural home away from the conurbations of Manchester and Merseyside has had the effect of increasing the proportion of professional, articulate, and middle-class households in the attractive villages of North Cheshire. Moreover, many residents were, or had been, themselves employed in the chemical industry. It is not surprising, therefore, that they were able to prepare and present an informed and well-argued case.

However, as UKF were not slow to remark, no written objections had been received from individual residents of Ince and Elton. Elton Parish Council had made its opposition clear in a letter, but they had not been able to organize a campaign comparable with those in Helsby and Frodsham. Elton was an expanding village, with a programme of development designed to meet the housing needs of young first-time buyers, many of whom worked in the chemical industry locally. Elton is overshadowed to the east by the Ince Power Stations, which tend to obscure from sight (and presumably from mind) the existing UKF plant. Nevertheless, the Ratepayers' Association opposed the development. If there was doubt about the opinions of Elton residents, there was none about those of Helsby and Frodsham. A consensus of local views had emerged from public meetings: in these two communities, at least, the position was quite simple—the original Shellstar plant should never have been sited at Ince and no expansion should now be permitted.

Led by a Helsby parish councillor (a lecturer in pharmaceutics at Liverpool Polytechnic) the objectors followed the now traditional strategy of amenity groups at public inquiries: firstly, they argued that the proposed development was not needed at all; secondly, if it were to be built, it should be placed elsewhere. The company's own targets for fertilizer production showed, the objectors claimed, that the existing plant was capable of supplying the necessary amount of ammonia. While they did not disagree that there would be a shortfall in indigenous ammonia supply over demand by 1981, it could be argued that this was better met by importing rather than by using as feedstock all too finite supplies of North Sea gas, which might be more prudently reserved for other chemical processes. However, if natural gas had to be the primary input, then it was only reasonable to site any new plant near to the gas terminals which were, of course, on the East Coast: Teesside, with unemployment rates even greater than in Merseyside, was an obvious candidate. As for visual impact, the view from Helsby would be worsened not only by the process and cooling towers but also by the plumes issuing from them. In addition, the objectors were not satisfied with the assurances on safety given earlier in the inquiry: memories of the Flixborough disaster (in June 1974) were still fresh in the minds of local residents.

With regard to atmospheric pollution from the existing plant, the residents' spokesman was particularly critical. Helsby, situated immediately beneath a 120 m escarpment, was peculiarly vulnerable to the accumulation of atmospheric pollutants. The frequently detectable odour of ammonia occurred in conjunction with a visible plume from the 'prill' tower. He then gave a lengthy account of the present, albeit incomplete, knowledge of the cancer risk associated with dietary nitrate. This evidence was challenged by the developers as being irrelevant but the Inspector was later to write in his report that, in view of possible risks to health and in spite of the developers' accusations of scaremongering, he 'did not accept that it was irresponsible of the local organisations to bring this matter to the inquiry'.[17]

The outcome

The Inspector's report, presented to the Secretary of State in April 1976, reveals a considerable sympathy with the concern for the environmental implications of the proposals expressed by the local authorities and the objectors at the inquiry. Most of the objectors' case, the Inspector recalled, referred to the disappointing performance of the existing works; nevertheless, these considerations were relevant since they could, by and large, be taken as an indication of the likely effects of any new development. Should this application be granted, then it was very likely that further development on Ince Marshes would ensue. Such a possibility should be given full weight in the preparation of the Cheshire Structure Plan; but any future proposal should still be taken on its merits and with particular reference to its environmental impact.

The Assessor, too, was very conscious of the pollution potential of the new plant. Moreover, he expressed the hope that an alternative to the 'prilling' process could soon be found, since this technique generally gave rise to considerable pollution problems. He also shared some of the objectors' doubts on the wisdom, with regard to long-term energy conservation, of using precious supplies of natural gas in the manufacture of ammonia.[21]

On the contentious condition requiring the applicants to undertake a programme of continuous monitoring of atmospheric discharges of ammonia and particulate matter, the Inspector wrote:

> The Assessor and I have considered the arguments for and against such a condition and we suggest that monitoring would be of value. Having regard to the submissions advanced on behalf of the applicants and the views expressed in the Fifth Report of the Royal Commission on Environmental Pollution, it is for legal consideration whether such a condition should be imposed. I would comment that the powers of the Alkali Inspectorate relate to individual works; in my opinion only planning authorities can control the cumulative build-up of atmospheric pollution in industrial areas.[17]

In his final paragraph, the Inspector recommended that outline permission be granted, but granted subject to the conditions agreed between the planning authorities and the applicant and to a condition 'requiring the monitoring of chemical emissions from the proposed ammonia plant in a manner to be agreed by the local planning authorities'.

The Secretary of State's decision to grant planning approval for the UKF extension was announced in a letter of May 1977. Planning permission was granted conditionally; but the conditions finally imposed by the Secretary of State bore little resemblance to those which were sought by the local planning authorities, which were recommended by the Planning Inspector and which, with a solitary exception, were agreed by the developers.

Not only did the Minister not accept the aim underlying the local authorities' proposed conditions, he also criticized their form: 'it is thought that as they are drafted, many are not sufficiently certain or precise to be reasonably capable of enforcement; others are unnecessary or otherwise in a form not suitable for use as planning conditions'.[22] While the Secretary of State appreciated the value of a programme of monitoring, such an exercise should not be made mandatory under a planning condition:

> it is considered wrong to impose conditions requiring the monitoring of noise or emissions to the atmosphere but it is agreed with the Inspector that there is a need for and value in monitoring. It is hoped that the local liaison committee will provide a forum in which the whole question of monitoring can be discussed and in which the results can be examined.[22]

The decision letter relating to the UKF application makes the view of the Department of the Environment perfectly clear: matters which are covered by specific legislation should not form the substance of planning conditions. This is a view with which officers of the local planning authorities involved in this development would not necessarily disagree. They would, however, argue that the planning conditions, which they hoped to see applied to any approval for UKF's proposals, were intended not to duplicate but rather to complement specific pollution control legislation.

The Minister's refusal to impose any conditions relating to air pollution served to reinforce the existing policy that the Alkali Inspectorate alone should impose and enforce controls over atmospheric emissions from scheduled processes. Yet Cheshire's planning department would insist that the condition requiring monitoring was not a covert attempt to secure some form of control over emissions to the atmosphere from either the existing or proposed plants; it was simply another contribution to the County's continuing programme of charting the distribution of atmospheric pollutants around the industrial areas on the south bank of the Mersey. As such, this requirement did not impinge on the Inspectorate's statutory duties, since these are confined to limiting specific emissions from individual sources: in contrast, the local planning authority has a responsibility for the quality of the atmosphere in general.

It is, of course, possible that UKF, advised as they were by an eminent QC, had, from the very beginning, correctly anticipated that the Secretary of State would ultimately delete any planning condition which appeared to encroach on the province of other legislation. If so, their steadfast refusal to agree to monitor is understandable. UKF's subsidiary reason for refusing to monitor, namely that it would involve the uneconomical use of skilled operatives' time, is somewhat less comprehensible. The cost of any monitoring exercise would be infinitesimal in comparison with the £50,000,000 investment represented by the proposed plant. Moreover, having produced technical experts to give evidence to the effect that there would be no conceivable risk to health from the plant, their reluctance to monitor could raise the suspicion that a possibility of nuisance, albeit harmless to health, remained.

The key to UKF's intransigence on the one outstanding point of disagreement may have been associated with the feelings of mistrust and hostility shown by some local residents and those in Helsby in particular, UKF feared that any published figures on emissions, no matter how low they might be in comparison with those from similar works or when related to objective, scientific criteria, would be used by their more implacable opponents to fuel groundless fears and to generate further opposition to petrochemical industry on the Mersey Estuary, perhaps jeopardizing the long-term future of UKF itself.

The refusal of the Secretary of State to retain the requested condition on monitoring could be interpreted as a breach of the 'polluter-pays' principle. The implication behind his decision is that if monitoring is required (and the Secretary of State agreed with the Inspector that monitoring would be useful and valuable) then it should be carried out by the local authorities and at the expense of the ratepayers, including those who are subject to pollution nuisance attributable to the plant in question. This would clearly not be in accord with the principle: while the externalities arising from the plant's operations would be borne by the local population, the economic benefits (the profits of the shareholders as well as the value gained by the consumers of the ammonia and its derivatives) would be distributed at the national, indeed, the international level.

The Cheshire Structure Plan

Many of the issues raised during the local inquiry into the UKF extension were discussed again at the Examination in Public (EIP) of Cheshire's Structure Plan in November 1977. Following a review of atmospheric pollution within the county in 1975[23] Cheshire's report of survey of the environment gave considerable attention to pollution of the atmosphere, land, and inland waters.[24] During this time, both officers and elected members were made aware of the public's desire to see the reduction of pollution among the higher priorities of County planning policy.

The written statement of the structure plan[25] included policies on hazard, noise, and water pollution; however, it was the three policy statements on air pollution which proved to be most controversial. These policies incurred the disapproval of the Department of the Environment even before the EIP was convened:

The Department welcomes the explicit recognition in the structure plan of the importance of ambient air quality. It is concerned, however, that an over-rigorous adherence to a particular quantified level of air quality universally applied in reaching planning decisions may be unsupported on scientific evidence, unworkable in practice and may unjustifiably obstruct the achievement of other policy objectives. ... The Department therefore proposes that policy statements 9.39 and 9.54 should be modified. ... The Department welcomes [policy] statement [9.40] which is in accord with good planning practice.[26]

The Department's proposed modifications to the two policies in question removed the reference to World Health Organization standards[27] as indicators of an acceptable atmospheric quality (Table 3.1).

The use of air quality standards was the subject of a lively and well-informed debate at one session of the EIP. Opposition to the County's proposals was expressed by representatives of the Departments of Industry and of the Environment, the Alkali Inspectorate, the Confederation of British Industry, and by an *ad hoc* group of oil and petrochemical companies with interests in and around Stanlow. A local trade unionist (who had voiced similar sentiments at the UKF inquiry in the previous year) declared his members' hostility to policies which, he averred, could jeopardize employment opportunities. Not unexpectedly, the local amenity groups were vocal in their support for the County's policies, which, they claimed, should be extended beyond smoke and sulphur dioxide to include all the various pollutants to which this part of Cheshire was prone.

While some speakers were opposed to the World Health Organization standards in particular, it was to the principles of using air quality standards as a form of pollution control that most opposition was directed. The industrialists objected to the inflexible nature of standards; such standards could be enforced only if imposed nationwide, for airborne pollutants had little respect for county boundaries. The Alkali Inspectorate agreed and pointed to the virtues of the pragmatism and flexibility implicit in the existing 'best practicable means' approach, in which a constant pressure for reduced emissions was tempered by a consideration of the environmental effects of the discharges and the economic implications of the control measures. In addition, the District Alkali Inspector maintained that the technical difficulties (e.g. in assessing the contribution of individual emissions from stacks to the ambient pollutant concentrations) would make the enforcement of standards almost impossible.

Policy 9.40 (Table 3.1) received the approbation of all the representatives. In discussing the siting of vulnerable development in the vicinity of existing pollution sources, the Chairman of the Panel was moved to describe the expansion of Elton village as the 'height of folly'.[28]

In summing up, Cheshire made few concessions to their opponents: the county planning authority had a right to adopt a yardstick by which to judge progress towards a cleaner atmosphere. The County's concern was with the general quality of the atmosphere; it was not, like the Inspectorate's responsibility, confined to certain gaseous pollutants from scheduled sources. If progress toward the target levels were to be prejudiced by an especially pollution-prone development, then planning consent would normally be refused.

When the Panel's report was published it revealed a sympathy with Cheshire's aims, but not with their methods. The members could not endorse the proposed use of air quality targets in Policies 9.39 and 9.54. Instead, they recommended the adoption of a single policy (Table 3.1) which would make reference to the need to consider

TABLE 3.1
Cheshire Structure Plan air pollution policies

CCC Policy	Reasons and explanations
9.39 In those parts of the County where pollution of the air does not exceed the target levels suggested by the World Health Organization development which is likely to cause these levels to be exceeded will not normally be permitted.	These parts of the County are relatively free of pollution and it is important for health and amenity reasons to ensure that they remain so. The World Health Organization has defined suitable levels which pollution should not exceed and it is unreasonable to allow significant deterioration of areas with already good standards.
9.40 There will be a general presumption against the introduction of land uses which are sensitive to pollution into areas around existing sources of air pollution if unacceptable nuisance to the new use is likely to result. Exceptions may be made for proposals where the new development would not materially delay general redevelopment, and which are not likely to give rise to additional causes for complaints.	To prevent the creation of situations where uses which are incompatible are located close together. Many such situations already exist and it is the aim of good planning to eliminate these as soon as possible, usually at the time of redevelopment. In the meantime it would be unreasonable to prevent efficient use of existing developments by refusing permission for minor development or to make the situation more enduring and costly to remedy by permitting major developments.
9.54 In those parts of the County where the pollution of the air exceeds the target levels of the World Health Organization new developments which are likely to cause additional pollution will only be allowed where both the following conditions are met: (a) where they are in themselves compatible with the achievements of the target figures suggested by the World Health Organization within ten years; (b) where, in the meantime, they do not cause unacceptable air pollution, nuisance or damage to health of local residents viewed against current national levels of pollution.	In these polluted areas it is important that residents' amenities are not made worse by further polluting industries. In some cases pollution levels are expected to improve as the normal process of industrial modernization brings lower pollution levels and it may therefore be reasonable to allow some new development where the general situation is likely to improve in the long term. It is possible that within a factory complex the World Health Organization targets may never be reached.

Source: References 25, 26, 29, and 30.

DOE proposed modification	Panel's recommendation	DOE final modification
In those parts of the County where the level of pollution of the atmosphere is believed to be acceptable, development which is likely to result in unacceptable levels of pollution will not normally be permitted. In deciding on the acceptability of a given level of pollution, the planning authority will have regard to available scientific evidence, and where appropriate will seek the advice of the authorities responsible for controlling air pollution.	Development which in the view of the County Council is likely to increase levels of air pollution to an unacceptable extent will not normally be allowed. In deciding on the acceptability of a given level of pollution, the planning authority will have regard to available scientific evidence and will seek the advice of the authorities responsible for controlling air pollution.	Development which in the opinion of the local planning authority is likely to increase levels of air pollution to an unacceptable extent will not normally be allowed. In deciding on the acceptability of a given level of pollution the planning authority will have regard to available scientific evidence and will seek the advice of the authorities responsible for controlling air pollution.
—	—	—
In those parts of the County where the level of pollution of the air is believed to be unacceptable, new developments which are likely to cause additional pollution will only be allowed where both the following conditions are met: (a) the development should be compatible with the achievement of acceptable air quality in the long term. (b) it should not itself lead to significant deterioration of air quality, nuisance or damage to health of local residents.	Delete (Replace by new 9.39)	Delete

'available scientific evidence' and to heed the advice of the 'authorities responsible for controlling air pollution' (i.e. the Alkali Inspectorate).[29] These recommendations amounted to a restatement of the existing situation under which a local planning authority, with the advice of its environmental health department or the comments of the Alkali Inspectorate, must make an intuitive judgment of the acceptability of polluting industry.

The Department of the Environment accepted the Panel's recommendation and adopted their suggested policy. The departmental attitude to the use of standards in structure plans was summed up:

> The Secretary of State accepts the Panel's recommendation that in deciding on the acceptability of a given level of air pollution the planning authority should have regard to available scientific evidence. It would however be inappropriate for him to approve policies based on standards which have not been accepted nationally and which are likely to give rise to difficulties in implementation.[30]

The disputes described in this chapter lend weight to the view that existing air pollution legislation is too fragmented: local authorities exercise control over smoke and dust emissions from combustion processes under the Clean Air Acts; the Alkali Inspectorate regulates processes scheduled under the Alkali Act; the Control of Pollution Act empowers the Secretary of State to regulate the lead and sulphur contents of motor spirit and fuel oils. When account is taken of the powers of the Minister of Agriculture, Fisheries and Food and the Secretary of State for the Environment in respect of radioactive emissions (such as those from the enrichment plant at Capenhurst near Chester) then it is clear that there is no single body with an overall responsibility to co-ordinate control over different discharges to the atmosphere, as the Royal Commission on Environmental Pollution reported.[20]

It should not be assumed that Cheshire's planners were seeking to fill this arguably vacant role (which may be compared with that of the water authorities in regard to river pollution). Chesire had chosen to view the atmosphere as part of the physical environment and to see atmospheric pollution as no less worthy of consideration in development control or strategic planning than mineral extraction or waste disposal.

Targets for atmospheric quality are necessary, Cheshire would argue, because the powers of the pollution control authorities (the Alkali Inspectorate and the environmental health departments) entail regulation of emissions at source and do not relate explicitly to their effect upon ambient concentrations. If there exists within an area a sufficient number of sources, each of which observes 'best practicable means', they could nevertheless combine to give unsatisfactory concentrations of pollutants within that area. In the absence of an alternative vehicle for introducing such targets, Cheshire chose to incorporate them within its structure plan.

While it is perhaps reasonable to question the effectiveness of Cheshire's policies as regulators of pollution, their force as planning controls cannot be denied. Indeed, the number of counsel and technical experts representing the petrochemical companies at the EIP readily attested to the gravity which the industrialists attached to the proposals. For them, the threat posed by air quality standards was real—if enforced they could well jeopardize the development of the south bank of the Mersey Estuary. That such development was contemplated was evidenced by the industrialists' active participation in the EIP debates on the land use designation of the remaining undeveloped areas of Ince Marshes and land around Thornton-le-Moors, currently in the ownership or the control of the petrochemical companies.

Should the county planning authority choose to refuse planning consent for any future development on the grounds that its atmospheric discharges would cause the air quality standards to be exceeded then, of course, the Secretary of State could resind that decision on appeal. However, his power to quash such a decision could only be compromised if it were supported by a structure plan policy which he, or a predecessor, had earlier endorsed.

Cheshire, dissatisfied with existing legislation on pollution, has sought to use planning powers to improve and maintain atmospheric quality. By its responses to Cheshire's recent initiatives, the Department of the Environment has revealed itself to be unwilling to concede such formidable powers to a local body. It would appear that where regulation of the pollution generated by a large industrial concern, whether proposed or established, is such as might endanger the economic viability of that concern, then such powers must be not only discretionary but also enforceable by a central body which takes adequate account of the national economic interest as well as of the local environment.

REFERENCES AND NOTES

[1] The designation 'white land' indicates a presumption that the existing land use (in this particular case, agriculture) shall be retained.

[2] Since ammonia manufacture is a scheduled process, the developers had consulted the Alkali Inspectorate on the pollution controls to be installed, quite independently of the planning process. It was subsequently felt by some objectors that it was improper for an Alkali Inspector to act as an Assessor at a planning inquiry when the Inspectorate

had earlier sanctioned technical aspects of the proposals. A complaint was made to the Council on Tribunals. It is now accepted that members of the Alkali Inspectorate should not act as Assessors in inquiries relating to development for which they have their own statutory responsibilities under the Alkali Act. See also R. E. Wrath and G. B. Lamb, *Public Inquiries as an Instrument of Government,* Allen & Unwin, London, 1971.

[3] 'Inspector's Report of the Local Inquiry into the Planning Application by Shell-star Ltd', Ministry of Housing and Local Government, London, 1966.

[4] This and other information about planning decisions was supplied from the files of Cheshire County Council Planning Department.

[5] 'Inspector's Report of the Local Inquiry into the Appeal by Mr J. E. Littler', APP/1993/A/36309, Dept. of the Environment, London, 1972.

[6] 'Decision Letter on Appeal by Bovis Homes', APP/1993/A/68613, Dept. of the Environment, Manchester, 1973.

[7] Cremer and Warner, 'Cheshire: Chemical and Allied Industries Survey', Cheshire County Council, Chester, 1976.

[8] 'Borough Planning Officer's Report 24/6/75', (TP/276), Ellesmere Port and Neston Borough Planning Department, Ellesmere Port, 1975.

[9] Any covenant in an agreement under s. 15 of the Cheshire County Council Act, 1968, is binding on successive owners of the land; with agreements made under s. 52 of the Town and Country Planning Act, 1971, this is true only of covenants of a negative or restrictive nature.

[10] Town and Country Planning General Development Order, 1977 (SI 1977, No. 289), Art. 4(1).

[11] Vale Royal District Council, formed in 1974 by the amalgamation of Northwich UDC, Northwich RDC and others, includes the parishes of Helsby and Fordsham.

[12] Chester RDC, together with Chester County Borough Council, formed the City of Chester District Council in 1974.

[13] Planning Officer, Chester City Council, 'Personal Communcation', 1979.

[14] Town and Country Planning Act, 1971, s. 14.

[15] Ibid., s. 37.

[16] This statement somewhat understates the hazard associated with a large-scale release of ammonia from, for instance, a ruptured storage tank.

[17] 'Inspector's Report of the Local Inquiry into the Planning Application by UKF Ltd', PNW/5146/219/1, Dept. of the Environment, London, 1977.

[18] Cheshire had an established post of Chief Environmental Health Officer within the structure of the County Planning Department. Five other county councils were listed in *Municipal Year Book, 1979,* Municipal Publications, London, as having similar posts. The presence of this officer in the Planning Department was undoubtedly very influential in determining both Chesire's attitude and response to the pollution implications of the UKF application and the County's stance on the pollution policies in the structure plan.

[19] 'The use of conditions in planning permissions', Ministry of Housing and Local Government, Circular 5/68, HMSO, London, 1968.

[20] Royal Commission on Environmental Pollution, *Fifth Report. Air Pollution Control: An Integrated Approach,* Cmnd. 6371, HMSO, London, 1976.

[21] It could be argued that fertilizer manufacture, which accounts for only 4 per cent of UK natural gas consumption, is a far more value-adding use than burning the gas in domestic heating and cooking appliances.

[22] 'Decision Letter on the Planning Application by UKF Ltd.', PNW/5146/219/1, Dept. of the Environment, Manchester, 1977.

[23] 'Cheshire—A Review of Atmospheric Pollution', Cheshire County Council, Chester, 1975. A second edition was published in 1977.

[24] 'Report of Survey: Environment', Cheshire County Structure Plan, Cheshire County Council, Chester, 1976.

[25] 'Structure Plan: Written Statement of Policies and Proposals', Cheshire County Council, Chester, 1977.

[26] 'Statement of Policy on Air Pollution Objectives and Planning: Cheshire Structure Plan EIP', Noise, Clean Air and Coast Protection Division, Dept. of the Environment, London, 1977.

[27] *Air Quality Criteria and Guides for Urban Air Pollutants,* Technical Report Series, No. 506, World Health Organization, Geneva, 1972.

[28] 'Transcript of Proceedings of the Examination in Public of the Structure Plan for Cheshire', 23 November 1977, Dept. of the Environment, Manchester, 1977.

[29] 'Cheshire County Structure Plan Examination in Public: Report of the Panel', Dept. of the Environment, Manchester, 1978.

[30] 'Decision Letter on Cheshire Structure Plan', PNW/137/6W, Dept. of the Environment, Manchester, 1979.

4

THE SULPHURIC ACID WORKS

The names of the mayors of St Helens, since its incorporation as a Borough in 1868, are inscribed on a brass plaque in the entrance of the town hall. Among the earlier entries, such names as Pilkington, Beecham, and Gamble are prominent, and their presence reflects the expansion of the glass and chemical industries in the latter half of the nineteenth century. These industries, together with the exploitation of the rich Lancashire coal seams, remain the principal sources of employment for St. Helens's present population of 194,000. St Helens, historically part of Lancashire, is now a district of the new county of Merseyside.

This chapter is concerned with atmospheric pollution arising from a chemical works in Sutton, an area of mixed residential and industrial development to the south-east of the centre of St Helens (Fig. 4.1). British Sidac Ltd, now a subsidiary of a Belgian company, moved into Sutton in 1934: its present site covers about 17 ha and it employs some 1,400 people, most of whom live in the vicinity. Sidac manufactures and converts transparent cellulose film used for packaging a wide variety of goods, particularly foodstuffs.

The sulphuric acid plant, owned and operated by the Leathers Chemical Company Ltd, covers just over 1 ha of land adjacent to, and leased from, British Sidac (Plate 2). Leathers, now owned by Occidental Petroleum of America, has been associated with the production of sulphuric acid since its establishment in 1750. The St Helens plant is one of a number operated by this company, which is also involved in the transportation of bulk supplies of sulphuric acid.

The planning application

In September 1968, British Sidac Ltd sought permission from the St Helens County Borough Council for the development of land in their possession for the construction of a plant to manufacture sulphuric acid, sulphur trioxide, and oleum.

Since the chemical processes involved in the manufacture of sulphuric acid from sulphur are net producers of heat, this energy, which would otherwise be wasted, would be utilized by Sidac in the form of high-pressure steam. At that time Sidac required three oil-fired boilers to raise steam for its plant: by using steam from the sulphuric acid plant, fewer boilers would suffice, thereby reducing the net discharge of sulphur dioxide from the burning of oil.[1] The

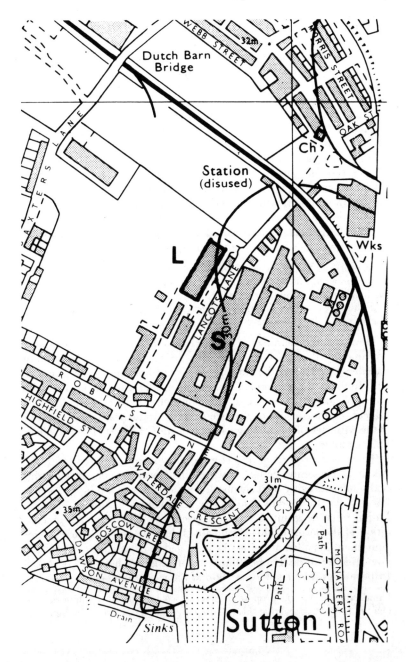

FIG. 4.1 Sutton, St Helens: Leathers sulphuric acid works

L: Leathers,   S: British Sidac,   1 : 5,000 ▲N·   Crown copyright reserved

high-pressure steam from the acid plant would also be used to generate electricity in Sidac's turbine; part of the output of this generator
would be sold back to the sulphuric acid plant operators, together
with low-pressure steam which could be utilized in the acid manufacture. In addition, Sidac would consume a sizeable proportion of
the total sulphuric acid output.

While the economic advantages to Sidac of having a sulphuric acid
plant in close proximity to its own works are apparent, there were
obvious environmental benefits to be gained from Sidac's scheme.
With the proposed effluent treatment plant, Sidac could reduce by
75 per cent the amount of sulphide discharged to Sutton Brook—
a watercourse long notorious in the area for its pollution and offensive
odour. In addition, with the acid plant operating as planned (i.e. in
conjunction with the treatment plant and with waste steam being
exploited by Sidac) there would be a significant net decrease in
sulphur dioxide emission to the atmosphere:

If the proposed Sulphuric Acid Plant is installed the Sulphur Gases generated
by the proposed Effluent Treatment System could be used as raw material for
the manufacture of Sulphuric Acid.

In this way a further significant reduction in the quantity of Sulphur Gases
discharged to the atmosphere would be achieved.[2]

However, the members of the St Helens Planning Committee were
not unaware that a pollution-free sulphuric acid plant is a fiction; nor
had they overlooked the close proximity of housing to the proposed
site. In view of the complex technical considerations associated with
the application before them, the Borough Engineer and Planning
Officer sought consultancy advice from the Industrial Liaison Officer
of the Ministry of Technology and from staff of the St Helens College
of Technology.

There is no record of any communication by St Helens with the
Alkali Inspectorate. Sidac, however, had been in contact with this
body independently of their discussions with the planning authority;
for in order to operate a sulphuric acid plant a certificate of registration must be granted by the Inspectorate. The principal precondition of the grant of this certificate is that the pollution-arrestment
equipment installed at the works is judged to be satisfactory and that
any chimney to discharge effluents is of sufficient height. The Alkali
Inspector, in a letter of June 1968 to Sidac, commented:

I understand that you propose to erect a 600 tons per day sulphuric acid
plant in St Helens, and that this will use, as part of the sulphur requirements,

the SO_2 from the incineration of H_2S derived from a new effluent treatment plant. ...

If you choose to erect the double contact plant, in view of the overall reducation in atmospheric pollution we will accept reluctantly, and without prejudice, a lower height of 140 ft, [43 m] provided the foundations are such as to support a stack of 200 ft [61 m] if operation conditions were found to require an increase in stack height.[3]

In their report, the planning authority's consultants from the College of Technology concluded that, if the plant operated to full efficiency in the manner claimed by the applicant, the benefits (in terms of pollution reduction) could be achieved. On the likelihood of increases in ground-level concentrations of sulphur dioxide arising from the normal runnning of the plant: 'it is very unlikely in our opinion that the new plant will contribute materially any increases in these levels.' With reference to the sulphur dioxide from oxidation of the hydrogen sulphide, they added:

The alternative [to linking with the acid plant] scheme of treating the pollutant, by burning and ejecting the sulphur dioxide waste, would contribute substantially to the level of sulphur dioxide in the atmosphere.

On the question of pollution arising from plant breakdowns, the report reads:

The second type of pollution is due to a sudden breakdown, such as a burst pipe or leaking valve on the plant. Such a breakdown is unlikely in a plant of this type, but could happen. It is to prevent problems due to sudden breakdown that the following safeguards are proposed.[4]

These safeguards consisted of requiring that the plant operators should install equipment to monitor emission levels of sulphur dioxide and trioxide. Concentrations of sulphur dioxide in excess of 0.2 per cent and sulphur trioxide in excess of 1.5 mg/cu.ft (53 mg/m^3) in the gases in the chimney would mean that the firm 'would be deemed to have violated planning permission'.[4]

The consultant's generally favourable appraisal proved influential in tilting the balance in favour of granting permission. In December 1968, British Sidac were granted conditional outline planning permission by the St Helens Planning Committee. Some four weeks later and after the submission of detailed plans, detailed planning consent, with identical conditions, was granted to Simon-Carves Ltd, who were to erect a 'double contact' sulphuric acid plant on behalf of Leathers Chemical Co. Ltd, who would own and operate the plant on a site leased from British Sidac.

The planning conditions

The planning conditions with direct pollution control significance were as follows:

3. Continuous monitors for the measurement of sulphur dioxide and sulphur trioxide shall be affixed on the effluent chimney; such monitors to be connected to an audible alarm in such manner that the alarm will be sounded when the permitted level of pollution is exceeded, and one further monitor for the measurement of sulphur trioxide/sulphuric acid shall be affixed in a position to be agreed by the local planning authority, the monitors being of types to the satisfaction of the local planning authority.

4. The atmospheric pollution levels as recorded on the monitors installed on the effluent chimney shall not be allowed to exceed 0.2% SO_2 or 1.5 mg SO_3 per cu. ft [53 mg/m^3].

5. In the event of the monitors referred to in condition 4 above recording pollution levels higher than the maximum levels stated in such conditions immediate remedial measures shall be taken to reduce the level of atmospheric pollution and the plant shall not continue to operate for longer than 30 minutes with the chimney effluent containing more than the permitted level of sulphur compounds.

6. The read-out from the monitors shall be in the form of a continuous inkline recorded on paper, such record to be stored and kept available for inspection.

7. Authorized officers of the council shall have access at all times to the monitors and to the records of the previous readings.

8. From the date of coming into operation of the sulphuric acid producing plant, all discharge of effluent to the Mill Brook shall comply with standards and conditions of the Mersey and Weaver River Authority and a continuous monitor shall be provided to record the measurement of sulphide in the effluent.

9. The sulphate settling beds which form part of the existing effluent plant shall be removed to preclude further discharge to Mill Brook and the land shall be reclaimed to the satisfaction of the Council.

12. The operation of the plant shall be such that sulphur only is burnt for the production of sulphur dioxide. Iron pyrites or other sulphide ores shall not be used for the preparation of sulphur dioxide without prior approval of the local planning authority.[5]

Conditions 8 and 9 represented an attempt by St Helens to secure some control over Sidac's contribution to the pollution of Sutton Brook. (There is no record of any consultations between the County Borough and the River Authority over these rather unrealistic conditions before they were imposed. After some discussion, the Planning Committee acceded to a request[6] from Sidac to withdraw condition 9 at their meeting in January 1969.)

Conditions 3 - 7 and 12 represented an attempt by the local planning authority to impose controls (in addition to those enforced by the

Alkali Inspectorate) to minimize discharges to the atmospheres from the proposed sulphuric acid plant. Condition 12 was intended to preclude the possibility of nuisance in the form of dust from the handling of spent sulphide ores. In a letter of December 1968 to St Helens, Leathers wrote with reference to condition 5:

We agree in principle with setting a time limit and we have asked the plant manufacturers to investigate immediately the technical implications of imposing a limit of 30 mins. ... As a result of the investigation it may be necesssary for us to ask you to consider some variation in the time limit.[6]

In the event, Leathers did not object to this or any other condition. However, in June 1969, the new District Alkali Inspector protested to St Helens that the Inspectorate had not been consulted about the planning consent and that it could not be responsible for the enforcement of the planning conditions.

Following the granting of planning permission for the sulphuric acid plant, St Helens Planning Committee began to grow concerned at the absence of any planning application from Sidac for the effluent treatment plant. However, Sidac were able to assure St Helens at a meeting in February 1969 that 'the sulphide burning plant could be made operative at any time'.[7]

In a letter dated October 1969, Sidac informed St Helens that they were about to seek planning permission for the effluent treatment plant but that it would not now be linked to the sulphuric acid plant. Sidac's reasons for this decision were stated thus:

1. The plant necessary to prepare the sulphur dioxide for presentation to the sulphuric acid plant is open to technical doubt.
2. The commissioning of the sulphuric acid plant and its early history must not be complicated by a minor feedstock from a different source. A guarantee cannot be obtained from Simon-Carves with such a feedstock.

This decision does not entirely eliminate the possibility of using the output of the treatment plant as feedstock for the sulphuric acid plant at a future date, when the operation of both plants has been stabilised and reappraisal of the technical difficulties can be made.[8]

St Helens Council were somewhat disturbed at this apparent change of mind. A meeting of all the parties concerned was arranged in November 1969 at which the Borough Engineer expressed his council's misgivings. In reply, Sidac explained that since the grant of planning permission in 1968, they and Simon-Carves had continued to work on the design of the effluent treatment plant and its link with the acid plant. However, while the chemistry of the process was understood, severe problems of chemical engineering remained in relation to the difficulty of finding appropriate materials and of finding a process 'which would give a stable gas fit for supply to the sulphuric acid plant even though this only comprised some 2 per cent of feedstock'.[9] At this meeting, the Alkali Inspector reported that he had accepted the discharge of sulphur dioxide to the atmosphere from the effluent treatment plant (which used a scheduled process) since it was consequent upon an improvement in water quality in Sutton Brook. However, he added that this discharge to the air must cease as soon as further research enabled the link to the acid plant to be made satisfactory.

Whether the planning authority were justified in their resentment at Sidac's failure to implement their original scheme; whether Sidac were morally obliged to do so; and whether the Alkali Inspector was entitled to place water pollution above atmospheric pollution are all open to debate. Irrespective of the technicalities of integration, it is curious that the stated objections were not apparent, or at least suspected, at an earlier stage, especially by a company with the expertise and experience of Simon-Carves. (There was at least one small sulphuric acid plant using sulphur dioxide produced by the combustion of hydrogen sulphide working successfully at a steelworks in the United Kingdom.) It is even more difficult to accept that the non-technical objection, that integration could prejudice performance guarantees, was not fully appreciated from the outset.

Although it was originally intended that the sulphuric acid plant and the effluent treatment plant should be brought into operation together, it was in January 1970 that the latter was given planning permission while, only a month later, the acid plant went into commission with a 43 m (140 ft) chimney. Shortly afterwards, pollution from the new plant provoked the first of a series of public complaints. St Helens later compiled a list of forty-five incidents attributable to Leathers between May 1970 and November 1975.[10] These incidents varied in intensity and form of emission and in the degree of nuisance caused. Incident 3, in July 1970, involved the release of what was later confirmed by laboratory test to be sulphuric acid mist. People in Sutton Road and Morris Street were affected, some requiring medical treatment. Some vegetation in the area was killed. An enforcement notice was subsequently served on Leathers by St Helens for their failure to fix sulphur dioxide and trioxide monitors to their stack, in breach of condition 3.

Incident 4 occurred in August 1970: a major plant breakdown caused an excessive emission of sulphur dioxide which affected people in Robins Lane and Monastery Lane, some of whom required hospital attention. A measure of the seriousness of this particular incident can be gained from the fact that Leathers evacuated their office block. There were graphic newspaper reports of the event:

Police moved in as dozens of children were reported violently ill.

Passers-by hammered on doors begging for water as factory plants were evacuated and one man collapsed.

Three other men were given emergency oxygen supplies and several old people thought they were the victims of heart attacks.

A gas mask was clamped on the face of a schoolgirl as she choked on the pavement from sulphur dioxide fumes.[11]

Leathers restarted their plant in September 1970, by which time the monitors were installed (as required by the enforcement notice). The start-up was observed by an officer from St Helens and another excessive emission of sulphur dioxide was reported.[12] In October 1971, Sidac's effluent treatment plant was finally commissioned; 1971 saw three, and 1972 nine, incidents associated with the acid plants. Two of these incidents were later to become notorious, involving as they did the sudden appearance of holes in ladies' hosiery caused by acid droplets. Public protest against these incidents had become vociferous and St Helens were forced to attempt to improve the situation.

At a meeting in September 1972, another new District Alkali Inspector advised Sidac against feeding sulphur dioxide from their effluent treatment plant to Leathers because the latter 'had enough problems'.[13] The Alkali Inspector was the principal speaker at another meeting in September at which elected members and senior officers were present. He stated that Leathers did not shut down their plant rapidly enough when malfunctions occurred: they (Leathers) strove to maintain steam for Sidac, who would otherwise have to engage their full boiler capacity; and if this were done rapidly, as would be necessary to ensure continuous production, black smoke could be emitted. As for acid leaks in the plant and the emission of acid spray which they caused, the Inspector declared that he was 'of the opinion that the situation is not serious from the health point of view'.[14] However, he went on to point out that he would recommend prosecution if the plant ran for more than a few minutes after a leak had been discovered. The Alkali Inspector stated that Leathers were unlikely to persist in such actions because: 'I do not think that a firm would operate in this way and allow themselves to be fined repeatedly, for their certificate of registration would not be renewed at the end of the year and they would not be able to operate.'[14]

A further meeting in September was attended by the Managing Director, Works Director and Works Manager of Leathers, while St Helens was represented by four members and six senior officers. The Alkali Inspector was also present. Leathers maintained that the incidents which had occurred were typical of the 'teething troubles' to be expected from such plants. They stressed the amount of money which had already been spent on remedial work to the acid-cooling system from which the leaks had arisen and the further alterations to be made.[15]

This meeting did nothing to allay local anxieties and public demands for action against the company grew. In March 1973, the local Member of Parliament tabled a parliamentary question asking a minister of the Department of the Environment to set up an inquiry into Leathers.

The enforcement proceedings

Incident 23, in March 1973, involved the emission of excessive amounts of sulphur dioxide. People were affected in a works 1,200 m north of the plant. Part of this factory was evacuated and one woman had to be taken to hospital. The incident was described by the Alkali Inspectorate as follows:

A new double contact plant, designed for an efficiency of 99.5% has been plagued with numerous teething troubles and minor incidents. It is located in an urban area where even the smallest of incidents causes complaint. During a start-up from cold, a heavy emission of sulphur dioxide occurred when an operator positioned a valve incorrectly despite its being clearly marked. It was also found that a gas flow measuring device was out of service. It was regarded as an infraction. The operator was disciplined and the gas flow measuring device was repaired the next day.[16]

The plant was shut down half an hour after the abortive attempt to start up. The next morning, the monitor readings were examined by a planning officer of St Helens, who observed that the emission had been in excess of the permitted level for one hour. Later that month, St. Helens served an enforcement notice on Leathers for violation of condition 4 of the planning permission. This notice required Leathers:

Within one week ... to take the following steps to comply with the said condition ... [viz] not to allow the atmospheric pollution levels as recorded on the monitors installed on the effluent chimney to exceed 0.2% SO_2 [*sic*].[17]

Leathers appealed to the Secretary of State for the Environment against this notice.

St Helens's account of incident 26 reveals that excessive sulphur dioxide emissions for six minutes and, later, another thirteen minutes during two attempted start-ups,[18] affected people in a shopping centre some 500 m south-east of the plant. In August 1973 St Helens served a second enforcement notice in respect of this later violation. The wording was identical to the first, as was Leathers's appeal.

Before this appeal was considered, there occurred a third incident (32) which was potentially more serious in so far as it involved a low level discharge of sulphur trioxide. Again attributed to negligence, this incident was held to be a breach of 'best practicable means' and incurred the censure of the Alkali Inspectorate:

Another infraction occurred at the same works later in the year during the loading of a road tanker with 65% oleum. The incident was caused by an ill-fitting flange on a vent pipe to draw off displaced fumes to an acid scrubber. It transpired that this was a new tanker with a non-standard connection and the operator, instead of seeking management advice, proceeded to fill the tanker with the leaking flange, causing a heavy emission of sulphur trioxide for 10-15 minutes. Infraction conditions were recorded and a notice of intended prosecution was also served.[16]

Leathers' response to this prosecution may be inferred from the following passage:

Last year, I reported that we were taking legal action against a works for allowing fumes of sulphur trioxide to be emitted whilst filling a road tanker with oleum. The company pleaded not guilty at the trial, but they lost their case and were fined £100 plus costs. The company appealed against the findings of the Magistrates' Court and a retrial was held at a Crown Court. The decision of the lower court was upheld, but the fine was reduced to £25.[19]

In reaching this decision, the judge adhered to the principle that a maximum fine should not be imposed in the case of a first offence.

The local inquiry into the appeals by Leathers against the two enforcement notices took place on 18 and 19 December 1973 in St Helens Town Hall. A retired district Alkali Inspector sat as the Technical Assessor. Represented by a QC, Leathers were appealing on the grounds that they were not, in fact, in violation of condition 4, and that this condition should be deleted from the planning permission. Much of Leathers' case consisted of contesting the legal status of the condition and arguing that it could not be considered in isolation.[18]

Leathers' counsel criticized the enforcement notices in so far as they required only compliance with the condition, but specified no positive measure to be adopted in order to achieve this compliance. If, contrary to their submission, conditions 3 - 5 were not to be taken as a whole, and condition 4 was to stand alone, then it should be discharged as unreasonable since it encroached on specific legislation, namely the Alkali Act. The Leathers plant was registered and atmospheric pollution control was effected by the application of 'best practicble means'—a precept which embraced not only the provision of pollution control apparatus but also maintenance, running, and supervision of the plant as a whole. In addition to visits by the Alkali Inspectorate, the St Helens Public Health Department made daily visits to the installation.[18]

With reference to the two incidents resulting in the enforcement notices, Leathers conceded that the stack monitor had recorded sulphur dioxide emissions in excess of 0.2 per cent. However, remedial actions had been taken and in neither case did the plant continue to run for more than thrity minutes. They went on to point out that the presumptive limit contained in the 'best practicable means' for this process was in fact more stringent than that specified in the condition at issue. (It is equivalent to 0.06 per cent sulphur dioxide by volume.[16] They added that a higher chimney might help to reduce ground-level concentrations of sulphur dioxide.

St Helens had also briefed a QC to present their case at this inquiry. He began by rebutting the legal arguments made earlier by the appellants. Condition 4 had been intended to be taken as absolute; and condition 5 was included in order to ameliorate the effects of an emission in contravention of condition 4. It was a breach of condition 4 that was at issue here: it was not the responsibility of a local planning authority to tell a company how to run its affairs, but merely to ensure that it complied with any planning conditions laid down.[18]

He went on to observe that the Alkali Inspectorate's powers were very old and that planning law is 'more pertinent now to the preservation of public health'.[18] With 'expert advice' the local planning authority had thought that, with safeguards in the form of the planning conditions which Leathers had accepted in 1968 without appeal, the plant could be operated to their satisfaction. If St Helens had not considered condition 4 to be absolute, the authority would not have granted planning consent.

During the hearing of evidence from the local authority, it was revealed that there existed no knowledge of atmospheric behaviour patterns in the area (e.g. prevailing winds, fogs, etc.) that the 43 m stack was in the immediate neighbourhood of large high buildings which could cause eddy currents and backwash conditions under certain circumstances and that the chimney had foundations sufficient for a stack of 61 m. It was also learnt that the monitors were less than satisfactory.

The Member of Parliament whose constituency included Leathers's site, and who had been active in the opposition to Leathers for some time, presented two public petitions dated August 1972 and August 1973 containing 438 and 101 signatures respectively. He drew attention to the distress which had been caused to local residents by various discharges from Leathers, not only those at issue at the current inquiry.[18]

A founder member of the East Sutton Residents' Association (which had been formed with the expressed aim of bringing about the closure of Leathers) described and submitted documentary evidence on the effects of the two discharges which had given rise to the enforcement notices on local residents and workers. Another local resident referred to a newspaper statement[20] by the St Helens Medical Officer of Health, to the effect that 'anyone with bronchial complaints could die if caught in an emission of the nature experienced from the works'.[18] This officer, however, did not present evidence at the inquiry.

The conclusions of the Inspector's report related principally to the debate on the legal status of the planning conditions. In his opinion, it was hard 'to avoid the conclusion that conditions 3 to 7 inclusive were not only intended but are, in fact, inextricably associated and form a logical sequence'.[18] He went on to question the validity of an enforcement notice which merely repeated the (negative) requirements of the allegedly violated condition. He also observed that the Alkali Act contained the statutory and specific controls for atmospheric emissions from sulphuric acid plants, and that in these circumstances planning conditions were both 'superfluous and of no assistance'.[18]

The Inspector commented further that 'there must be grave doubt about the suitability of this location for a plant of this nature albeit the site lies within an area allocated for industry.'[18] He drew attention to the absence of an effective monitor for sulphur trioxide. He was advised by his Assessor that the principal source of nuisance to local residents arose from leakages of sulphur trioxide and spillages of oleum during tanker loading, but this aspect had apparently been neglected by the local planning authority.

In his report, the Assessor generally supported the view that control should reside in the hands of the Alkali Inspectorate and that planning conditions were inappropriate. He did, however, suggest that serious attention be given to the desirability of raising the height of the chimney stack from 43 m to 61 m.

In his final statement, the Inspector left the problem of the legal status of condition 4 to the Secretary of State. If condition 4 was considered absolute (in which case Leathers would have violated it) then it should be discharged as unreasonable. In reaching this conclusion, he referred to his Assessor's report in which it was stated that abnormally high emissions were inevitable when contact plants were started up. If, however, conditions 4 and 5 were to be read as one (in which case there had been no violation) then the Inspector saw no objection to their retention, since, conjointly, they imposed no unreasonable demands on the company.

It must be emphasized that the opposition of the Alkali Inspectorate to the use of planning conditions which seek to apply controls over pollution from scheduled processes is a matter of principle. The conditions which St Helens imposed were, in the Inspectorate's

terms, perfect exemplars of the misuse of planning powers to which
they had for so long opposed: these planning conditions were misconceived, ill-advised, and quite simply ineffective. If conditions
3–5 were taken together, they were technically unrealistic and offered
little real environmental protection. If condition 4 were to be taken
in isolation, as St Helens had argued, the Alkali Inspectorate's
opposition remained; in fact it was more emphatic. For alone,
condition 4 was tantamount to a demand that the plant should
operate without any failure, accident, or breakdown: such a requirement when applied to any chemical engineering system was, at the
very least, impracticable. Whilst no member of the Inspectorate was
summoned to give evidence at this inquiry, its view was made manifestly clear in yet another reference to Leathers:

A works operating a double-contact plant was served with an enforcement
notice by the local authority for contravention of planning conditions put in
the consent. The company's appeal to the Secretary of State resulted in a
Public Inquiry which was held on the 18 December. The decision is awaited.
We deprecate the insertion into planning consents of conditions which
impinge on our statutory duties.[16]

In his decision letter of May 1974, the Secretary of State for the
Environment echoed these views: planning conditions which encroached on the province of the Alkali Inspectorate were undesirable,
since they could give rise to 'conflicting requirements and procedures'.[21] The Secretary of State accepted his Inspector's recommendation that conditions 4 and 5 were to be read as one. The
appeal was thus upheld on the grounds that the matters alleged in the
notice did not constitute a breach of the planning consent (thus
interpreted). In addition, he stated that had he been involved in the
grant of the planning consent, he would have been inclined to discharge any conditions of this nature. Lastly, the Secretary of State
expressed the opinion that, contrary to Leathers' contention, the
enforcement notices were not valid in that they specified no particular
remedial action: where a breach of a planning condition was 'an
occasional one which recurs or might recur', he did not consider it
necessary for the planning authority 'to do more than require that
the conditions be complied with'.[21]

The discontinuance proceedings

The ministerial decision on Leathers' appeal against the enforcement
notices meant that St Helens Metropolitan Borough Council (as it
became on 1 April 1974) were left with no effective control over the
plant. Nevertheless, their concern continued, as did the incidents.
 With incident 39, in May 1974, there occurred two excessive emis-

sions of sulphur dioxide on start-up. Unusual wind conditions brought the gas to ground within 100 m of the plant; although no one was reported to be seriously affected, there was some panic since the likely duration of the emission was unknown. The continuing anxiety of local residents was expressed to members of the Planning and Development Committee when they met representatives of the East Sutton Residents Association in July. At that time, this group had organized a picket of Leathers' factory: local residents were joined by some nurses from the nearby hospital and by trade unionists in an attempt to disrupt Leathers' production by exhorting tanker drivers not to enter the works. Additional trade union support for the campaign against the acid plant is apparent from a newspaper article:

Members of St Helens Trades Council have been invited to tonight's meeting of East Sutton Residents' Association to hear about a scheme to close Leathers Chemicals ... trades unionists might agree to a penny-a-week levy to maintain the wages of any worker prepared to leave the plant.[22]

Meanwhile, the deliberations of the St Helens councillors continued. When it was learned that an appeal against the decision on the enforcement notices (which they had been intending to take to the High Court) would not be heard for many months, during which time the Minister would be unable to discuss the Leathers issue further, the Planning Committee voted to terminate this course of action. Later in July, a deputation from St Helens, including the Chairman of the Committee and the leader of the Association (who was also a local councillor for East Sutton by this time) met the Parliamentary Under-Secretary of State at the Department of the Environment. At this meeting, which was attended by the Deputy Chief Alkali Inspector, the Minister 'was astonished to hear that St Helens never consulted the Alkali Inspectorate when they considered the Leathers application in 1968'.[23] The Minister informed the St Helens deputation that there was no provision under which the Secretary of State could order an investigation into the Leathers issue;[24] furthermore, St Helens could 'expect no government aid in paying compensation if they closed the plant'.[23]

Although the closing of the Leathers' plant had been mooted much earlier, it was as a result of this meeting that the Planning Committee decided that they had only two choices: either to accept the existence of Leathers and urge the Alkali Inspector to take all steps to ensure the plant's least offensive operation; or to take the drastic measure of serving a discontinuance order, and meeting the considerable payment in compensation should the order be confirmed by the Secretary of State.

At a meeting of the Planning Committee held in September 1974, a motion proposed by the Association councillor calling for a discontinuance order to be imposed on the Leathers' plant was defeated by 10 votes to 4. However, it was agreed that a comprehensive report should be prepared on Leathers. This report contained no specific recommendations but listed a series of policy options, including those of creating a 'buffer zone' around the plant by demolishing housing and of serving a discontinuance order: the estimates of the compensation payable ranged from £2,000,000 to £3,000,000.

The report was discussed at a meeting of the Planning Committee held *in camera* in December 1974. Again, a motion calling for a discontinuance order was defeated, this time by 8 votes to 6. However, the following full Council meeting referred the minutes back to the Committee for further consideration.[25] In January 1975, the Planning Committee again rejected—again by 8 votes to 6—a motion calling for a discontinuance order. However, at the next meeting of the Council, the minute from the Planning Committee was once more not confirmed and, at the following Council meeting in March, with the majority Labour group under a 'whip', a motion calling for a discontinuance order against the Leathers Chemicals sulphuric acid plant was carried by 34 votes to 7.

In March 1974, the District Alkali Inspector had written to Leathers suggesting that it might be prudent to increase the range of sulphur dioxide monitors to 1.5 per cent and to raise the chimney height to 61 m. In July, Leathers duly submitted an application to St Helens for planning permission to extend the chimney. No action on this application was taken and, in November 1974, the Alkali Inspector was moved to inform St Helens of his concern. In their reply, St Helens explained that a comprehensive report on Leathers was then in preparation and that the question of planning consent to the extension of the chimney would be included therein.

Leathers eventually appealed to the Secretary of State against St Helens's failure to offer a decision. However, the appeal was rejected on a technicality: the proposal to increase the chimney had not been advertised in the local press. Leathers subsequently submitted a second application and advertised it.

Following repeated deferment of a decision on this application by the Planning Committee, the Alkali Inspector wrote again in July 1975. While there was no danger to public health from the existing chimney, he declared:

Increasing the chimney height will provide additional protection to people in Sutton from unforeseeable emissions during start-up or breakdown conditions. Should any serious incident occur which would have been alleviated by a taller chimney, it is my view that St Helens Borough Council must accept full responsibility because of their failure to expedite this application.[26]

In September 1975, shortly after the publication of this letter, planning permission to raise the stack was finally given:

At a works operating a double-contact plant, where numerous teething troubles have been reported in these Reports, major modifications were carried out, during a prolonged stoppage, with the object of avoiding serious heat exchanger corrosion problems. At the same time the chimney height was increased from 140 ft [43 m] to 200 ft [61 m], after considerable difficulty in persuading the local planning committee to grant permission, with the Company at one stage lodging an appeal to the Secretary of State for the Environment. Earlier, the local authority decided to place a discontinuance order on the plant. The Company has lodged an appeal against the order and a public inquiry is due to be held in January 1976.[27]

Clearly, the planning authority was reluctant to assist Leathers in making a belated improvement to their plant when such an action could only benefit the company's case in opposing the discontinuance order. Indeed, the Alkali Inspector's concern about St Helens's inactivity is somewhat curious when it is recalled that the lower chimney height was accepted by his predecessor albeit 'reluctantly' but nevertheless 'without prejudice', more than seven years earlier.

Of the five incidents which occurred in 1975, that in August, (43) is particularly significant because it was the first in which a St Helens officer was able to measure sulphur dioxide levels using a newly acquired portable monitor: a concentration downwind of $3,990 \, \mu g/m^3$ was recorded; whereas upwind, a level of $142 \, \mu g/m^3$ was detected.[13] St Helens reported that the emission giving rise to this high level was due to a gas leak from a worn-out heat exchanger. Passers-by and the environmental health inspector operating the monitor were affected by the fumes.

Despite the threat of a discontinuance order, the overhaul began three days later and involved a reported expenditure of £340,000. Between August and November 1975, numerous renewals and modifications were carried out, the chimney was finally raised to 61 m, and the range of the sulphur dioxide stack monitor was increased.

While this work was being carried out at Leathers, St Helens were preparing their case for the forthcoming local inquiry. However, it would appear from a newspaper report that their QC was less than confident that the order would eventually be confirmed:

Councillors in top-secret session have scotched a scheme for a truce with Leathers Chemicals.

The suggestion from the Barrister Iain Glidewell was rejected when the Planning Committee went into private session on Tuesday afternoon.[28]

The local inquiry

Having sought the Secretary of State's confirmation of the order requiring discontinuance of the use of land for the purposes of the manufacture of sulphuric acid and its by-products by Leathers Chemicals Ltd, St Helens duly informed Leathers and British Sidac, respectively the occupier and owner of the land in question. Both companies lodged an objection within the statutory twenty-eight days. The Minister instituted a local inquiry, which was held in St Helens Town Hall on 6-9 and 14-16 January 1976. The Inspector was assisted by a chemical engineer sitting as the Technical Assessor.

At the inquiry, the local planning authority was seeking to demonstrate that a discontinuance order was necessary because the original decision to grant planning permission for the purpose of sulphuric acid manufacture had been an error. Although the site in question was within an area allocated in the relevant Development Plan for industrial use, the type of use had not been specified. It was not to be supposed, as Leathers suggested, that the proximity of another registered works (Sidac) implied that the site was suitable for acid manufacture.[13]

It was contended by St Helens that when their predecessors, the County Borough, granted planning consent in 1968, they did so without full knowledge of the implications of their decision. The advice given by the two consultants had proved misguided. Although Simon-Carves had told the local planning authority that the double contact process was new, they had not explained that this would be a 'pioneer' project—the first of its type and, at that time, the largest sulphuric acid plant in the country. Finally, the expectation that Sidac's effluent treatment plant would be linked to the acid plant had been a 'material consideration' in granting planning permission.

These considerations had motivated the Council to take the extreme measure of seeking a discontinuance order. In addition, this action had been prompted by the doubts, cast by the earlier decision of the Secretary of State, on the 'validity of the planning conditions that the County Borough Council thought necessary for the protection of the public'.[13] The Council accepted that there had been no incident of acid spray since 1973 and that the situation had improved since the major overhaul a few months earlier. Nevertheless, the potential for breakdown, and hence pollution and nuisance, remained. Controls under the Alkali Act, the Public Health Act, and actions in nuisance at civil law provided redress only after an incident had occurred—a discontinuance order ensured that there would be no such incidents.

Counsel for St Helens declared that it was recognized that amenity considerations, including atmospheric pollution, were legitimate grounds for refusing planning permission, despite their being covered by other statutes. He explained that it was not necessary for the local planning authority to demonstrate 'a serious and unavoidable risk' from the acid plant. Visual amenity might constitute adequate grounds for an order: the Town and Country Planning Act made no reference to health. It followed that a discontinuance order could be made on the same grounds.

With reference to the Health and Safety at Work Act, 1974, he submitted that 'other persons' related to non-employees on the premises, not to the public at large. In a slighting reference to the Alkali Act, he considered that one prosecution in forty-five incidents was a measure of the control that could be exercised with this particular piece of legislation. As for civil proceedings, 'an injunction would not be granted for a single incident or infrequent incidents.'[13]

In seeking confirmation of the order, St Helens were fully aware that the compensation involved would amount to a substantial sum. This, however, was a matter for the councillors and their electorate. As for the effect of Leathers' closure on neighbouring Sidac, they could find alternative sources of acid, especially if Leathers set up production elsewhere. Lastly, St Helens did not accept that time should be allowed for the recent improvements to be seen to be effective: the area had suffered from the Leathers plant for more than five years and that was enough. It was to be recorded that the local authority were supported in their endeavours by the local Trades Council, despite the latter's great concern with unemployment.[13]

It emerged during the hearing of evidence from St Helens that much of the housing in the vicinity of the plant was owned by the local authority. Ironically, some of this had been built or extensively renovated since the 1968 planning permission. Apparently, very few residents had taken the opportunity, when offered, of transferring to a new home in a different location. In addition, Sutton Primary School, to the east of the site, had been rebuilt between 1973 and 1974.

The District Alkali Inspector stated that, under normal operating conditions, the 'best practicable means' required that the sulphur dioxide concentration in emissions from the acid plant should not exceed 0.06 per cent by volume and he averred that ' 'best practicable means' for controlling emissions to the atmosphere are being used', but, 'at start-up the operation is abnormal'.[13] In the first three years of operation, he stated, there had been several public complaints, all of which had been thoroughly investigated by himself or by a colleague. The causes of these complaints had been, or were about to be, rectified. He also stated that, in September 1972, he had advised against feeding sulphur dioxide from Sidac's effluent treatment plant to Leathers.

The Alkali Inspector remarked on the resentment of his immediate predecessor at not being consulted over either the decision to grant planning permission or the imposition of planning conditions. In response to a direct question from the Inspector as to what his answer would have been, had he been asked in 1968 whether he considered the site suitable for a sulphuric acid plant, the Alkali Inspector replied that he would not have recommended planning refusal.[13]

Leathers were quite frank with regard to the early performance of their plant, admitting it to be 'underdesigned compared with older plants' and listing the defects in the acid-cooling system which had caused the notorious acid spray incidents. These, however, had ceased in September 1973 with the acquisition of new coolers. In November 1975, the company's figures, corroborated by those of the Alkali Inspector, showed the level of sulphur dioxide in the stack emission during start-up to be consistently lower then 0.04 per cent, and therefore in accordance with 'best practicable means'.[13] Leathers did not seriously challenge the list of incidents presented by St Helens. They pointed out that sulphur dioxide emissions in excess of 0.2 per cent were likely to occur after a shut-down of more than twelve hours' duration. St Helens Council must have been aware of the problems which 'cold start-ups' occasioned because this was 'implicit in the conditions imposed'.[13]

In arguing their case against the discontinuance order, the QC for Leathers considered that it was not enough to refute the wisdom of the 1968 planning consent. The order should be decided by the conditions which prevailed in 1975; while the Council might be justified in arguing that emissions were greater than they had been led to believe, these had been due to 'teething troubles', of which 'continuance is not to be expected', following the extensive over-haul.[13]

If the plant closed, Sidac would be forced to revert to three boilers with a consequent net increase in sulphur dioxide discharge. In addition, the loss in supplies of sulphuric acid to both the home market and to export would be serious. More especially, the St Helens plant was one of only four in the country capable of producing oleum and supplied half the home market. Similarly, the plant under threat supplied 40 per cent of the total liquid sulphur trioxide required by detergent, pharmaceutical, cosmetic and other manufacturers. It was doubtful whether importing would meet the deficit caused by closure at St Helens; the subsequent closure of oleum- and sulphur trioxide-using companies was possible.

Leathers' calculations on the compensation payable resulted in figures of the order of £6,500,000-£8,750,000. Thus, the benefit, if any, of closure to residents close to the plant was hardly commensurate with the financial burden to be borne by ratepayers throughout the district. Moreover, if the discontinuance order were confirmed, the workforce at Leathers would be made redundant, and with unemployment then standing at over 8 per cent in St Helens, few were likely to secure other work. There was also the possibility of a loss of jobs at Sidac.

Leathers' counsel went on to argue that Sidac's failure to feed sulphur dioxide from their effluent treatment plant to the sulphuric acid plant was not relevant at this inquiry. Furthermore, in seeking an absolute guarantee that sulphur dioxide would never exceed 0.2 per cent of emission gases, St Helens were demanding the impossible. Nevertheless, risk of such emissions would be kept to a minimum; in any event, there was no risk to health. In casting doubt on the real depth of public feeling against the plant, he drew attention to the fact that the East Sutton Residents' Association had only sixty members, of whom only fifteen attended the meeting at which their chairman and secretary were given terms of reference to represent the Association at the inquiry. All in all, he held that the Council, acting as they were against the recommendation of the Planning Committee, were behaving irresponsibly and unreasonably.[13]

Leathers maintained that St Helens's discontinuance order was 'misconceived, inappropriate and unnecessary'. Since there existed specific remedies in statute and common law, the use of general planning powers should not be entertained—a precept endorsed by government circulars relating to the use of conditions. In addition to an action in nuisance at common law, the Local Government Act, 1972, enabled a local authority to institute proceedings 'for the promotion or protection of the interests of the inhabitants of their area'. Finally, there was, more recently, the Health and Safety Act, which was 'designed to protect the safety of people not only at work but arising from work'.[13]

British Sidac's QC presented figures which showed that disposing of the sulphur dioxide from the effluent treatment plant by discharge to the atmosphere, rather than by feeding to the acid plant, had not led to a detectable change in ground-level concentrations. Moreover, their main objective, reducing sulphides in Sutton Brook, had been achieved. Sidac admitted that the possibility of exploiting waste sulphur dioxide, rather than simply releasing it to the atmosphere, had been 'an inducement to grant planning permission'. However, the importance which the County Borough had attached to this possibility was now imponderable; they certainly had not attempted to ensure integration by the use of planning conditions.[13]

Sidac went on to explain that, despite the original advice that an integrated scheme was feasible, it had proved impracticable. In the absence of integration, adequate dispersion of the sulphur dioxide could be achieved using a sufficiently tall chimney; in any event, this would be required in order to dispose of the sulphur dioxide when the acid plant was not operating. It was generally understood that integration would be reconsidered if it were ever to become technologically possible. They emphasized that a net reduction of emissions of sulphurous gases had been made possible by exploiting Leathers' waste steam. With regard to the incidents, Sidac supported Leathers' contention that the new 'failsafe' acid coolers would lead to no further low-level emissions. With the new chimney, even emissions on start-up would be unlikely to cause offence, unless they coincided with unusual meteorological conditions.[13]

Sidac's counsel sought to cast doubt on the relevance of the evidence produced by St Helens. It was not a question of whether there would never again be emissions, spillages, etc., but whether such emissions seriously endangered public health. In past incidents, affected residents had visited their doctors or the hospital. However, no specific treatment seemed to have been given and no medical evidence had been adduced to show any damage to health. Moreover, the Council was apparently suggesting that the Alkali Inspectorate was not competent to control the plant.

Sidac agreed that the plant appeared to have been inadequately installed, inadequately staffed, and only belatedly modified. However, there was no reason to assume that a properly run acid plant would not be an appropriate use for the site, situated, as it was, next to Sidac, who were large consumers of sulphuric acid. Finally, Sidac listed the financial losses they were likely to incur in the event of a closure by Leathers. These included: loss of £1,200,000 revenue over the following four years from selling electricity and low-pressure steam to Leathers; loss of £200,000 investment in the generator and ancillary plant; and extra costs involved in obtaining and storing alternative supplies of acid.

The chairman of East Sutton Residents' Association explained that the people of Sutton were not, as the list of incidents attributable to Leathers might suggest, hysterical but simply hard-working men and women, who were used to a poor environment but who deeply resented the deterioration of that environment, especially when earlier promises of improvement had been broken. The secretary of the Association (the elected councillor) compared the sixty or more complaints against Leathers with the handful arising from other industries in the same area.

A local resident, who was a senior lecturer at Liverpool Polytechnic, spoke of his fears for the health of young children and the aged living in the locality, which, being predominantly working class, contained an 'unusual number' of sufferers of respiratory disorders. He concluded by saying that there was no reason to expect better plant performance in the future. Of the other nine interested persons, most gave evidence on the distress which they or others had experienced as a result of various emissions from Leathers. The headmaster of the local secondary school described the adverse effects of fumes on his pupils.[13] Another gentleman displayed a pair of ladies' tights holed by acid mist in March 1972.

The outcome

Having listed his findings of fact, the Inspector began his conclusions, in his report of the inquiry, with his opinion that the local planning authority were entitled to seek an order against a works which they considered to have caused nuisance and to have been granted planning permission erroneously. (This view found support from the Royal Commission on Environmental Pollution.)[29] The Inspector further declared that 'the foremost consideration is the effect of this particular use on surrounding development.'[13]

However, the question of the failure to integrate the effluent treatment and sulphuric acid plants was, according to the Inspector, 'wholly irrelevant'. He rebuked the Alkali Inspectorate on two counts. Firstly, with reference to Leathers' chimney, they were 'extremely slow to recognise the practical desirability of the extension, having regard to the number of occasions when there were high sulphur dioxide ground level concentrations which gave rise to complaints'. Secondly, the Inspectorate were remiss in allowing Leathers to continue operating beyond the planned date of the overhaul in 1975 thereby 'risking possible serious failure'. The Inspectorate's action here was not consistent with the enforcement of 'the efficient maintenance criteria of best practicable means'.[13]

These comments notwithstanding, it seemed to the Inspector 'that the plant should now operate without giving rise to incidents which would justify complaint from the public, and that there is therefore no justification for confirming the discontinuance order.' In reaching this conclusion, the Inspector stressed the already improved performance of the plant following the modifications of 1973 and 1975. He suggested that a diminution of public concern was 'already apparent from the small membership of the residents' association considering the extent of residential development in Sutton and the surprisingly small public attendances at the inquiry.'

In addition, the adverse effect on the national economy of the loss of a supply of sulphuric acid, as well as oleum and sulphur trioxide, served to support the Inspector's view. Similarly, the question of compensation, 'the implications of which may not have been fully realised when the discontinuance order was made', was a material consideration. 'Expenditure of public funds of this large order for the limited benefit of comparatively few members of the public would not be defensible.'[13]

The Inspector's most important conclusion—that the discontinuance order be not confirmed—was endorsed by the Assessor. The latter supported the Inspector's conclusions but was disturbed at the high number (12) of incidents associated with spilled and leaking oleum. With reference to the requirements of the Control of Pollution Act, 1974, and the confused state of knowledge of the effects on health of sulphur dioxide and trioxide, he outlined the need for Leathers to undertake more effective and more comprehensive monitoring of their gaseous emissions.[13]

In his decision letter of November 1976, the Secretary of State for the Environment reiterated the conclusions of the Inspector and went on:

The Inspector's conclusions have been considered. The representations that the order is misconceived, inappropriate and unnecessary have been noted but it is considered that, once a local authority have decided to take action under Section 51 of the Act of 1971, it remains for the Secretary of State to decide only whether it is in the interests of the proper planning of the area, having regard to the development plan and to any other material considerations, that the order should be confirmed. On this it is agreed with the Inspector that the foremost consideration arising on the present order is the effect which the use has had on surrounding development, particularly residential development. It is noted, however, that modifications carried out in 1973 and 1975 have led to a marked reduction in the incidents and the Inspector's view that the plant is now up to modern standards is accepted. As the Inspector has commented, great care will be needed in the maintenance of the plant and to avoid spillages and leaks of oleum. Nevertheless, whilst it must be accepted, having regard to the process involved, that there is some risk of adverse conditions arising in the future, it is considered that the powers of the Alkali and Clean Air Inspectorate are sufficient to ensure that such risk is kept to an acceptable minimum. It is agreed with the Inspector that the other considerations referred to in his conclusions support the view that the order should not be confirmed.

For reasons given therefore, the Secretary of State has accepted the Inspector's recommendations and has decided not to confirm the order.[30]

The seeking of a discontinuance order for such a large works is extremely uncommon. Where such an order has been imposed against industrial premises, it has usually related to small-scale, back-street, scrap metal and other, similar works situated in areas where such uses are incompatible with proposed redevelopment schemes. The decision to proceed was clearly the result of intense political pressure brought by members of the public. The residents of this predominantly working-class area used every legitimate weapon at their disposal against the works about which they still complained bitterly, in response to continuing incidents. They even elected an officer of the local action group (campaigning solely against Leathers) to the Council. He proved to be very active within the ruling Labour group in seeking the order. Lobbying by the public and newspaper debate (assisted by a number of 'leaked' documents) were very important factors. It would appear that the order was sought against the advice of the Council's officers (who take part in debates by the Planning Committee but not in full Council meetings such as that at which the decision was taken).

Among the options considered was the possibility of creating a 'buffer zone' around the Leathers plant. This would have involved the demolition of existing housing and been in direct conflict with the rehabilitation and rebuilding which had been taking place. This remedy would be very expensive and politically sensitive—not least because the expense falls upon the ratepayers, in breach of the 'polluter-pays' principle. However, these considerations apply no less to the payment of compensation in the event of confirmation of a discontinuance order on the offending pollution source. In addition, the 'externalities', or social costs, of the buffer zone in terms of the upheaval suffered by the resettled inhabitants would hardly be less than those, such as the loss of some sixty jobs, incurred by closing the plant. That the councillors were prepared to pay the financial costs and see these jobs lost was a measure of the intensity of feeling against the company. Certainly, Leathers' actions and public relations gave the local residents the impression that they were determined to maintain production and profitability by playing down the incidents and doing little to rectify the problems.

It is apparent that St Helens were of the opinion that, as their QC stated, a discontinuance order was preferable to any legal action leading to an injunction. The reason may have been that St Helens would be satisfied with nothing less than closure, as the public demanded: a discontinuance order, by definition, fulfils this requirement. There was no guarantee that an injunction, if granted, would go so far as to require closure.

However, the Public Health Act, 1936, has been used to obtain redress against nuisance from a registered works (see Chapter 2). In this case, as at Leathers, the District Alkali Inspector contended that the best practicable means (which is not a sufficient defence for actions in the High Court) had been observed. Nevertheless, the local authority eventually secured the closure of the works. A High Court judge, when considering an action in 'statutory nuisance', unlike the Minister in deciding whether to confirm a discontinuance order, is not obliged to consider wider, national implications. His deliberations are confined to deciding whether nuisance has occurred and what the remedy should be. Furthermore, a local authority which secures an injunction entailing the closure of an offending works is not obliged to pay compensation.

There is no means of identifying which factor was most influential in the final decision not to confirm the discontinuance order against Leathers. However, given the Minister's endorsement of his Inspector's opinion 'that the foremost consideration ... is the effect which the use [sulphuric acid] manufacture has had on surrounding development, particularly residential development', then it is reasonable to infer that the Alkali Inspectorate's assertions (that 'best practicable means' had been observed and that their powers would be sufficient to minimize the risk of public nuisance in future) was of considerable importance. If so, it must have outweighed the profound concern of the residents and their elected representatives.

Remedies

In July 1976, fractured pipework caused two Leathers' workers to be showered in sulphuric acid: one man died and the other was seriously injured. A report on another incident at the works is contained in the Alkali Inspectorate's report for 1976:

In last year's report, reference was made to a local authority's discontinuance order. The District Alkali Inspector gave evidence to the public inquiry on behalf of the Health and Safety Executive. The appeal was upheld and the discontinuance order was quashed. Operations at the plant throughout the year were trouble-free and without complaint until 27th December. On this date, for the first time since 1973, there was a serious emission of oleum fume when a seal on an oleum recirculating pump failed, causing spillage of some twenty gallons [90 litres] of 65% oleum. An operator was in attendance at the time and took immediate action to shut down the system. A more frequent pump maintenance schedule has been instituted.

The above passage does not suggest any obvious intention on the part of the Inspectorate to impose more rigorous control (at least, not in terms of prosecution) over the plant than hitherto. And since the use of planning powers has, on two occasions, proved woefully ineffective in safeguarding the residents of East Sutton, they would take little comfort in the observation that prevention is better than cure and that they are the unfortunate victims of a palpable planning error. Nevertheless, it is necessary to list some of the changes in procedures and policies of those bodies principally involved in the Leathers' issue, since the planning application in 1968, which might prevent the recurrence of such an error.

In the County Borough, senior officers of the Planning Department exerted considerable influence over their colleagues in other departments and, indeed, over the councillors. This departmental jurisdiction resulted in an officer from the Planning, and not the Public Health, Department reading Leathers' pollution monitors. With local government reorganization in 1974 St Helens, along with many other local authorities, adopted the corporate management approach in which a team of heads of departments exercise a collective responsibility for the preparation of policies and, once they are approved by the Council, for their execution. This fundamental change in procedure has gone a long way to remove the petty inter-departmental rivalries which had led to a situation in which technical advice on a pioneer industrial plant was sought from a source clearly lacking in the necessary expertise and in which the Public Health Department was excluded from involvement for nearly four years. Liaison between the Planning and the Environmental Health Department is now an established routine in St Helens; and as an additional safeguard, an environmental health officer attends all meetings of the Planning Committee to offer technical advice on planning matters with pollution significance.

In addition, officers of the Environmental Health Department will now readily consult the Alkali Inspectorate over matters relating to registered works within the Borough. However, in this connection, it must be observed that communication alone is not sufficient to ensure that a planning error of the Leathers' order can never again arise. The Alkali Inspector's reply to the Inspector's question at the local inquiry suggests that advice to refuse planning consent might well not have been given had he, or his predecessor, been consulted by the planning authority at the very outset. This conclusion is supported by the Inspectorate's failure to communicate with the Council, though it was aware of Sidac's proposals at least six weeks before the planning application was received by St Helens.

Whilst the Inspectorate frequently urges the refusal of planning consent for new housing in the vicinity of existing registered works,[32] there are few examples of the converse. Although the Inspectorate could, at least in theory, withhold the certificate of registration in such circumstances, its usual practice is to register the new works and to consider the proximity of housing as another 'local circumstance' and one requiring a more demanding interpretation of 'best practicable means' to be observed by the operators. The Inspectorate's customary response to calls for improved protection for neighbouring residents is to demand a higher stack. In the absence of data about atmospheric conditions, and consequently about dispersion, it is perhaps surprising that the decision to raise the chimney height at Leathers was so belated. However, the District Inspector did, in addition, require the installation of new coolers and improved maintenance procedures.

When the developers first sought planning consent for the Leathers plant, the metropolitan county of Merseyside did not exist. When, in 1975, officers of the new county planning authority began to analyse the results of a survey of public attitudes to the local environment, it soon became clear that considerable weight needed to be given to policies on pollution in the structure plan then in preparation:

> The greatest benefit to the community can be derived by making a concentrated effort to improve overall air quality through an accelerated programme of smoke control ... and complement this by improvements in the operation of commercial and industrial premises.[33]

Of the industrial pollution policies contained in the finally approved structure plan (which, unlike that of Cheshire (Chapter 3) suffered only minor amendment by the Secretary of State), it is the policy contained in paragraph 9.53 (Table 4.1) which is most germane to the issues illustrated by the Leathers episode. This policy recognizes that, with certain industrial processes, a threat of pollution of surrounding areas is inevitable even where controls beyond those required by 'best practicable means' are enforced. It is not enough, it argues, to allow these 'special category industries' to be sited in an area designated for industrial use in the revelant development plan. The plan advocates the reservation of sites which are well removed from existing housing and other sensitive uses and which allow natural dispersion of atmospheric pollutants for those processes, such as sulphuric acid manufacture, from which polluting discharges can be anticipated.

During the preparation of the structure plan, the County engaged a firm of consultants who compiled a schedule of some seventy sites which might prove suitable for special category industry. However, some boroughs, including the relatively affluent Wirral (until 1974, part of Cheshire), were reluctant to see sites within their areas named within any published plan or document. Nevertheless, the County has retained this schedule and reference is to be made to it in the event of informal inquiries from potential developers. In addition, should a district planning authority refuse consent for special development at an unsuitable location, the schedule might offer an alternative site where the application might be viewed with more favour.

TABLE 4.1
Merseyside Structure Plan industrial pollution control policies

9.49   How it arises

Outside older industrial areas, industry may take the form of isolated works, single firms, industrial complexes, or modern purpose-built industrial estates. Pollution, where it occurs, tends to result from isolated lapses or difficulties in control. In the older areas, by contrast, factors such as poor services, obsolescent plant and the proximity of housing tend to aggravate the effect of basically quite minor pollution problems. These problems—of dust and smuts, bad smells, noise and vibration— tend, however, to be localised and are dealt with by the environmental health authorities. Unpleasant and pervasive smells are more acute in the docklands and common in many other areas: they are technically difficult to control.

9.50   Avoiding future pollution problems

When considering proposals for new development, local planning authorities should try to ensure that sensitive land-uses are not sited so as to be exposed to serious industrial pollution; and they need to take considerable care that, in redevelopment of older urban areas, they do not perpetuate such injurious relationships.

9.51   Policy

Local planning authorities:
  (i) will not normally permit residential development where the proximity of existing industry would pose a risk to health or seriously restrict the quality of environment achievable;
  (ii) will seek reductions in environmental pollution from industrial and commercial sources, through the pollution control authorities, especially where such pollution adversely affects existing residential neighbourhoods.

9.52   Sites for pollution-prone industries

Provided that sites can be found for them within existing industrial areas and away from such sensitive land-uses as housing or hospitals, Merseyside can probably accommodate some firms whose processes potentially give rise to pollution, and can do so with minimal risk or nuisance to the community and reasonable cost to the firms concerned. This is because pollution control technology has advanced in step with pollution control legislation and enforcement. 'Special Category Industry' as defined by the Town and Country Planning (Use Classes) Order, 1972, poses potential problems such as gases and dust discharged into the atmosphere, odour nuisance and liquid effluents, which are difficult to handle. Planning authorities will define locations within existing industrial areas and away from sensitive land-uses, each of which can acceptably accommodate at least one of the emission problems, e.g. dust or liquids. Waste treatment and disposal and certain chemical and pharmaceutical manufacturers, though not ranking as special category industry, will be considered for these locations.

9.53   Policy

Local planning authorities:
  (i) will consider on their merits applications by special category industry to develop on land allocated for industrial use;
  (ii) in those locations defined for special category industry, will normally give more favourable consideration to development difficult to accommodate elsewhere for environmental reasons.

90   *Planning and Pollution*

9.54   Wider impact to be considered

When a District Council receives a proposal to establish or extend special category industry, the County Council will ask to be consulted. This should ensure consideration of any wider environmental impact; and also enable planning authorities to recommend other sites better able to accommodate the type of industry proposed.

9.55   Small firms, pollution and jobs

Redevelopment in older industrial areas and in inner urban areas often displace small firms who may have difficulty in finding replacement premises. This will probably apply especially to special category works. In other cases, industrial processes may cause such severe nuisance on their present sites as to justify re-location for environmental reasons. Though such works are often small, they provide valuable employment. If need were shown to exist, the County Council could reserve or prepare and service sites specifically for industry with particular waste management problems.

9.56   Helping firms with problems

The County Council will consider assisting firms with waste management problems causing pollution or nuisance, where need for such assistance is proven. Ways in which the County may help include assisting the improvement of premises relocating the process or providing serviced sites for special category industrial operations.

Source: Reference 34.

Whilst offering no guarantee that local opposition to special industry can be totally avoided, the implementation of such a scheme could do a great deal to reduce this risk of planning errors such as permitting the Leathers works.

It is possible, however, that the most significant change which has occurred in recent years relates, not to the policies and procedures of local authorities and the control agencies, but to public awareness and expectations of the environment. No longer is there a passive acceptance of decisions, whether taken by members of local or central government, which inflict upon those living in the vicinity the unacknowledged costs of polluting industries, whilst the benefits accrue to those who frequently do not reside in their vicinity. Moreover, even in a period of high unemployment, few will accept that occasional acid mists are part of the price to be paid for having an employer close to their home, even if he is utilizing 'best practicable means'. It seems likely that, nowadays, public participation might well result in the identification of likely pollution problems and in lobbying strong enough to ensure the use of the strongest local authority power in the prevention of atmospheric pollution—the refusal of planning permission for eminently inappropriate developments such as Leathers'.

REFERENCES AND NOTES

[1] 'Local Inquiry into an Application by the St Helens Borough Council for Confirmation of the St Helens (Lancots Lane) Discontinuance Order 1975', PNW/5093/15/1, Dept. of the Environment, Manchester, 1976, Document 3.

[2] Ibid., Document 4.

[3] Ibid., Document 6.

[4] Ibid., Document 7.

[5] Ibid., Document 10.

[6] Ibid., Document 9.

[7] Ibid., Document 12.

[8] Ibid., Document 13.

[9] Ibid., Document 15.

[10] Ibid., Document 41.

[11] *St Helens Reporter*, 4 September 1970.

[12] 'Local Inquiry into an Application by the St Helens Borough Council ...', Document 20.

[13] 'Inspector's Report of the Local Inquiry into an Application by the St Helens Borough Council for Confirmation of the St Helens (Lancots Lane) Discontinuance Order 1975', PNW/5093/15/1, Dept. of the Environment, Manchester, 1976.

[14] 'Local Inquiry into an Application by the St Helens Borough Council ...', Document 24.

[15] Ibid., Document 25.

[16] *110th Annual Report on Alkali etc. Works 1973*, Dept. of the Environment, HMSO, London, 1974.

[17] 'Local Inquiry into an Application by the St Helens Borough Council ...', Document 28.

[18] 'Inspector's Report of the Local Inquiry into the Appeal by Leathers Chemicals Ltd, against Enforcement Notices Served by St Helens County Borough Council', APP/1586/C/73/870, Dept. of the Environment, Manchester, 1974.

[19] *111th Annual Report on Alkali etc. Works 1974*, Department of the Environment, HMSO, London, 1975.

[20] *St Helens Reporter*, 19 September 1972.

[21] 'Local Inquiry into an Application by the St Helens Borough Council ...', Document 36.

[22] *St Helens Reporter*, 5 July 1974.

[23] *St Helens Reporter*, 6 Sept. 1974.

[24] It is perhaps surprising that no reference was (apparently) made to an inquiry under s. 22 of the Alkali Act (see Chapter 2).

[25] 'Local Inquiry into an Application by the St Helens Borough Council ...', Document 54.

[26] *St Helens Reporter*, 5 September 1975.

[27] *Industrial Air Pollution 1975*, Health and Safety Executive, HMSO, London, 1977.

[28] *St Helens Reporter*, 28 Nov. 1975.

[29] Royal Commission on Environmental Pollution, *Fifth Report. Air Pollution Control: An Integrated Approach*, Cmnd. 6371, HMSO, London, 1976.

[30] 'Decision Letter on St Helens (Lancots Lane) Discontinuance Order' 1975, PNW/5093/15/1, Dept. of the Environment, Manchester, 1976.

[31] *Industrial Air Pollution 1976*, Health and Safety Executive, HMSO, London, 1978.

[32] C. Wood, and N. Pendleton, 'Land Use Planning and Pollution Control in Practice', Occasional Paper 4, Department of Town and Country Planning, University of Manchester, 1979.

[33] 'Environmental Pollution and Condition of Land', Draft Report of Survey, Merseyside Structure Plan, Merseyside County Council, Liverpool, 1976. The final version of this report of survey was published, unaltered, in 1979.

[34] 'Structure Plan: Written Statement', Merseyside County Council, Liverpool, 1980.

5
PLANNING AND WATER POLLUTION

Since 1974 control over the pollution of inland waters in England and
Wales has been one of the responsibilities of the ten regional water
authorities. Created by the Water Act of 1973, these bodies are
involved in all phases of the hydrological cycle and, in addition to
the regulation of pollution, their duties include water supply, sewage
disposal, fisheries and assisting water-based recreation.

From Fig. 5.1 a definite trend towards improved river water

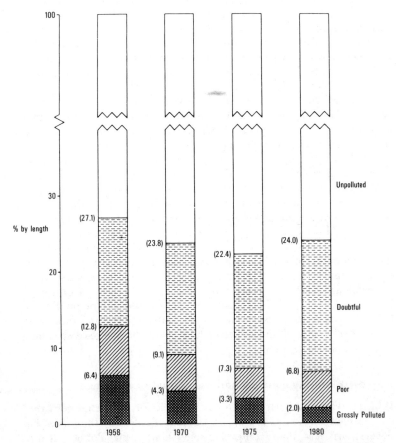

FIG. 5.1   Non-tidal river water quality by class, England and Wales, 1958-80
Source: Reference 2

quality is discernible. Nevertheless, 24 per cent of the total length of over 26,000 km of rivers still suffer some degree of pollution, a significant proportion of which must be attributed to over 2,000 outfalls from sewage treatment plants which regularly discharge an effluent which is less than satisfactory or which does not meet the standard specified within the discharge consent.[1,2] Over 60 per cent of the 4500 discharges from sewage works in England and Wales were, however, satisfactory in 1975, compared with 50 per cent of the 2000 industrial effluent discharges. Over 400 discharges of untreated sewage are principally responsible for the polluted state (Class 2 or below) of half the total length of tidal rivers and estuaries, though the trend again shows marginal improvement.[2]

Sewerage and sewage disposal, formerly within the remit of local authorities, are now among the responsibilities of the water authorities. Allowing a sewage treatment works to discharge a substandard effluent to a watercourse conflicts with an authority's general duty to maintain water quality. This inherent conflict between the authority's roles as both poacher and gamekeeper is taken very seriously; the North West Water Authority, for example, has developed a structure in which no member of the Water Management Subcommittee (approving discharges from treatment works) may at the same time sit on the Water Quality Panel (the duties of which relate to the maintenance and improvement of river water quality).[3]

Where a discharge from a sewage disposal works causes detectable pollution, a riparian owner downstream of the outfall could take action against the water authority in order to defend his common law right to receive the water of his stream 'without sensible diminution or increase and without sensible alteration in character or quality'.[4] Moreover, in a celebrated case brought by an angling association against Derby Corporation in respect of pollution from one of the latter's sewage works, Lord Denning held that it was not a defence to claim that exceeding the works capacity caused the effluent to be sub-standard.[5] More significantly, when Part II of the Control of Pollution Act, 1974, is fully implemented, members of the public will have the power to prosecute any water authority (or any industrial discharger) whose effluent to river falls below the standard specified in the published consent.

Planning controls and residential development

Whilst a water authority is fully answerable for what emerges from its treatment works, its powers to regulate what enters them (via the sewers) are less than comprehensive. Under the Public Health

(Drainage of Trade Premises) Act, 1937, it may refuse, or allow with conditions, the discharge of industrial or trade wastes into the public sewers but, under the Public Health Act, 1936, the owner of any residential property has a right, firmly established in the courts, to discharge domestic waste to sewers.

To test this right, the North West Water Authority attempted to deny the developer of a housing estate permission to connect a private sewer to the public system in 1976. Planning permission for the development had been granted many years earlier, before the creation of the multi-purpose water authorities. The sewerage in the village in question (Disley, in the Borough of Macclesfield) was already grossly overloaded and additional discharge could have led to the deposit of raw sewage on to the highway during periods of heavy rainfall. The developer's appeal against the authority's action was upheld in the Magistrates' Court and subsequently in the Crown Court. This case tends to confirm that, provided the connection is structurally satisfactory, a property owner's right to connect to the public sewer and discharge domestic waste is absolute.

The water authority's dilemma can be mitigated if local planning authorities can be persuaded to withhold planning permission for development, especially housing, in the catchment area of any overloaded treatment plant. Hampshire County Council, for example, has for some time been in consultation with the Southern Water Authority over the amount of development which might be permitted in the drainage area of one overloaded works discharging into Langstone Harbour which, being almost land-locked, enjoys relatively little natural dispersion of pollutants. Similarly, since 1974 the North West Water Authority, in common with other water authorities, has occasionally and reluctantly requested local planning authorities to ban development in areas where sewage disposal facilities were judged to be inadequate and where limited capital resources were more urgently required elsewhere.

Planning powers may also be used to forestall pollution which results from the overwhelming of inadequate sewerage. In areas drained by combined foul/storm water sewers, it is possible in times of heavy storm for overflow from sewers to reach the local watercourse, causing contamination by raw sewage. Again, the local planning authority may reduce the risk of such occurrences, by withholding consent for development, particularly housing, in the affected areas until an adequate system of sewerage is installed.

Such action is not always taken at the instigation of the regional water authority. Until recently, additional development in the village of Haslington, within the area of the Crewe and Nantwich Borough

Council, has been deferred pending the construction of a sewer to relieve the existing drainage which, during periods of heavy storm, could be as much as 200 per cent overloaded. The local watercourse into which the sewer overflowed could become visibly contaminated with faecal matter. Sewerage is the responsibility of the Council under delegated powers and the planning officers accepted the advice of engineering officers that planning consent for any development which would drain to the already overloaded public sewer should be refused. The policy of refusing development in Haslington was enforced from the time of local government reorganization but without the support of the North West Water Authority. The Authority declined to appear at appeals against planning refusal on the grounds of overloading this sewer because, it argued, worse cases of nuisance existed in its area and a too liberal resort to this expedient would, once planning appeals began to be upheld, render it in-effective in cases where it was more imperative. In this case, since the storm water which caused the problem also served to dilute the sewage, the pollution was deemed by the Authority to be acceptably low, given that it only occurred intermittently.[6]

The intervention of local planning authorities is not confined to refusing planning consent in such circumstances. It is possible for a planning authority to require a developer to install a private sewer; such an arrangement could take the form of a planning condition or be included within a planning agreement. At Haslington, for example, the local authority's embargo did not apply to housing development which incorporated private sewerage. The existence of a private sewer bypassing the section of the public sewer prone to overflow enabled one sizeable development to proceed. Crewe and Nantwich Borough Council employed both a planning condition and a planning agreement to ensure that the sewerage provision was satisfactory.[6]

This practice is not uncommon, nor is that of appending to any consent for housing in areas devoid of main sewerage a planning condition specifying the design and overflow characteristics of any septic tank.[7] Fenland District Council, in East Anglia, for example, has a particular concern for the risk of pollution of small water-courses which may result from the effluent from the 'soakaway' type of septic tank overflow. This particular district is characterized by isolated small clusters of dwellings, far removed from main drainage; the land is low lying and the water-table is relatively high, and some care is needed by the planning department to prevent pollution of the many small streams and ditches.

Planning controls and non-residential development

The second largest category of discharge consents in Table 5.1 refers to industrial effluents. The water authorities now allow the direct discharge of trade wastes to rivers only with reluctance; wherever possible, they encourage discharge to sewer and hence to the treatment plant where, given sufficient dilution with domestic sewage, all but the most toxic effluents can be treated. The principal role of the local planning authority in controlling water pollution remains that of deciding upon the location of industrial development, notwithstanding the right of the water authorities to refuse to accept trade discharges or to impose conditions upon them. This role can conflict with the authority's other objectives.

TABLE 5.1

Merseyside Structure Plan Water Pollution Control Policies

10.8 Planning authorities will reserve land for screening stations at locations along the water-front on both banks of the lower Mersey estuary, in order to help the North West Water Authority to improve the condition of foreshores.

10.11 Planning authorities will reserve land for sewage treatment at suitable locations in Liverpool and Wirral.

10.13 There will be a presumption against development proposals which, in the opinion of the local planning authorities, after consultation with the North West Water Authority, would prejudice water quality in the Ribble or Dee estuaries, so that it might fall below the standard which allows the passage of migratory fish at all stages of the tide.

10.16 Planning permission will normally be refused for development which would, in the view of the local planning authorities, after consultation with the Water Authorities, contribute to a further deterioration in the condition of inland waters, either directly or indirectly by over-loading sewage treatment systems which are above or close to capacity.

10.18 Priority should be given to the improvement of grossly polluted rivers and the elimination of nuisance at:
Fine Jane's Brook, Sefton
Sutton Brook, St Helens
Netherley Brook, Liverpool
River Alt below Liverpool North Sewage Works, Liverpool, Knowsley and Sefton
Sankey Brook, St Helens

10.21 Planning authorities will not normally give planning permission for development which, after consultation with the British Waterways Board and the North West Water Authority, they consider would prejudice the quality of water in the St Helens and Leeds-Liverpool canals.

Source: Reference 21.

At Crewe, for example, a long-term aim of the North West Water Authority to improve the quality of the River Weaver could have jeopardized the development of a 40 ha industrial site. The effluent from the Crewe sewage treatment works, although meeting Royal Commission standards in terms of biological oxygen demand and suspended solids,[8] contained ammonia in quantities which could adversely affect freshwater fish. The works' notional surplus capacity was reduced from 10,000 to 2,000 population equivalent by the water authority in order to forestall further deterioration of the river. Crewe and Nantwich Borough Council did not accept this reduction as it was actively seeking the development of the industrial site (which it owned and where it had provided the necessary infrastructure, including a trunk sewer). If one of the vacant plots on this industrial estate had been occupied by a firm which made large demands on effluent treatment, then the notional spare capacity of 2,000 population equivalent could well be exhausted and further expansion would have been ruled out. In the event, following informal meetings between officers of the local and the water authorities, the expansion of the sewage works was brought forward and no development had to be delayed or refused.[6]

In principle, a planning authority anxious to protect waters within its area could apply planning controls to this end: wherever planning consent is sought for a new industrial development, a planning condition could be imposed regulating the quantity, temperature, or chemical composition of any waste discharged to a watercourse. Similarly, a planning authority, when granting consent for any pipeline discharging waste to the seas, might limit wastes to those which would not occasion nuisance if returned by the tide to the shore.[9] The use of such conditions, of course, would run counter to central government advice as they would duplicate controls imposed by the water authorities. However, these considerations are somewhat hypothetical, as no instances of planning powers being used to regulate the nature of discharges of industrial effluent to coastal or inland waters in England and Wales have been reported. [7,10]

It should not be inferred from this observation that land use planning has no part to play in mitigating water pollution arising from industrial sources; for there is one area in which planning authorities are considered to have a role. This is in the imposition of planning conditions which require the developers of land near watercourses to take measures to reduce the risk of the accidental entry of materials which could cause pollution, either directly or by impeding the flow of the river. Equivalent powers are available to County Courts on the application of the water authorities under the Rivers (Prevention of Pollution) Act, 1951. However, the water authorities, and their predecessors (the river authorities) have been reluctant to use these anticipatory powers because of the difficulty of satisfying the County Court that pollution is 'reasonably' apprehended.[11]

Chapter 6 furnishes an example of a planning authority acting with the full support of the water authority to reduce the risk of the entry of potentially harmful materials to a river. In this particular case, the river was Class 1 and the materials were organic herbicides—the output of a small formulation plant. On successive planning consents for development on the site, the local planning authority imposed conditions relating to the handling and storage of chemicals which, in addition to reducing the risk of the airborne dispersal of the defoliating substances, would serve to protect the river which lay only a few metres from where raw materials were stored.

When Part II of the Control of Pollution Act, 1974, is fully implemented the anticipatory powers of the water authorities will be strengthened; in particular, the taking of measures to remedy existing pollution or to forestall accidental water pollution will not require an order in the County Court and, in certain circumstances, it will be possible to recover the cost of such operations.[12] The 1974 Act also confers upon the Secretary of State the power to make regulations designating areas wherein certain activities posing a threat of water pollution may be undertaken only with the consent of the water authority.[13] Until these provisions are brought into force, however, planning powers will remain the most effective means of anticipating and hence forestalling river pollution from accidental entries.

Even with the full implementation of the 1974 Act, there is one significant respect in which the powers conferred upon the water authorities will still fall short of the equivalent powers of Alkali Inspectors. The latter may specify not only the pollution-arrestment equipment to be installed but also the operating procedures to be observed in order to minimize atmospheric emissions. Officers of the water authorities (and their predecessors) have always been prepared to offer industrialists advice on the treatment of effluents prior to their discharge to river; nevertheless their statutory powers over routine discharges (as distinct from accidental entries) are confined to imposing, and then enforcing, quantitative limits on what emerges from the outfall.

The generality of the power of planning authorities to impose planning conditions could, in principle, be invoked to give these bodies, perhaps with technical assistance from water authority personnel, a means of demanding that certain effluent treatment processes be carried out. Again, however, there appear to be very few instances in which this practice has been adopted.[7] In addition, it is arguable that, even with Part II of the Control of Pollution Act, 1974, in force, site-specific planning conditions, or agreements, will continue to provide a more flexible and more effective means of requiring, and enabling prior approval of, measures to mitigate the danger of accidental pollution of rivers. (See the chemical formulation plant case study described in Chapter 6.)

The principal sources of discharge to inland waters are sewage works and industry; however, pollution may arise from other sources, which cannot be regulated in the normal way. Perhaps the most important of these is water pollution arising from certain agricultural activities. This has been of growing concern in recent years. Attention is now being paid to the run-off from fields treated with nitrogenous fertilizers into waters, from which potable supplies are eventually abstracted, as a consequence of the possibility that certain forms of cancer may be linked with rising concentrations of nitrates.[14] In addition, copper and other metallic ions, originating from pig-feed additives, have been found in watercourses which drain fields where slurries from pig-rearing units have been spread.

In the event of proceedings taken as a result of an entry of polluting matter into a watercourse, it is a defence to demonstrate that the entry 'is in accordance with good agricultural practice'. However, this defence is not available when the Secretary of State, on the application of the water authority, has served on the farmer in question a notice specifying (with a reasoned justification) those steps which he must take to prevent the occurrence or recurrence of an entry.

The role which land use planning can play in limiting such pollution has been restricted by successive General Development Orders which have designated most development associated with agriculture as 'permitted development'. However, there is evidence of at least one planning authority withdrawing permitted development rights from an intensive livestock unit which had been the source of a polluting discharge to a stream as well as the origin of odour nuisance.[7]

As mentioned in Chapter 2, the Royal Commission on Environmental Pollution has recommended that all such units should now require planning permission (the largest units already do).[14] The Commission made a number of suggestions relating to improving the control of water pollution from agricultural sources. It recommended mandatory consultation of the water authorities by planning authorities on development proposals which might have significant water pollution implications, including intensive livestock unit developments, where these required planning permission.

The Royal Commission took a somewhat equivocal position on the use of planning conditions to control pollution:

we regard intensive livestock units as industrial in character and we consider it reasonable to require the observance of operational practices designed to reduce pollution risks. One approach to this that has been adopted by some planning authorities is to attach conditions to planning consents which relate to the operation of these units. ...

We believe that where development control is needed on pollution grounds it is understandable and proper that planning authorities should wish to obtain assurances, as a condition of consent, that the operating practices adopted will be such as to reduce pollution risks to an acceptable level. We think, therefore, that the question of whether planning conditions should be used to control pollution cannot be answered in isolation. It is necessary to consider the other means that are available to ensure that good practices are observed from the pollution viewpoint. ...

We see a need to set constraints on operating practices, in advance, where nuisance conditions may be caused: while we are agreed that the imposition of planning conditions is an inappropriate method for seeking to control the day-to-day management of an enterprise, the practice appears logical and defensible where no other means of achieving this aim are available. This is not to say that the practice is legitimate or effective; we are not aware that the validity of such conditions has been tested or that they could be enforced. Nevertheless, we would suppose that the attachment of conditions to planning consents would increase the likelihood that they will be observed.[14]

It is apparent, therefore, that the Royal Commission sees local planning authorities playing a useful role in the siting of certain agricultural activities, should they be subject to planning permission. In the absence of alternative anticipatory controls (Chapter 2), the Commission accepts that planning conditions can be used to ensure some limitation of potential pollution. At the time of writing, no response to these observations has been made by the Government.

It is appropriate to conclude this discussion of unsewered pollution sources by referring to the transportation of chemicals and to leaching. More care in the bulk transport of hazardous chemicals can perhaps be encouraged only by heavy, deterrent fines on the owners or drivers of road-tankers which, through negligent handling, overturn and spill their loads (via the storm sewers) into watercourses, often causing considerable pollution. Leaching of toxic materials from solid waste tips can also cause significant pollution of surface and underground waters (Chapter 7).

Development plans and water pollution control

The form and content of references to water pollution in development plans show a wide variation. Nevertheless, the majority of structure plans contain a commitment to withhold development in areas where sewage disposal or sewerage systems are such that an additional burden would lead to pollution of watercourses. In this respect, policies contained in the approved structure plan for South Hampshire are typical:

> No development will be permitted which would overload existing or proposed facilities such as to cause harmful pollution ...
> No industrial or other uses will be permitted unless local planning authorities are first satisfied that effective steps will be taken to avoid the discharge of harmful waste or effluent.[15]

Policies with a similar purpose were included in the approved structure plan for Staffordshire:

> The County Council will not permit:
> (a) development which would overload existing facilities so as to cause harmful pollution;
> (b) industrial or other land use which would discharge harmful wastes or effluents.[16]

Withholding planning consent for development, principally housing, in order to forestall pollution is not uncommon and thus the incorporation of this indirect means of pollution control within a structure plan policy is unsurprising. However, the reference in the policies quoted above to industrial land uses and the commitment to refuse consent, should any effluent be thought to lead to deterioration of water quality, is more remarkable. Arguably, such a policy, by implication, pre-empts the power of the water authority to refuse consent to discharge under specific water pollution control legislation. The true effectiveness of such a policy can only be judged once it has been cited in support of a decision to refuse planning consent. The views of the Secretary of State, in the event of an appeal by the aggrieved applicant, would then determine the utility of such pollution control policies.

A policy included in the draft structure plan prepared by Humberside County Council is salient:

> The County Council, with the many agencies involved, will investigate existing levels of pollution with a view to establishing standards with which development will be required to comply so that atmospheric and water quality are not adversely affected.[17]

The reference to atmospheric quality standards can be compared with that contained in Cheshire's structure plan (Chapter 3); however, Humberside's intention to judge development in terms of its potential effect on a standard of river quality is perhaps unique.[7] The quantitative standard would have been enforced only with the support of the three water authorities (Yorkshire, Anglian, and Severn-Trent) within whose areas the county lies.[18] In view of observations recorded in Chapters 2 and 3, it is not suprising that this particular policy, although not deleted, failed to receive the endorsement of the Secretary of State for the Environment.

Humberside's structure plan also made reference to a 'subject' plan[19] which the county planning Authority had prepared on intensive livestock units. This plan was prepared by a working party of representatives of *inter alia* the county and district councils, the Ministry of Agriculture, Fisheries and Food, the National Farmers' Union, and the Yorkshire Water Authority. In order to mitigate the problems which arise when intensive livestock units are located in the urban fringe, the plan designated areas around existing settlements as 'protected areas' within which new units would not be permitted.[20]

Humberside's policies on the maximum rate of animal waste spreading were advisory in character and took account of current Ministry of Agriculture advice. For instance: 'there should not be applied a quantity greater than 225,000 litres per hectare ... of undiluted slurry per year.' It was further proposed that animal wastes should be neither spread nor stored in the vicinity of abstraction points for potable water supplies, both from surface and underground sources. Whilst the Yorkshire Water Authority was fully involved in the preparation of the plan, it was emphasized that 'water pollution problems are not intended to be dealt with in this plan and consultations on individual developments should still take place with the appropriate Water Authority.'[20] Nevertheless, the Secretary of State apparently held that a subject plan was not an appropriate medium for the expression of policies on the environmental problems posed by intensive livestock units, and 'the local authorities have agreed that the policy to be adopted on this matter should be separately developed.'[14]

The discharge of untreated sewage from a surrounding population of about 1,000,000 is the principal reason why the Mersey has one of the most polluted estuaries in Europe. Merseyside County Council's structure plan commits the planning authorities to reserving suitable areas of land for screening stations in order to reduce the contamination of the foreshores by crude sewage and by solids and fats from industrial effluents. In contrast, the estuaries of the Dee and the Ribble are among the cleanest in Britain; nevertheless the structure plan includes a presumption against any development which might prejudice the maintenance of this high quality. For watercourses like Sankey Brook (which at times consists of 60 per cent by volume of industrial and sewage effluents) the presumption against development is aimed at preventing further deterioration of this grossly polluted tributary of the Mersey, which has long been a source of nuisance in St Helens (see Chapter 4).[21]

The emphasis which Merseyside's plan has placed on pollution, and water pollution in particular, is remarkable. Nevertheless, the policies remain firmly in the realms of the possible and the practicable; they make no reference to quantative standards of environmental quality nor does their attainment require vast amounts of investment (see Table 5.1). The proposals were drawn up by a working party of officers in which all the relevant pollution control bodies were fully represented, and they implicitly recognize the separate but complementary roles of the water and the planning authorities. Inter-authority collaboration has been assisted by the presence within the county planning department of a number of senior officers with scientific backgrounds. Given the pragmatic approach adopted by Merseyside, it is perhaps unsurprising that their structure plan was approved by the Secretary of State with only very minor amendments.

A number of planning authorities have devoted subject plans to improving the amenity potential of river valleys. Often, in plans of this type, water quality can become subordinate in priority to visual amenity, preventing fly-tipping, reclaiming derelict land, and enabling access to the river bank. However, a subject plan for the River Tees, prepared by Cleveland County Council, calls for an upgrading in the quality of this river not only by the installation of a new sewage disposal plant but also by more stringent conditions on industrial discharge consents.[22]

Gross pollution is recognized in Greater Manchester's structure plan as an impediment to the recreational potential of rivers such as the Tame, the Irwell, and the Mersey.[23] The North West Water Authority has collaborated with the county and district planning authorities on a number of schemes to improve water quality in valleys throughout the conurbation. Notwithstanding the Secretary of State for the Environment's approval of similar policies in other structure plans, the following policy was deleted from Greater Manchester's plan as being too detailed and insufficiently concerned with structural planning:

In granting planning permission for new industrial and residential development the County Council will have regard to the impact it may have on existing river quality standards in the local water courses in those areas where sewage disposal facilities are inadequate.[23]

Whether this decision by the Secretary of State is anomalous or is a response to the changing relationship between county and district planning authorities is unclear.

PLATE 2. Leathers sulphuric acid works. View from Baxters Lane, Sutton, St Helens.

PLATE 3. Grosvenor chemical formulation works. View from the north towards Linthwaite. The River Colne is clearly visible, as are the disputed storage tanks to the left of the works. The Thornton and Ross premises are some distance to the left of the edge of the photograph.

PLATE 4. Penketh Hall Estate and Gatewarth Farm tip. View of phase 3 from the west. The housing estate and the waste disposal site are separated by a railway line (just visible) and the derelict St Helens canal. Tipping was proceeding well to the right of the mound at the time the photograph was taken.

PLATE 5. Chloride lead battery works. View from Cutacre Tip looking north. The building in the foreground is the effluent treatment block and beyond that is the amenities block, to the right of the main production building. The thin stack breaching the skyline serves the registered oxide mill.

It could well be that a water authority's primary interest when examining any development plan submitted for comment lies, not in the
environment section, but in those chapters which discuss population,
housing and industrial trends. A knowledge of the preferred location
of housing expansion and of new industrial estates is of obvious
importance to a water authority in its corporate planning of capital
expenditure on water supply, sewage treatment, and sewerage.
However, it is not the practice of the North West Authority to com-
mit resources solely on the basis of statements in a structure plan;
evidence of a proven, rather than a predicted, need is required
before finances are allocated toward, for instance, a new sewage
disposal works.[3] Generally, it might be argued that an element of
optimism is inherent in the discipline of town and country planning
and that strategic planning is often predicated upon the assumption
of continued growth rather than recession. The water authorities are
sometimes obliged to adopt a degree of circumspection in their
reactions to the prognostications contained in structure plan, in
order to reduce the risk of scarce resources being prematurely
devoted to the servicing of development which subsequently fails to
materialize.

In this context, it should be remembered that a water authority is
required, under the Water Act, 1973, to undertake its own survey of
the waters within its area and to prepare an estimate of the future
(twenty-year) demand for water. In addition, a plan is to be drawn up
outlining the authority's proposals for meeting its various statutory
responsibilities, including 'restoring or maintaining the wholesome-
ness of rivers and other inland and coastal waters'. The survey and
plan are to be kept under continuous review and in a period of not
more than seven years, the water authority is required to prepare,
and submit to the Secretary of State for approval, a programme 'of a
general nature for the discharge of its functions'. In the preparation
of these programmes, plans and surveys, a water authority must not
only consult every local authority within its area but 'have regard to'
any development plan in force within part of its area. Such consultation is willingly undertaken since structure plans contain information which might corroborate the water authority's own estimates of
population, and hence, the demand for water and water-related
services.

The relationship between planning and water authorities

The General Development Order, 1977, lists five categories of
development for which a planning authority, having received a
planning application, is obliged to consult the appropriate water

authority.[24] Each of these categories relates to development which poses an implicit threat of water pollution. One category relates to refuse or waste tips, where the implied threat takes the form of long-term 'leaching' of polluting matter to underground water sources or of percolation through soil to surface waters. Another relates to sewage treatment and sludge disposal and a third to oil refining or storage. It is not difficult to postulate a much wider range of developments for which a more direct threat of pollution of surface waters is posed.

Indeed, a circular issued by the Department of the Environment, in conjunction with an earlier General Development Order, suggested that consultation (with the river authorities) would be 'desirable' over developments which 'appear likely to give rise to pollution' and in particular over:

applications for planning permission relating to or involving the erection of buildings or installation of plant for the compounding, manufacture, storage or significant use of toxic chemicals and proposals to change the use of existing buildings to use for that purpose. Authorities are asked to let river authorities know of any proposals which appear to them likely to give rise to pollution.[25]

It was to just such a change of use to chemical manufacture that the events described in Chapter 6 relate.

It would appear that liaison with the appropriate water authority is now established routine for *any* planning application with water-related implications.[7] The North West Water Authority, for example, has issued a manual on planning liaison to assist local planning authorities in considering planning applications with water pollution or drainage implications.[3]

In the case of residential development, liaison is principally concerned with water supply and drainage considerations but, as noted above, pollution becomes an issue wherever sewerage and sewage disposal are inadequate. Whenever development is proposed in areas where potable water supplies might be threatened (over aquifers or in the catchment areas of reservoirs) then the water authorities are most concerned to have details of the proposals as early as possible. The threat might be such that they would wish to urge planning refusal, or alternatively they might choose to invoke powers of their own.[26]

Only in a small fraction of the planning applications submitted to the water authorities does the liaison process lead to the use of planning powers to limit or forestall water pollution. The principal circumstances in which planning controls are of value have been outlined above: to supplement the 'apprehension' powers of the Rivers (Prevention of Pollution) Act, 1951, and to prohibit development in areas with adequate sewage treatment facilities. Some local planning authorities do append to planning consents conditions which they derive from the comments received from the water authority. The chemical formulation case (Chapter 6) affords an example: the planning authority replicated, as a planning condition, the water authority's refusal to allow wastes to be discharged either to the river or to the sewer. However, this case was to some extent exceptional, given the resolve of the pollution prevention officer of the water authority to protect both the river and the sewage treatment plant (with its biological filters) from herbicidal chemicals.

Whilst it would be an exaggeration to say that relations between planning and water authorities are universally cordial, there are few fundamental differences in attitude comparable with those which have arisen between certain planning authorities and the Alkali Inspectorate. Moreover, there is no evidence of instances in which planning powers have been used, against the wishes of the water authority, to secure control over the discharge of an effluent to a watercourse.[7.27] On the contrary, planning intervention as an indirect means of maintaining river water quality is made, in the great majority of cases, at the request of the water authorities.

The establishment of generally good liaison between water and planning authorities is at first sight a little suprising when it is recalled that before 1974 sewerage and sewage disposal were the responsibility of public health authorities (namely the county boroughs, the municipal boroughs, and the urban and rural district councils). Indeed, these were the original and definitive duties of local authorities under the first public health legislation of the nineteenth century. However, the control of river pollution was not a local authority function but the duty of the river authorities (and their predecessors, the river boards). The local bodies have therefore lost the role of polluter; and the record of many of them in investing in sewage treatment facilities was such that they cannot now make excessive demands on their successors. Resentment at the transfer of functions has been partially mitigated by the fact that the local authority representatives constitute a majority (over central government nominees) in each water authority. In addition, the great majority of district councils act as agents of the water authority in the provision of sewerage in their areas.[28]

Unlike the control of air pollution where there remain many problems of a purely technical nature, there are few forms of water pollution which cannot be solved given sufficient expenditure on the appropriate treatment plant. The demand for a cleaner atmosphere, and for a smoke control programme in particular, was motivated by a recognition of the adverse affect of smoke and sulphur dioxide on the public health. Whilst an individual must perforce breathe notwithstanding the quality of the atmosphere, he is not obliged to drink from, or bathe in, a Class 4 river. Moreover, while such bodies as the National Anglers' Council have an interest in encouraging cleaner rivers and exert considerable pressure to achieve this end, there is no pressure group (analogous to and comparable in influence with the National Society for Clean Air) devoted solely and specifically to this aim.

Although local authorities are no less anxious than the water authorities themselves to see an improvement in water quality, their concern stems, not from public health grounds, but from a recognition of the amenity and recreational potential than clean rivers can offer. However, local councillors are not unaware of the problematic nature of the cost-benefit calculus of clean rivers; while the high costs of effluent treatment are well known, the benefits, in terms of the satisfaction to be gained from boating on, fishing in, or walking beside a restored river, are less tangible.

It remains to be seen whether the publication of a register of consents to discharge,[29] coupled with the right of individuals to prosecute dischargers who violate their consent conditions,[30] will lead to a greater public concern over river water quality. The water authorities are well aware that they could face legal proceedings themselves in respect of the many sewage treatment works which, owing to overloading, fail to comply with their consents. This regretted state of affairs denies the water authorities the opportunity of demanding more stringent standards from industry since the Secretary of State and the National Water Council require that trade effluent and sewage effluent should be treated to the same standard. Apprehension as to the effect of extending the power of prosecution is one reason why Part II of the 1974 Act remains substantially unimplemented at the time of writing.

Effluent treatment plants must compete for scarce funds with water supply and sewerage provision, and while it is central government policy to curb public sector borrowing, the priority must be to maintain the quality of the cleaner rivers rather than to seek improvement of the worse. In these circumstances, the co-operation of planning authorities in phasing development, both residential and industrial, to the available infrastructure will continue to be important.

REFERENCES AND NOTES

[1] The discharge of industrial or sewage effluent to surface waters requires the consent of the appropriate water authority under the Rivers (Prevention of Pollution) Acts, 1951 and 1961, or, in the case of discharge to tidal waters, the Clean Rivers (Estuaries and Tidal Waters) Act, 1960. Where discharge is to underground waters via 'a well, borehole or pipe' then the Water Resources Act, 1963, applies. Under all these various statutes appeal against refusal or consent or against any condition (on quantity, chemical composition, temperature) imposed is to the Secretary of State.

[2] *Digest of Environmental Statistics, 4,* Department of the Environment, HMSO, London, 1982.

[3] C. E. Miller, C. Wood, and J. McLoughlin, 'Land Use Planning and Pollution Control', Report to the Social Science Research Council, Pollution Research Unit, University of Manchester, 1980, vol. iii.

[4] John Young v. Bankier Distillery [1893] AC 691.

[5] Pride of Derby v. British Celanese and Others [1953] Ch. 159, [1953] 1 All ER 179.

[6] C. E. Miller *et al.*, op. cit., vol. II.

[7] Questionnaire returns, reported in C. E. Miller, *et al.*, op. cit., vol. I.

[8] The Royal Commission on Sewage Disposal recommended a 'normal standard for effluents' of a maximum of 20 parts per million for biological oxygen demand and 30 parts per million for suspended solids; this standard presumes a dilution by the receiving watercourse of at least 1 : 8 (Royal Commission on Sewage Disposal, *Eighth Report* HMSO, London, 1912).

[9] There are eleven Sea Fisheries Committees in England and Wales. Limited powers to restrict the disposal of wastes to coastal waters are conferred upon these committees by the Sea Fisheries Regulation Act, 1966. Part II of the Control of Pollution Act, 1974, gives the water authorities powers to control discharge to waters within three miles from any point on the coast.

[10] However, the Secretary of State for Scotland, when granting outline planning consent for the construction of the oil-rig at Nigg Bay in Ross and Cromarty imposed seventy conditions, one of which specified limits on total amounts and concentrations of phenols, oils, biological oxygen demand, sulphides, etc., to be discharged to the sea.

[11] G. Newsom and J. G. Sherratt, *Water Pollution,* Sherratt & Son, Altrincham, 1972.

[12] Control of Pollution Act, 1974, s. 46(4).

[13] Ibid., s. 31(5).

[14] Royal Commission on Environmental Pollution, *Seventh Report. Agriculture and Pollution,* Cmnd. 7644, HMSO, London, 1979.

[15] 'South Hampshire Structure Plan: Written Statement', Hampshire County Council, Winchester, 1975.

[16] 'Structure Plan: Written Statement', Staffordshire County Council, Stafford, 1979.

[17] 'Structure Plan: Policies', Humberside County Council, Beverley, 1979.

[18] Planning Officer, Humberside County Council, 'Personal Communication', 1979.

[19] Town and Country Planning Act, 1971, s. 11(4).

[20] 'Intensive Livestock Units Subjects Plan', Humberside County Council, Beverley, 1979.

[21] 'Structure Plan: Written Statement', Merseyside County Council, Liverpool, 1980.

[22] 'River Tees Plan for Recreation and Amenity', Cleveland County Council, Middlesbrough, 1978.

[23] 'Structure Plan: Written Statement', Greater Manchester County Council, Manchester, 1979.

[24] Town and Country Planning General Development Order, 1977 (SI 1977, No. 289), Art. 15(1)(f).

[25] 'Town and Country Planning General Development Order 1973', Department of Environment, Circular 12/73, HMSO, London, 1973.

[26] Section 18 of the Water Act, 1945, enables the statutory water undertakers to make bye laws to prevent *inter alia* the combination of water supplies. This section is to be repealed by Part II of the Control of Pollution Act, 1974, whereupon equivalent powers will be available in regulations passed by the Secretary of State, under ss. 31, 34 and 35.

[27] C. E. Miller, *et al.*, op. cit., vol. IV.

[28] Water Act, 1973, s. 15.

[29] Control of Pollution Act, 1974, s. 41. Under s. 42 a discharger may apply to the Secretary of State for exemption from the register, on the grounds that a trade secret might be prejudiced by disclosure of the consent conditions.

[30] Under s. 11 of the Rivers (Prevention of Pollution) Act, 1961, a private citizen must obtain the consent of the Attorney-General to bring a private prosecution.

6

THE CHEMICAL FORMULATION WORKS

Colne Valley, like other formerly prosperous parts of the old West Riding of Yorkshire, is visibly scarred by the decline of the traditional woollen and associated textile industries. Many of the mills lie empty and derelict; some have been converted to other uses. It was to such a building, Grosvenor Works, formerly occupied by a rug manu-facturer, that the Formulation Division of Crewe Chemicals Ltd went in 1976.

The site comprises some 2 ha of flat land at Linthwaite, at the bottom of the steep-sided Colne Valley (Plate 3). It lies about 6 km south-west of Huddersfield and is bounded to the south by a loop of the River Colne, which is only metres from the works itself, and to the north by the now disused Huddersfield Narrow Canal, a popular haunt for anglers. Although there is a mill occupied by Thornton and Ross, pharmaceutical manufacturers, a few hundred metres from Crewe Chemicals' building, land immediately to the east and west is in agricultural use. The site is approached from the A62 trunk road from Huddersfield to Manchester; a single-track lane descends a 1 : 8 gradient and crosses the river. The building is nearly midway between, and approximately 400 m from, parallel lines of ribbon development on the shoulders of the valley (Fig. 6.1).

Crewe Chemicals Ltd was formed in 1972 at Sandbach in Cheshire by a businessman who was, by 1978, the Chairman of a company with a reported[1] annual turnover of £5,800,000, with associated works at Linthwaite and Workington, in addition to the original in Cheshire.

The Works Manager, who joined Crewe Chemicals in 1976, had commenced his career in the chemical industry on the shop floor; and later he too had founded his own company. He began work at Lin-thwaite (in 1976) with one labourer and capital of £1,500. The works, which had a reported turnover of £1,300,000 per annum[1] by 1978 and £2,000,000 per annum by 1980,[2] had been involved in the formulation of a wide variety of chemical products including agri-cultural chemicals, herbicides, pesticides, paints, lacquers, and food additives, often responding to orders at very short notice. As a result of the manager's aggressive sales policy and numerous trips abroad in search of new markets, the works exported some 85 per cent of its output in 1978. By that time, the plant was in operation for twenty-four hours per day, seven days a week, and employed some thirty-

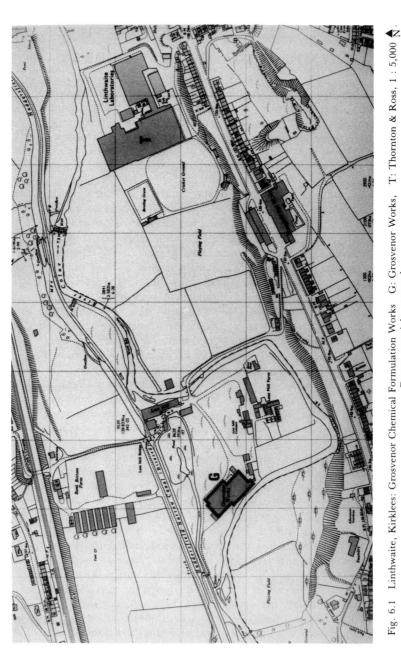

Fig. 6.1   Linthwaite, Kirklees: Grosvenor Chemical Formulation Works   G: Grosvenor Works,   T: Thornton & Ross, 1 : 5,000

two operatives, who earned wages above the local average for unskilled labour.

The Works Manager took pride in an achievement which, in a short time, had created jobs in an area of high unemployment; had contributed to the export drive; and, in the manufacture of pesticides, had assisted agriculture. Occasionally, he would concede,[1] such intensive, innovative, and enterpreneurial endeavour was not totally compatible with the vigorous enforcement of either town and country planning or pollution control legislation.

The original planning applications

In May 1976, Crewe Chemicals applied to Kirklees Metropolitan Borough Council for planning permission for the change of use of Grosvenor Works, Linthwaite, from 'rug manufacture to the manufacture, processing and packaging of chemicals'. In considering this application, Kirklees Planning Department undertook a series of consultations with a number of bodies, including the Yorkshire Water Authority, the British Waterways Board, the County Council, and the Department of the Environment (which at that time embraced the Department of Transport), the Factory Inspectorate, and Kirklees Environmental Health Department, which sought the specialist advice of the Alkali Inspectorate in Manchester.

The local planning authority was aware of the potential water pollution hazards associated with the proposed use. Indeed, a planning application for the change of use of a building situated near a watercourse to chemical manufacture was explicitly cited in a circular as being one for which consultation with the water authority was 'desirable'.[3] The danger of the accidental entry to the river and the canal of chemicals, whether in liquid or solid form, was obvious; as was the possibility of the discharge of chemicals to the atmosphere. Further, consideration was given to the question of noise, both from the operation of the plant within the building and from the lorries serving the plant.

Having discovered no compelling objections to the development during the various consultations, the Kirklees Development Control Subcommittee granted permission for Crewe Chemicals' application. The Grosvenor Works site was within an area designated for industry under the Colne Valley Town Map approved in 1963; in addition, it was Kirklees' policy to encourage industry to move into the Colne Valley to relieve the high unemployment there. Granting the application was therefore in accordance with Council policy. The permission was subject to fifteen planning conditions, many of which were included on the advice of the various consulted bodies. Those relating to pollution control were:

2. Before the commencement of the development, details of any manu-facturing or formulating process or plant shall be submitted to and approved in writing by the District Planning Authority.
8. No goods, plant or machinery (including motor vehicles) shall be stored or displayed for sale in the open without the written consent of the District Planning Authority.
9. Before the development commences, full details of any trade effluent, and the proposed methods of disposal of drainage and of any alter-ations to the existing drainage from the premises shall be submitted to and approved in writing by the District Planning Authority.
10. No work other than the movement of containers and work incidental to the storage of materials shall take place in the open air.
11. Suitable and efficient dust extraction and collecting equipment shall be installed in the building allowing also for adequate ventilation thereof, so as to prevent emissions of pollutants to the atmosphere.
12. All vapours and odours shall be collected and passed through suitable scrubbing towers (either Alkaline or Acid Solution to be used), and finally deodorised by the installation of suitable and efficient plant and discharged at a height of at least 10 feet above the highest point of the building.
13. The noise level measured at a point 1 metre from the external wall of the building shall not exceed 65 dB (A) during daytime and 55dB (A) at night time. (Between the hours of 10.00 p.m. and 7.00 a.m.).
14. No vehicle over 2 tons [tonnes] unladen weight shall be permitted to enter or leave the premises before 7.00 a.m. or after 10.00 p.m. on week-days and at no time on Sundays.
15. All effluent including toxic wastes shall be disposed of in accordance with the provisions of the Control of Pollution Act, 1974.[4]

The minutes of the meeting of the Subcommittee of July 1976 record the resolution:

That in respect of [Crewe Chemicals'] application, a joint meeting of the Executive Sub-Committee of the Development and Technical Services and Environmental Health and Control Committees be convened to consider the detailed matters reserved by Condition 2 when these are received.

It should be noted that the 'development' involved relates, not to the construction of a building, but to the change of use of an existing building. However, for the types of processes carried out by Crewe Chemicals at Grosvenor Works, the company contended that they were not obliged to seek planning permission because the uses to which they put the building fell within the same use class of the Use Classes Order, 1972,[5] as that of the building's previous occupant. Both rug manufacture and the formulation processes initially operated by Crewe Chemicals could classify the works as 'a general industrial building' (Class IV). It is only when a process is specifically cited under Classes V to IX of the Order that the building in which it is operated carries the designation of 'special industrial building'. The company later stated that they had chosen to seek planning permission in anticipation of operating processes which would entail, in the particular meaning of planning legislation, a change of use.[2]

Kirklees Planning Department, however, had inferred from the list of processes and materials submitted with the planning application, that the building could become a 'special industrial building by virtue of the presence of processes, either registrable under the Alkali Act (1906) or using chlorphenols or chlorcresols as intermediates (Classes V and VII respectively).[6] A meeting with the Alkali Inspectorate in August 1977, however, confirmed that the works were not registrable and hence did not fall within Class V. Kirklees subsequently made substantial efforts to prove that the works could be classed as a special industrial building but the company denied this until 1980, when a new and registrable process was installed. Only then did the planning consent and its attendant conditions come into effect.

In August 1976, the Works Manager submitted a second planning application for:

use of land for parking, loading and unloading of vehicles and storage of materials ancillary to the manufacture, processing and packaging of chemicals at: Land adjacent to Grosvenor Works, Linthwaite.

This application related to land which had been omitted from the previous one. Further consultations were carried out by the local planning authority and permission was granted in January 1977, again with conditions which sought to protect the local environment from various forms of pollution:

7. Bunding of storage vessels shall be provided to the satisfaction of the District Planning Authority and all such vessels shall be kept well clear of flammable materials.
12. The area adjacent to the site boundary shall incorporate flood defences to minimise the risk of flooding to the satisfaction of the District Planning Authority; details of these shall be submitted ... and the works shall be carried out before the development is completed.
16. No drainage to, or pollution of, the Huddersfield Narrow Canal shall take place.
17. The sites shall be developed with a separate system of drainage connected to the existing public sewer, and surface water to the River Colne.
[Condition 4 was virtually identical to condition 8 of the first permission and conditions 13, 14, and 15 reproduced the requirements of the identically numbered conditions.]

Condition 7 was included at the request of the Yorkshire Water Authority and sought to prevent the spread, to the river in particular, but also to the sewer, of any materials in the event of damage to a storage vessel. The risk of an accidental entry of chemicals to the channel of the River Colne was an obvious cause for concern. A drum or sack of raw material, especially any herbicidal compound used at the works, if inadvertently allowed to enter the stream, could have had a serious and, perhaps, lasting effect on the ecology of the river. An incident of this nature could have resulted from the mishandling of materials during loading or unloading, or perhaps could have occurred during a period of flooding. The danger might have been partially allayed by requiring secure storage of all materials. Of course, it was neither practicable nor possible to anticipate or forestall all sources of accident; but planning conditions, such as condition 7 of the permission, might have served to mitigate the danger. Conversely, condition 12 recognized the danger posed by flood waters from the River Colne reaching the stored chemicals. In such circumstances, however remote, not only could the river be disastrously contaminated but land over a wide area of the flood plain could be adversely affected.

Of course, once an entry of polluting matter to the river had occurred then the water authority would have been empowered to prosecute under the Rivers (Prevention of Pollution) Act, 1951. Anticipatory powers also exist under the Act (Chapter 5) but the need to demonstrate that pollution is 'reasonably apprehended' has resulted in this procedure being used only rarely.[8] As mentioned in Chapter 5, when Part II of the Control of Pollution Act, 1974, comes into force it will be possible for a water authority to carry out measures to prevent anticipated pollution.[9] Nevertheless, site-specific planning conditions (or agreements) may well continue to provide a more flexible means of requiring measures to mitigate the danger of accidental pollution of rivers. This is particularly true where, as with Crewe Chemicals, the potential danger might be averted simply by demanding bunding of any vessels containing liquids, by requiring secure storage and careful handling of solid materials, and by demanding fencing of the nearby river bank.

A regional water authority's principal means of forestalling non-accidental contamination lies in the right to refuse, or to allow conditionally, the discharge of trade effluent either directly to the river (under the Rivers (Prevention of Pollution) Act, 1951), or indirectly, via the sewage disposal system (under the Public Health (Drainage of Trade Premises) Act, 1937). The Yorkshire Water Authority had taken some pains to make it quite clear in discussions with Crewe Chemicals that no discharge of trade effluent to the sewer, far less to the river, would be permitted. Only domestic sewage could be discharged to the public sewer. All trade effluent was to be removed by tanker to a licensed waste disposal site. In addition, any surface water from areas such as the roof of the building which might be vulnerable to contamination from chemicals was similarly to be collected and tankered away for disposal elsewhere. As for less vulnerable surface runoff from the car parking area, this could be drained ultimately to the river provided that a 'soakaway' of sufficient depth was constructed.

These stringent requirements, which formed the substance of a number of conditions in the planning consents, must be seen in the context of the classification of the River Colne at Linthwaite. From its source in the Pennines, through Colne Valley as far as its confluence with the River Holme at Huddersfield, the Colne falls within the water quality Class 1 (clean)[10] and has a fair population of trout and other freshwater fish. The water authority would view with extreme disfavour any discharge which would reduce the quality of any stretch of water from Class 1 to Class 2 (poor or doubtful). However, discharge of process effluent from Crewe Chemicals even to the sewer had been proscribed; for the herbicidal chemicals used at Linthwaite works, if present in the effluent, could have destroyed the biological filtration system of the sewage treatment works.

Having refused permission to discharge to the sewer, and to the river, the water authority had no statutory right to specify alternative means of process waste disposal. Yet the local planning authority could require that liquid wastes be stored and removed by road tanker for disposal at a waste disposal site. Condition 15 of the two permissions gave the district planning authority a power equivalent to that of the waste disposal authority because to dispose of Crewe Chemicals' waste, other than 'in accordance with the Control of Pollution Act, 1974', would automatically entail an offence under that Act.

Conditions 13 and 14, which related to noise pollution were, unlike many of the water pollution conditions, retrospective: enforcement would follow the existence, rather than the possibility, of the polluting incident. However, it is likely that a number of violations of the conditions (i.e. either frequent nocturnal movement of lorries or repeated exceeding of the noise limits) would have to have been demonstrated before the local authority would have considered taking action.

It could be argued that conditions of this nature replicated powers available to the local authority under other legislation.[11] But in summary proceedings under the Control of Pollution Act, 1974, relating to noise nuisance from trade premises, it is a defence to show that 'best practicable means' have been used to prevent noise. More importantly, it lies to the Magistrates' Court to decide whether the noise in question constitutes, whether by quality or quantity, 'nuisance'.

With the above planning conditions, however, should the owner have appealed against any enforcement notice then the subjectivity of the concept of 'nuisance' would not have arisen since a violation of the condition could be unequivocally demonstrated either from the records of noise-measuring equipment or by corroborated evidence of traffic movements within the proscribed periods. It does not follow, however, that an appeal against enforcement would automatically be dismissed in the light of such evidence: it could be that the original condition would be discharged as unreasonable, given the availability of alternative means of redress against noise pollution under other legislation.

While the use of specifically worded planning conditions to control noise avoids, at least in theory, the interpretation of 'nuisance', the very objectivity of such conditions can serve to reduce their intended effect. It is possible that the operations of Crewe Chemicals could have occasioned noise nuisance to local residents without involving either violation of the noise limits or nocturnal movement of lorries. In such circumstances, the planning conditions would have afforded no redress and resort to other legislation would have been necessary.

However, since this second planning consent was for the 'use of land ... ancilliary' to a change of use which had not yet been made, it remained similarly outstanding and its seventeen conditions were equally inoperative.[6]

Local reaction

When Crewe Chemicals' original planning application had been publicized, a local amenity group, the Colne Valley Society, had been somewhat concerned at the prospect of another chemical works within the area. In order to learn more of Crewe Chemicals' intentions for the Linthwaite site, two members of this society, both polytechnic lecturers, had visited the company's parent division at Sandbach and received assurances from the chairman that the works would operate with little adverse effect on the surrounding areas. As the operations of Crewe Chemicals at the Grosvenor Works progressed, the hostility of the Colne Valley Society grew more pronounced. The society, in conjunction with the Friends of the Earth, organized a protest demonstration at the site attended by some seventy people, many of whom were residents of nearby houses. Protest letters began to appear in the local press and complaints were delivered to local councillors and to the Kirklees Environmental Health Department.

It was alleged that noise from the works was a source of nuisance, causing frequent disturbance of sleep. The cause was not only the movement of heavy lorries but also the operatives' practice of hammering the sides of grinding equipment jammed by the accumulation of chemicals being processed. In addition, residents complained that the chemicals used at the works had a distinct and unpleasant odour, which was frequently detected in the vicinity of the works.

Nevertheless, the principal source of complaint related to the defoliation of vegetation around the site caused, it was claimed, by herbicide dust originating from Crewe Chemicals. Large areas of grass on the adjoining recreation and cricket grounds, for example, had been completely destroyed.[12] Observing this, Thornton and Ross, who have occupied their site near Crewe Chemicals since 1936, grew alarmed at the prospect of pollutants from Crewe Chemicals contaminating their pharmaceutical output. The possibility of such an occurrence could lead to the Medicines Inspectorate of the Department of Health and Social Security withdrawing their licence, thereby imperilling the jobs of the workforce of 350.[13]

In response to the growing opposition to Crewe Chemicals, Kirklees decided to undertake environmental monitoring around the site. After seeking advice from the West Yorkshire County Analyst's Department, the Alkali Inspectorate, and other authorities, the Environmental Health Department decided to examine rain-water. Deposit gauges were set up at various points around the works and left in place for over eight months. At monthly intervals samples were sent to the County Analyst's Department for examination. These tests proved negative; if the rain-water did contain compounds released by Crewe Chemicals, they were in quantities too small to be measurable. (Atrazine, the compound later shown to be responsible, is quite difficult to detect in water at low concentrations.) Other tests, on locally grown vegetables alleged to have been contaminated by fall-out, also proved negative.

Environmental health officers reported[11] that they had observed 'discoloration of trees' some 200-300 m from the Grosvenor Works, but they could find no direct evidence to link this occurrence with Crewe Chemicals. A meeting between environmental health officers investigating these complaints and the company took place in August 1977. The Works Manager agreed that scorching of vegetation (taking the form of various plants and trees dying or foliage becoming damaged) on land owned by the company—but confined to it—had taken place as a result of the herbicide atrazine, in powder form, being discharged while loading a vehicle. He stated that an enclosed loading bay was to be constructed to prevent further emissions.[14]

The involvement of the Alkali Inspectorate as a result of local representations about pollution was recorded:

> Considerable complaint arose concerning a works carrying out grinding and formulation of herbicide-type materials. Two incidents of scorching of vegetation occurred close to the works. A joint investigation was made involving the Factory Inspectorate, Alkali Inspectorate, Employment Medical Advisory Service and the local authority. It was concluded that site emissions were mainly an amenity problem to the neighbourhood but that due attention to the control of the process was necessary.[15]

Quite apart from Kirklees' reference to this body, the Works Manager stated that he had worked closely with the District Alkali Inspector and that it had been suggested that a local liaison committee be set up.[2]

The environmental health officers also investigated a number of complaints arising from the operation at night of a diesel-powered compressor. An amicable resolution of the problem was achieved by insulating the compressor by surrounding it with bags of chemicals. Other noise problems were also easily ameliorated. Overall, the officers could find no substantive grounds to warrant taking action in nuisance.

The Colne Valley Society viewed the various claims of both the Environmental Health Department and Crewe Chemicals with derision: the fact that the tests commissioned by the local authority proved negative served only to cast doubt on the scientific validity of the procedure and on the technical competence of those undertaking it. The effects of the presence of Crewe Chemicals, the Society maintained, were all too obvious: trees and vegetation around the site, which were alive before the firm's arrival, were now dead or dying.

Subsequent planning applications

In August 1977, Crewe Chemicals submitted a planning application for the 'erection of a steel framed building for chemical manufacture on land adjacent to Grosvenor Works'. In considering this application, the local planning authority again consulted a variety of agencies. A press release by the company in October 1977 referred to products Kirklees knew nothing of and the authority therefore wrote to the company seeking more information. Crewe Chemicals replied, giving details of the company's products and agreeing with the assessment by the Council that the processes carried out at Grosvenor Works all fell within Class IV of the Use Classes Order.[7]

In October 1977, Kirklees received a letter from Thornton and Ross which described the company's fears at the prospect of the expansion of Crewe Chemicals' activities which the development, if permitted, would allow. Thornton and Ross also lent their support to a letter,[16] written by the Colne Valley Society in November, in which they urged the Secretary of State for the Environment to exercise his power to 'call in' the application and determine it himself. This letter expressed fears for the health and safety of Crewe Chemicals' workforce as well as the anxieties of local residents. In particular, it drew attention to:

(a) the effects of air pollution on the health of persons living in the area;
(b) damage to vegetation and contamination of the river and canal by effluent or accidental escape of dust;
(c) the degree of increased noise from traffic and operation of machinery which would result from the extension being built;
(d) the effect of the operation of the plant on the activities of Thornton and Ross;
(e) potential hazards from fire, explosion or flood.

A note accompanying this letter indicated that its purpose was endorsed by, among others, the MP for Colne Valley, a lady who was both a county and district councillor for the area, a local magistrate, a local doctor, and the Huddersfield branch of the Friends of the Earth. The Society also organized a petition bearing 170 names. However, before a reply from the Department of the Environment was received, the local planning authority decided, in November 1977, to refuse the application for the following reasons:

The District Planning Authority is satisfied that the proposed development would result in·an unacceptable increase in environmental pollution, and, furthermore, that the environment could not be satisfactorily protected by the imposition of conditions.

At the same time, the authority decided to take enforcement action against several storage tanks which had been erected without planning permission. They were persuaded to delay by the company, pending the submission of a retrospective planning application.

This refusal was explained as follows.[6] There had been incidents of scorching of foliage around the site and, while none of these incidents could be incontrovertibly attributed to Crewe Chemicals, the expansion of the company's activities, which the proposed development would foster, could only add to pre-existing pollution from a variety of sources in the area. In addition, it was the view of Kirklees Borough Council that, in order to forestall this possibility, a refusal rather than a conditional approval of planning permission was necessary, since even the maximum enforcement penalty would be incommensurate with the damage which could be caused and hence would afford insufficient safeguard.

A subsequent planning application, submitted in December 1977, proved no more successful. This application sought retrospective planning consent for the construction of ten bulk storage tanks which had already been erected. The views of various agencies were sought and the Yorkshire Water Authority reiterated that any storage vessels, and these tanks in particular, should be adequately bunded. The Colne Valley Society organized a second petition, this time signed by some 250 persons, against the application in March 1978.

In June 1978, Kirklees chose once again to withhold planning approval. On this occasion, their reasons were:

The proposed [*sic*] development would allow for an intensification of the existing use at Grosvenor Works, and the District Planning Authority is not satisfied that such an intensification would not result in environmental pollution.

In comparison with the previous explanatory statement the above justification was not only more cautious in tone, but also more explicit, in so far as it explained that it was the possibility of intensification of use, and hence a greater risk of pollution, which necessitated planning refusal.

This decision on the storage tanks coincided with the decision on yet another application, submitted on behalf of Crewe Chemicals in April 1978, which sought permission for the addition of an enclosed loading bay to the entrance of the existing building, for the erection of a warehouse and for further parking space. However, the plans relating to the warehouse were identical to those submitted with the earlier, unsuccessful, application for the 'steel framed building for chemical manufacture'.

Permission for the loading bay alone was granted by the full committee with nineteen conditions, many of which related to the control of potential pollution:

12. Except with the written approval of the District Planning Authority, domestic foul sewage shall be taken to the foul sewer, surface water from uncontaminated roofs shall be disposed of via a soakaway, and chemical waste and surface water runoff from the yard areas around the premises shall be taken to a chemical waste effluent tank for disposal by a road tanker.
13. Before development commences full details of drainage proposals to satisfy the requirements of Condition No. 12 above shall be submitted to and approved in writing by the District Planning Authority.
14. No goods, plant or machinery including chemical products and raw materials shall be stored in the open, and no work other than the movement of containers and other suitably packaged or contained materials shall take place in the open air without the written consent of the District Planning Authority.

18. No material shall be permitted to enter the channel of the River Colne.
19. All loading and unloading of materials shall take place in the loading bay, and not in the open air.
[Condition 15 was identical to the two previous conditions numbered 14.]

Conditions 14 and 19 allowing, in the open air, only the movement of adequately sealed containers, represented an elaboration of earlier conditions designed to minimize the release of potentially harmful materials. The most stringent conditions were, yet again, aimed at reducing the risk of pollution of the River Colne. Condition 18 gave the local planning authority a power comparable with that vested in the regional water authority under the Rivers (Prevention of Pollution) Acts.

Under this condition there was no obligation upon the local planning authority to demonstrate that any entry caused or might cause, pollution either directly or indirectly by impeding the flow of the river. Thus, in theory, Crewe Chemicals would have been open to enforcement action should any 'material', whether harmful or innocuous, have entered, whether by accident or by intent by some person, the River Colne. However, it is again by no means clear that, in the event of an appeal against an enforcement of this condition, so literal an interpretation would be accepted.

Perhaps the true importance of this condition lay in the fact that its potential enforcement, following an entry of pollutants from Crewe Chemicals to the river, lay at the discretion, not of the water authority, but of Kirklees Borough Council. Thus it afforded the local authority a rare opportunity to be seen to take a positive step, as distinct from making representations to the water authority, in seeking to deter would-be polluters of local watercourses. Condition 12 spelt out in more detail the requirements of the local planning authority (or, perhaps more accurately, the water authority) on drainage.

These planning decisions have been explained as being part of a consistent approach: it became the practice of Kirklees to oppose any development which could, either directly or indirectly, result in intensification of the land use, i.e. chemical formulation. In other words, any construction (such as the 'steel framed building', the 'warehouse', or the 'storage tanks') which would be necessary for increased output of finished products, entailing a greater throughput of raw materials and hence a greater risk of pollution of the surrounding area, would be refused. On the other hand, any application for an innocuous development, or for one, like the loading bay, which might serve to reduce the possibility of pollution, would be approved. However, any such planning approval would carry with it numerous planning conditions relating not merely to the particular development in question but to various aspects of Crewe Chemicals' site and operations.[7]

A meeting between the company and Kirklees, held in July 1978, resulted in the suggestion by the Works Manager that an independent inquiry should be set up at which the future of Crewe Chemicals operations could be reviewed. The Council members present affirmed their support for the encouragement of industrial development but confirmed that they had to have regard for environmental considerations and for the views of all the parties involved, including the people living and working in the area.[7]

In a newspaper article,[17] following a meeting of the Kirklees Development and Technical Services Committee in August, the Works Manager was quoted directly:

One of the biggest problems with our planning applications has been their technical aspects and the fact that nobody in Kirklees understands our operations [he went on]. Hence came the suggestion of an independent expert.

Pollution has been extremely slight. Of 19 compounds listed, tests carried out by environmental health have been unable to detect any measurable amounts of pollution.

In the same article, the Chairman of the Committee, who had not attended the meeting with Crewe Chemicals, was also quoted:

It is not the intention of Kirklees Council to join in any independent inquiry with Crewe Chemicals into their operations. It was agreed that the Council would take their advice if the firm made any further planning applications. If they choose to put applications in we have our own experts to deal with them.

In addition, the Chairman was reported as saying that the Council would 'go ahead' with action against the tanks built without planning permission.

Later in August, however, Crewe Chemicals submitted a second planning application with respect to the storage tanks. On this occasion, the plans submitted with the application indicated the presence of twelve tanks (not ten, as previously). A week later, Kirklees received a planning application seeking permission for the 'erection of a site perimeter fence' around the Crewe Chemicals site. In September 1978 a further application was submitted, on this occasion for the 'erection of electricity substation and customers' switchroom'.

A newspaper article revealed that the 'woven timber fence' was one part of Crewe Chemicals' scheme to give their site 'a face-lift before plans for the plant's future developments were discussed with council officials'.[18] The article continued, paraphrasing a company statement:

Work is still being done on plans for the drainage system. Once that stage has been reached outline plans for the firm's long-term development will be prepared for discussion with Kirklees.

In the statement Crewe Chemicals say that during the establishment of the new division they have had to concentrate entirely on the competitiveness of their operations. They had now entered the second phase of their growth when it was both possible and necessary to take much more account of factors outside the factory walls and to do as well environmentally as they had proved themselves able to do commercially.

The firm say that within the next few months six new jobs would be created by the establishment of a packaging department.

The Company are grateful for the tolerance of their neighbours during the first difficult two years, and now undertake to repay their kindness by putting right those aspects of their operations which have been, of necessity, somewhat makeshift.

The sentiments expressed by a resident (a member of the Colne Valley Society) in a letter published in a local journal were somewhat at odds with those contained in Crewe Chemicals' statement.[19] As well as the risk of an explosion similar to that which had occurred at the Sandbach works, there was, he alleged, the risk that 'even a few empty containers washed downstream could devastate plant, fish, insect and animal life' in the River Colne. Since the arrival of Crewe Chemicals at Linthwaite, it was asserted, 'all vegetation around the works has been killed, mature trees a quarter of a mile away are dead, local residents have been driven to distraction by the noise at night.'[19]

In a letter to the following issue of this journal,[20] Crewe Chemicals dismissed these claims as a 'farrago of nonsense'. The explosion at the Sandbach works was caused, not by chemical dust in the atmosphere, but by 'gas escaping from a leaking pipe'. While they were not unaware of the inherent danger posed by dispersed dust, the company had 'twenty years of experience in handling and grinding fine powders'. In addition, the company worked closely with the 'Chemical Inspectorate of Factories' (*sic*) and 'this, coupled with our own experience, gives a very satisfactory workable situation'. Finally, they drew attention to the programme of measures to improve the appearance of the site which had earlier been announced.[20]

The Development Control Subcommittee considered the three applications received from Crewe Chemicals at their meeting in October 1978. The decisions were issued in early November and were in accord with the strategy outlined above. Permission for the storage tanks was once again withheld. Consent was granted for the environmentally innocuous sub-station, and for the erection of a site perimeter fence. Since this fence might serve not only to improve the appearance of the site but also to act as a barrier to accidental entries into the river, it was received with approbation. Nevertheless, the local planning authority did not forgo the opportunity of reiterating a number of their earlier general planning conditions and adding some new ones designed to control pollution:

6. The details to be submitted ... shall include full details of the proposed berm along the riverside and additional landscape treatment within the remainder of the site, and details of the surface treatment proposed for the fenced compound and roadways.
7. No goods, plant or machinery including chemical products and raw materials shall be stored in the open other than within the area referred to as a fenced compound on the Approved Plan, and no work other than the movement of containers and other suitably packaged or contained material shall take place in the open air without the written consent of the District Planning Authority.

[Condition 9 was identical to the previous condition 18.]

It is possible that the fencing and proposed 'berm' (condition 6) might constitute adequate safeguards against accidental entries of polluting materials to the river.

The decision, yet again, to refuse planning permission for the storage tanks was reported in a newspaper article.[21] This suggested that the decision was contrary to the advice of the planning officers, who had recommended that approval should be granted, subject to adequate conditions. It was later revealed that the officer concerned did not regard these vessels as being linked to the pollution problem. He believed that by granting conditional planning approval for the tanks, the local planning authority would have secured conditions which, unlike those appended to the consents which had not yet been taken up, were readily and immediately enforceable.[22] Such conditions could have sought to minimize the risk of pollution (particularly water pollution) associated with the chemicals stored in the tanks.[6]

The newspaper article continued:

it is understood that the Council will tell the firm that if other work connected with the scheme is completed within a certain time, the Sub-Committee will look again 'without prejudice' at the application for the tanks.[21]

This latter point was a reference to suggestions that Kirklees officers and members would view an application for permission for the tanks with more favour if Crewe Chemicals were to engage a reputable architect to prepare a comprehensive plan, giving full details of their intentions for the future development of the site. In the past, planning applications had been submitted by Crewe Chemicals in a somewhat piecemeal manner; if, in contrast, the company were to offer the local planning authority a detailed master plan, together with an inventory of the materials and processes to be used at the works, then it was possible that Kirklees might adopt a more compliant attitude to Crewe Chemicals' enterprise. The last three applications and the plans submitted with them had, in fact, been drawn up by a firm of architects in Huddersfield, but no master plan or inventory had been presented.

A list of the materials used had been supplied at the time of the very first planning application and a revised list had been supplied in October 1977, but the Works Manager had intimated that other, unspecified, compounds would be required as the operation progressed and that these would be discussed with the local authority as and when the need arose. This response was considered unsatisfactory by planning and environmental health officers who were anxious that Crewe Chemicals should understand that they did not have 'carte blanche' to carry out any process whatever. Moreover, condition 2 of the first permission, although not yet in force, established the district planning authority's right of prior approval (in consultation with the Environmental Health Department) of 'details of any manufacturing or formulating process'.

Kirklees planning officers viewed the company's decision to recruit the services of an architect as an encouraging sign of a more open approach. They had been surprised at Crewe Chemicals' apparent reluctance to exercise their right of appeal against any of the various planning refusals as a resulting local inquiry would have provided the local planning authority with a great deal of information on the past and future activities of the company, armed with which they would be far better prepared to answer the complaints and assuage the fears of local residents.

The enforcement notice

The option of serving an enforcement notice with regard to the storage tanks had been available to the local planning authority for some time and had been considered previously.[17] The Colne Valley Society was also aware of this possible course of action and they wrote to Kirklees' Development Solicitor urging Kirklees to serve an enforcement notice 'with respect to the tanks unlawfully erected at Grosvenor Works' on Crewe Chemicals. They continued:

In view of the anomaly in the planning legislation relating to use classes orders, it is not possible without payment of compensation to stop use of the existing buildings. However, any expansion of the works can and should be checked by the council's use of planning powers.

A planning application has now been refused on two occasions because it would allow for an intensification of the existing use and create pollution problems.

The public have a right to expect that planning laws are enforced without fear or favour in both domestic and industrial cases.[23]

The 'anomaly in the planning legislation', by which chemical processing could succeed rug manufacture without the need for planning consent, was discussed further by the Society in another letter.[24] to the local journal. This letter gave an account of the various planning applications submitted by Crewe Chemicals since arriving in Linthwaite in 1976; it discussed the planning conditions imposed and the reasons why these had been found to be unenforceable; finally, it suggested that any enforcement notice serviced by the local planning authority 'must amount to removal of the tanks'.

The Colne Valley Society's call for enforcement action was reported in a newspaper article[25] which revealed that the enforcement notice had been drawn up and that the Development Solicitor was awaiting instructions to serve it. This article quoted a spokesman for the company as saying: 'We are trying to establish whether Kirklees want us to stay in business or whether they are intent on closing us down. This is the nub of the whole problem'.

Eventually, after some initial difficulty in discovering the address of the actual owner of the Grosvenor Works, enforcement notices were served by Kirklees Borough Council on the owner and on the occupier of the site in January 1979. These notices called for the removal of thirteen storage tanks within four months. Crewe Chemicals appealed to the Secretary of State for the Environment against the enforcement notice and against Kirklees' (second) refusal of planning approval for the vessels.

In July 1979, after the enclosed loading bay had been constructed, the Managing Director of Thornton and Ross complained to Kirklees that serious scorching of vegetation existed on land as far east of Grosvenor Works as the pharmaceutical company's ornamental garden. He requested the Council to consider taking out an injunction to stop Crewe Chemicals from handling powdered materials. The Environmental Health Department decided to conduct a detailed investigation of the problem and retained the services of consulting chemical engineers and of university ecologists. An air filter from Thornton and Ross was analysed and found to contain a small quantity of atrazine, the first time the presence of this chemical in the environment had been scientifically confirmed.[17]

The ecological consultants carried out detailed investigations of trees and herbaceous vegetation. They found that injury was localized in a distinctive manner and was most severe at sites adjacent to

Crewe Chemicals. Their view that the injury was caused by emissions from the works was confirmed by soil analyses which demonstrated heavy contamination with atrazine, which could only have escaped from the works.[26] The consulting engineers reported that the loss of herbicides to the environment from the works was of the order of 1.7 kg/week, sufficient to cause environmental damage (the normal single agricultural dosage is around 2-4 kg/ha).[27] As a result of their consultants' findings, Kirklees were now satisfied that nuisance had occurred and that statutory notices should be served.[14]

The public inquiry

The inquiry took place in Slaithwaite Civic Hall on 6-7 December 1979 and 3-4 January 1980. According to the local newspaper,[28] the inspector 'upset' the parties protesting against Crewe Chemicals by arguing that pollution from the Grosvenor Works did not come within the scope of the inquiry unless it could be directly linked to the issue of the storage tanks.

Crewe Chemicals retained an eminent QC specializing in planning law to present their case and called the Works Manager, his architect, and a consultant chemist as witnesses. The Works Manager stated that the water authority had been consulted about the tanks and had given their approval, which he had wrongly interpreted to be a planning permission. The company conceded that damage to vegetation around the works had been caused, but that this had nothing to do with the tank storage. Defoliation 'may have been caused by the escape of milled atrazine which was blown by the wind whilst loading was taking place. ... There may also have been some escape through the dust extraction not operating as efficiently as we desire.'[29] A neighbouring farmer had been compensated in both 1978 and 1979 for loss of hay arising from the blowing of dust on to his land downwind from the works. Atrazine, however, was no longer made and the works were now much better controlled.[29]

The firm's chemical consultant also admitted that the dust extraction system was inadequate and had led to pollution problems. He conceded that pollution from the spillage of liquids had occurred but stated that an effluent disposal tank had now been constructed and that the tanks enabled more liquid blending to take place. His evidence reinforced the argument that, if Crewe Chemicals were to continue on the site without the tanks, then part of the buildings used for liquid blending would be converted to the formulation of solids, giving a greater risk of pollution damage. He had made a number of recommendations to the company relating to the prevention of spillages, the construction of retaining walls, and the surfacing and grassing of the site.[30]

Somewhat belatedly (on the third day of the inquiry)[31] counsel for the company contended that the tanks could be classed as permitted development[28] as the external appearance of the site 'was not materially altered by their presence'. He also argued that the four-month compliance period specified in the enforcement notice was too short, that other firms would suffer from lack of supplies, and that a total of 350 jobs might be lost. In summing up his case on 3 January 1980, the QC stated: 'Crewe Chemicals are a successful and profitable business who should be encouraged.'[22]

The planning authority called seven witnesses: the planning and environmental health officers involved, a meteorologist, two vegetation experts, a consultant chemical engineer, and a public analyst. They were represented by a Council solicitor. Kirklees argued strongly that damage to vegetation, which had been shown to be due to the works, had grown steadily worse between 1977 and 1979 and that this increase had coincided with expanding capacity at Crewe Chemicals made possible by the erection of the tanks, by now numbering fourteen. They believed that the artificial distinction between the handling of liquids and solids was unacceptable. The inspector asked only one question after hearing the ecological evidence against Crewe Chemicals: 'Could this scorching of vegetation be attributed directly to the materials stored in the tanks?' The answer, of course, had to be 'no'.

The meteorologist explained that air was trapped in the valley bottom because of the incidence of thermal inversions, giving rise to elevated pollution levels. The chemical engineer stated that the standard of engineering at the site was rudimentary; the tanks (and much of the other equipment) had been installed with a philosophy of minimum capitalization.[27] The vessels had been bought second-hand without warranty or certification. Improvements were necessary to bring the installation up to a standard which the consulting engineers considered appropriate for a works of the size, and in the location, of Crewe Chemicals. He felt that further precautions should be taken against the risk of escape of a toxic or hazardous chemical from the works. Under cross-examination, it transpired that he felt that the activities at Grosvenor Works were part of a complete process involving Class V and Class VIII land uses, a view by now shared by the Council, though this was not at issue at the inquiry.[31]

The Colne Valley Society was represented by a barrister. The members were used to living in an industrial environment; they were not the sort of people to get upset about trifles. They contended that nothing had been done after all the promises made by Crewe

Chemicals. The loading bay, for example, had been constructed without doors. They formally objected to the inspector's refusal to consider the record of the company germane to the appeal:

> The way in which the company had disregarded the planning process over the storage tanks was symptomatic of their attitude generally. In the experience of the Society and the residents, statements by the firm about their future intentions were totally unreliable.[32]

They submitted that the risk of pollution must have been greater because of the presence of the tanks and that river pollution could result from filling or emptying them. More chemicals had been brought on to the site as a consequence of increased storage capacity and the company was expanding and becoming a greater potential danger.

Thornton and Ross, also represented by a barrister, were afraid of losing their licence from the Medicines Inspectorate:

> To protect our premises fully, by ultrafine filtration and washing, would be extremely expensive. Why should Thornton and Ross Limited be put either to the expense of special air treatment plant or to the continued fear of contamination by chemicals falling on our works from elsewhere? After all, we have been on the present site for 43 years.[13]

They believed that the installation of tanks had led to the possibility of further activities involving powders being carried out at the site and hence to an unacceptable risk of contamination. They felt that Crewe Chemicals had spent very little on dust control and that the Works Manager had displayed a lack of concern for the impact his operations might have.

The Inspector's findings of fact[31] included the statements that: 'the chemicals used do not require registration under Class V of the Use Classes Order', and that 'both parties are not sure whether a Class VIII use is now operative'. The following two findings were more significant: 'the tanks have not been suggested to have contributed to any of the vegetation damage' and 'the tanks ... not being prominent and appearing as part of the industrial scene'.

The Inspector's conclusions were that the appellant was operating 'special industrial processes' and that the enforcement notice was 'wrongly directed to development rather than properly to a breach of one of the conditions referred to':

> It is thought that the works here are identical to the manufacture of the end product which involved Class V and/or Class VIII uses. Whilst the site use in itself might be within Class IV this seems to be too narrow a view of the overall manufacturing process and, for this reason, the land use here is thought to be incidental to Class V and/or Class VIII activities requiring special considerations.[31]

Notwithstanding these comments, the Inspector felt that the storage tanks could be classed as permitted development and hence did not require planning permission. He therefore recommended that the enforcement notice be quashed. Some of the Inspector's other conclusions were of particular interest:

The objections by interested parties are sound particularly in respect of pollution but this is a matter to be dealt with under other powers.

As it stands, the site is allocated for industrial purposes in the statutory plans, there are no intentions of altering these provisions and there are no statutory limitations set out on the kind of industrial activities allowed for in the Town Map. Under these circumstances, it is not right for the council to say they want to encourage industrial usage here and, at the same time, seek to restrict it in respect of noise, disturbance and other effects which may give rise to local complaints.

A general industrial use is more than likely to create noise, smell, fumes, traffic and other effects which local residents and others would object to. If the complaints are cogent then the land allocation should be revised but until that is done, industrial use on land properly allocated for that purpose should not be unduly fettered.[31]

The Secretary of State for the Environment's decision letter, issued in April 1980, was brief.[33] While he refused to be drawn on the question of whether special industrial uses were involved, he rejected the Inspector's contention that, if Class V or Class VIII uses were undertaken, the enforcement notice had been wrongly directed: the erection of the tanks amounted to development whether or not the 1976 permissions were in force. The Secretary of State accepted, however, that the external appearance of the premises of the undertaking was not materially affected by the development and hence, that it was permitted by virtue of the Town and County Planning General Development Order, 1977. He made no observations on the Inspector's other conclusions.

Kirklees planning officers were very surprised by the appeal decision, not because the enforcement notice was quashed, but because the tanks were classed as permitted development. They took counsel's opinion and were informed that the Secretary of State's reasons were of very doubtful legality. Nevertheless, it was decided that an appeal to the High Court would not be advantageous, for even if the decision were to be quashed, the Secretary of State could simply grant planning permission for the tanks when directed by the Court to reconsider the decision.

The planners' surprise at the decision is easily understood: that the issue should finally be decided on a question of visual amenity, and not on any of the more substantive environmental impacts suffered by the local residents for several years, is ironical. The absence of a technical assessor at the inquiry was perhaps unfortunate. More significantly, the refusal of the Inspector, and later the Minister, to allow existing pollution from other parts of the works to be a material consideration in this case was in marked contrast to some precedents.[34,35]

Further, certain of the Inspector's conclusions, in effect, were suggesting that once a local planning authority has decided upon an industrial use, it should not attempt to mitigate the environmental consequences, except on payment of compensation. In other words, it could not pursue both economic and environmental objectives. This runs counter to much of the Department of the Environment's policy[36,37] so it is unsurprising that the Secretary of State ignored his Inspector's comments.

The designation of the storage tanks and associated structures as permitted development could be regarded as a dangerous precedent. If storage tanks were added to an existing works, and were deemed to constitute permitted development, the planning authority would be denied the opportunity to intervene. The tanks might be used to store highly toxic compounds but whether the elected representatives of the population most at risk could eliminate that risk, by refusing permission for the tanks, could depend, not on the toxicity of their intended contents, but on their external appearance!

Subsequent events

In May 1980 just five months after their QC's eloquent summing-up and less than two weeks after the ministerial decision, Crewe Chemicals were declared bankrupt. The Grosvenor Works operation was taken over by Mirfield Sales Services Limited, with whom the Works Manager had previously been associated. A new company, Pennine Chemical Services Limited, was formed with the Works Manager as one of the directors. He remains in charge at Grosvenor Works. Notwithstanding this change of ownership, Kirklees Environmental Health Department finally served a prohibition notice on the new company under the Public Health (Recurring Nuisances) Act, 1969, later that month.

In June 1980, the Alkali Inspectorate wrote to the local planning authority to inform them that the works were now registered by virtue of the operation of a newly installed bisulphite process. The District Inspector had already notified the Environmental Health Department that the addition of this very minor item of plant was to take place. The new company's solicitor and Kirklees agreed that the works were now classified as a special industrial building and that the original planning permissions now applied. For those parts of the works involving the scheduled process, the right of prior approval of any measures, whether in terms of plant maintenance, material handling or the fitting of dust-arresting equipment, adopted in pursuit of 'the best practicable means for preventing the escape of noxious or offensive gases', lay with the Alkali Inspectorate, though control of the remainder of the works, of course, lay with Kirklees Borough.

It might be argued that conditions 11 and 12 of the first permission conflicted with the requirements of 'best practicable means'. However, while the planning conditions require the installation of equipment 'to prevent emissions of pollutants to the atmosphere' and that 'all vapours and odours shall be collected' it could well be that the 'best practicable means', as prescribed by the District Alkali Inspector, would be less demanding, requiring measures 'for rendering such gases where discharged harmless and inoffensive'.[38] There is, however, no evidence of any disagreement between the planning authority and the Alkali Inspectorate over the application of these conditions.

The planning committee decided to give the new company time before serving enforcement notices requiring compliance with the original conditions and a number of meetings took place to discuss the authority's requirements. In 1980, the council's consultant ecologists were able to report some recovery of vegetation and there were no complaints about scorching from the company's operations during the year. The new company were no longer seen to be expanding (they had withdrawn their application for an extension) but the Council's strategy did not alter: they were determined to make Grosvenor Works as environmentally acceptable as possible. In a letter to the Council the company said they 'wanted to work in harmony with the authority and to develop their business at the site, having due regard to environmental and neighbouring safeguards.'[39]

Notwithstanding the company's intentions, in June 1981 the Planning Subcommittee decided to serve an enforcement notice on Pennine Chemicals requiring compliance with the original planning conditions. Later that summer, further scorching of vegetation was suspected.[40] The role of the local action group and other objectors and of the local newspapers (which gave some prominence to the debate about Grosvenor Works), in pressurizing Kirklees into enforcement action, cannot have been insubstantial.

It could be argued that this case lends support to the view that Class IV of the Use Classes Order, embracing a wide range of potentially pollution-prone chemical processes together with relatively harmless activities such as rug manufacture, is too broad in application. Of course, there is the option available to local planning authorities, when granting planning consent for a development, of imposing a planning condition restricting the use of land or a building to a specific process or activity. By this means, the local planning authority extends its power to intervene and to consider in more detail the most appropriate use of any building or land, having regard to the implications of the pollution risk to adjacent areas.

Here, however, the local planning authority demonstrated, by approving Crewe Chemicals' first application, that they were not opposed in principle to the existence of a chemical works in the Colne Valley. The subsequent withholding of planning approval stemmed from Kirklees' concern about the increased throughput of chemicals and hence the greater risk of environmental pollution. Again, it is theoretically possible for a local planning authority to append to any planning consent a planning condition limiting, or requiring prior approval of any increase of, the throughput of an industrial plant, to which the planning consent was in some way related. Of course, such a condition, like those actually applied, would remain inoperative until 'development' is undertaken.

The Works Manager has intimated that he would have considered a condition restricting the intensity of operations at Crewe Chemicals to have been categorically unacceptable. Had Kirklees attempted to impose such a condition, he would then have transferred his plant and capital to a site within the area of a more compliant local authority. The success of his Linthwaite enterprise, he has averred, lay in his ability to respond rapidly to short-term demands from larger chemical companies for a wide range of chemical products. Planning conditions which sought to restrict the type and quantitites of materials to be used could only have served to frustrate his efforts.[1]

Had the members of the planning committee accepted their officers' advice and granted consent for the tanks, then the environmental safeguards embodied in the planning conditions appended to a consent for the tanks could have been employed to regulate the use of the site as a whole.[34,35]

In the event, it was the conditions attached to the first two consents which come into force, by virtue of the registration of the works under the 1906 Alkali Act. The effectiveness of these conditions in reducing the environmental impact of the works can only be judged by the outcome of the enforcement proceedings authorized by Kirklees. Should the company appeal against any notice, it seems likely that the Secretary of State will be unwilling to support the planning authority in its attempt to minimize the external costs of an initially under-capitalized operation which has hitherto shown scant regard for its environmental impacts on its neighbours. Such an outcome would again lend weight to the view that enforcement is a fundamental weakness in land use planning controls over pollution, particularly as the ministerial decision in this case appears to illustrate a weakening of central government support for environmental quality objectives.

Had the planning authority attempted to solve the pollution problems described above by serving a discontinuance order, payment of compensation for the costs incurred by the company would have become necessary, had the Secretary of State approved the action. Removal of the company would thus involve a violation of the 'polluter-pays' principle even greater than that entailed by its operations.

REFERENCES AND NOTES

[1] Works Manager, Crewe Chemicals, 'Personal Communication', 1979.

[2] Works Manager, Crewe Chemicals, 'Proof of Evidence', Local Inquiry into Appeals Relating to Land at Grosvenor Works, Linthwaite, APP/5113/C/79/860 and A/78/11026, Department of the Environment, Bristol, 1979.

[3] 'Town and Country Planning General Development Order 1973', Department of the Enivornment, Circular 12/73, HMSO, London, 1973.

[4] This and other information about planning decisions was supplied from the files of Kirklees Planning Department.

[5] Town and Country Planning (Use Classes) Order, 1972 (SI 1972, No. 1385).

[6] Planning Officer, Kirklees Metropolitan Borough Council, 'Personal Communication', 1979.

[7] Planning Officer, Kirklees Metropolitan Borough Council, 'Proof of Evidence', Local Inquiry, loc. cit., 1980.

[8] G. Newsom and J. G. Sherratt, *Water Pollution,* Sherratt & Sons, Altrincham, 1972.

[9] Control of Pollution Act, 1974, s. 46.

[10] *River Pollution Survey, England and Wales, 1975,* Department of the Environment, HMSO, London, 1976.

[11] Control of Pollution Act, 1974, s. 58.

[12] Environmental Health Officer, Kirklees Metropolitan Borough Council, 'Personal Communication', 1981.

[13] Managing Director, Thornton and Ross, 'Proof of Evidence', Local Inquiry, loc. cit., 1980.

[14] Environmental Health Officer, Kirklees Metropolitan Borough Council, 'Proof of Evidence', Local Inquiry, loc. cit., 1980.

[15] *Industrial Air Pollution 1978,* Health and Safety Executive, HMSO, London, 1980.

[16] 'Letter to the Rt Hon. Peter Shore, MP, Secretary of State for the Environment', Colne Valley Society, Linthwaite, 19 November 1977.

[17] *Huddersfield Daily Examiner,* 8 Aug. 1978.

[18] *Huddersfield Daily Examiner,* 5 Sep. 1978.

[19] *Colne Valley News,* Sept. 1978.

[20] *Colne Valley News,* Oct. 1978.

[21] *Huddersfield Daily Examiner,* 25 Oct. 1978.

[22] *Huddersfield Daily Examiner,* 4 Jan. 1980.

[23] 'Letter to the Directorate of Technical Services, Kirklees District Council', Colne Valley Society, Linthwaite, 9 November 1978.

[24] *Colne Valley News,* Nov. 1978.

[25] *Bradford Telegraph and Argus,* 11 Nov. 1978.

[26] University Consulting Ecologist, 'Proof of Evidence', Local Inquiry, loc. cit., 1980.

[27] Consulting Engineer, 'Proof of Evidence', Public Inquiry, loc. cit., 1980.

[28] *Huddersfield Daily Examiner,* 6 Dec. 1979.

[29] Works Manager, Crewe Chemicals, Unread statements in the written 'Proof of Evidence', Local Inquiry, 1979 (see reference 2).

[30] Consulting Chemist, 'Proof of Evidence', Local Inquiry, loc. cit., 1979.

[31] 'Inspector's Report of the Local Inquiry into Appeals Relating to Land at Grosvenor Works, Linthwaite,' APP/5113/C/79/860 and A/78/11026, Dept. of the Environment, Bristol, 1980.

[32] *Huddersfield Daily Examiner,* 8 Dec. 1979.

[33] 'Decision Letter on Appeals Relating to Land at Grosvenor Works, Linthwaite', APP/5113/C/79/860 and A/78/11026, Dept. of the Environment, Bristol, 1980.

[34] *Pyx Granite Co.v. Ministry of Housing and Local Government* [1958] 1 QB, 554; [1959] 3 All ER 1.

[35] *Penwith District Council v. the Secretary of State for the Environment & Anr.* [1977] P & CR 269.

[36] 'Development Control: Policy and Practice', Department of the Environment, Circular 22/80, HMSO, London, 1980.

[37] 'Planning and Noise', Circular 10/73, Department of the Environment, HMSO, London, 1973.

[38] *Alkali, etc. Works Regulation Act, 1906,* s. 7(1).

[39] *Huddersfield Daily Examiner,* 17 Dec. 1980.

[40] The new company states that 'very substantial steps have been taken ... since 8 May 1980, to carry out on site improvements in management and control', Managing Director, Pennine Chemical Services Ltd, Personal Communication, 1982.

7

PLANNING AND LAND POLLUTION

For the greater proportion of solid waste generated in the United Kingdom, disposal is to land. Thus, in one sense, it is axiomatic that land use planning has a role in the disposal of solid waste. Table 7.1 gives a classification of areas of land in England used for the deposit of solid wastes in 1974.[1] This classification is not exhaustive: it makes no reference to derelict waste disposal sites, to areas of land devoted to the disposal of clinker and ash from power stations; to agricultural and forestry wastes; nor to the disposal on land of over 1,000,000 tonnes per annum of sludge from sewage treatment works. Nevertheless, Table 7.1 does indicate that the area of land dedicated to the active disposal of industrial, commercial, and domestic wastes is broadly comparable to that taken up in the tipping of mineral wastes, though it is, of course, far less than that devoted to the winning of mineral resources.[2] The table also shows that land used for mineral waste tipping is also less likely to be restored than that used for non-mineral waste disposal.

Land pollution arises from the deposit of wastes; where they are disposed of in an environmentally acceptable manner, there may be no more than a threat to amenity from the physical appearance of the wastes. All too often, however, the methods of disposal employed may lead to contamination of watercourses and aquifers by leachate or to air pollution from odours, fumes, and particulate matter. The threat of such potential problems, especially from toxic waste disposal, is one reason for the widespread antagonism to this land use.[3] In addition to the more obviously undesirable consequences, tipping waste on an area of land precludes, either temporarily or permanently, its use for a putatively more beneficial purpose, e.g. housing or agriculture. The restoration of land previously used for tipping solid wastes frequently leaves much to be desired, as the area of derelict spoil heaps and tips (13,000 ha in England) attests.[4]

Any solid waste tipping which amounts to 'building, engineering, mining or other operations in, on or under land or the making of any material change in the use of any buildings or other land' thereby constitutes 'development' and hence necessitates the approval of the local planning authority. However, the continuance of tipping activity on land already used for the purpose is not closely controlled by planning powers. Thus, in certain circumstances, tipping of colliery spoil by the National Coal Board and the disposal of wastes by mineral undertakers and others is designated 'permitted develop-

TABLE 7.1

Land used for mineral and non-mineral waste tipping, England, 1974

Type of waste	Area affected by active tipping (ha)	Proportion not subject to restoration conditions (%)
Chalk	93	17
China clay	776	54
Clay/shale	772	45
Coal	7,187	55
Gypsum/anhydrite	231	76
Igneous rock	417	37
Limestone	532	32
Sand and gravel	1,172	16
Sandstone	290	34
Slate	83	62
Vein minerals	459	10
Other minerals	248	6
Total mineral	12,260	46
Public refuse	5,773	20
Industrial and commercial	5,626	32
Total non-mineral	11,399	26
Total all wastes	23,659	36

Source: Reference 1

ment'. Nevertheless, in general, planning authorities have the power to refuse consent for the deposit of solid waste or for new mineral operations in areas where such activities are held to be environmentally unacceptable.

Planning controls and 'controlled' wastes

Perhaps the most important influence on the attitudes of local planning authorities toward their use of statutory powers in regulating solid waste tips is the recognition that local authorities themselves have responsibilities for ensuring the disposal of certain categories of waste. Under Part I of the Control of Pollution Act, 1974, a district council in England and Wales is the 'collection authority' for its area; it is responsible for collecting all household waste and, if requested, commercial waste arising in its area. The county council in England (and the district council in Wales) is the 'disposal authority' for its area; it must dispose of the waste collected. These responsibilities over collection and disposal mean that, in the context of solid waste, local authorities are, potentially if not actually, 'polluters' and not simply (as in the case of noise and air pollution) regulators of pollution. Waste disposal authorities may themselves operate sites for the disposal of domestic wastes, where industrial wastes may (at a cost) also be received. Alternatively, industrial concerns may engage in the business of waste disposal; in which case theire installations must be licensed by the disposal authority. In 1974, some 5,800 ha of land were devoted to the tipping of public refuse (mostly at sites operated by waste disposal authorities); whilst a further 5,600 ha were devoted to the tipping of industrial and commercial wastes (mostly at sites operated by private companies).[1]

Before the Local Government, Planning and Land Act, 1980, was passed, applications for the use of land for the disposal of solid waste were generally not statutorily 'county matters'. In some areas, West Yorkshire for example, the view was taken that, since the county council was the waste disposal authority and responsible for issuing the site licence, it should also determine planning applications for waste disposal sites; and the 'development control agreements' between these county and district councils were drafted accordingly. In the majority of cases, however, planning consent for waste disposal sites (whether landfill, incineration, pulverization, composting, chemical treatment, or whatever) was determined by the authority which first received the application, namely the district council. Now the receiving authority must forward the planning application to the County for determination, though the county planning authority is statutorily obliged to consult the district before reaching a decision.[5] The county planning authority must also, of course, decide by resolution whether or not to grant the county waste disposal authority permission to dispose of waste.

With planning applications for the use of land for solid waste disposal, there are certain specific requirements under the Town and Country Planning Act, 1971, and the General Development Order. An applicant must advertise his proposals in a local newspaper and must post, on the land in question, a notice indicating that planning permission is being sought.[6] Before granting permission, the county planning authority must consult with the appropriate regional water authority and, where proposals for new waste disposal sites entail the loss of more than ten acres of agricultural land, with the Minister of Agriculture, Fisheries and Food.[7]

The announcement of an intention to develop land for waste disposal almost invariably incurs opposition from neighbouring land users, especially residents. With proposals which pose a particular threat to the character and amenity of an area, natural justice requires that no interested party is denied the right to object through ignorance of the proposed development. The cost of additional publicity is met by the potential polluter. Mandatory consultation by the planning authority with the water authority is a recognition of the threat of contamination of surface and underground water posed by leachate from solid waste tips. In the past, it was common for planning consents for mineral extraction to be granted subject to conditions requiring filling and the restoring of the site. Often such conditions were imposed with no consideration of the geology of the site and with no restriction on the types of material to be allowed as 'fill' In too many instances the lucrative practice of disposing of toxic wastes in mine shafts and old quarry workings has proved to be environmentally hazardous.[8]

For example, an exhausted quarry in the catchment area of Cowm Reservoir near Rochdale was the subject of a planning consent for waste tipping. This consent did not exclude motor tyres. When, in 1975, the reported 300,000 tyres in the quarry were ignited (allegedly by hooligans) pyrolysis occurred under the high pressures and temperatures at the base of pile of tyres. An oily, noxious residue eventually reached the reservoir via a previously unknown shaft or 'drift' cut originally to drain the quarry workings. Samples taken from the reservoir, after it had been isolated from the water supply network, revealed some 650 organic compounds; many, including various phenols, were toxic. The extent and form of the contamination was such that Cowm Reservoir is unlikely to serve as a source of potable water again.

In addition to refusing disposal sites in unsuitable locations, planning powers can prevent the incursion of sensitive development upon existing waste tips. In this connection, a working party on refuse disposal has recommended 183 m as a minimum separation which should be sought between housing and tipping sites:

But we do not think a recommendation specifying the same minimum distance for all applications would be practicable. Much depends on the existing features of the site and its surroundings. A proposal to fill a deep hole as near as, say, 200 yards [183 m] from a residential area might be acceptable until filling approached near the top while a greater distance would be desirable where a positive visual screen (such as an embankment) was not available or could not be provided. These are some of the factors which should be borne in mind when considering the suitability of sites for the controlled tipping of untreated house and similar refuse; we think that, in general, tipping should not approach nearer than 200 yards [183 m] from the curtilage of any existing residential community. Conversely, new development should not, in general, be allowed to approach nearer than this distance to an established tip before it is completed.[9]

One member of the working party could not support the majority view on the desirability of a 183 m guideline. This, he argued, would be misinterpreted by prejudiced local residents as a rigid limit. Instead any proposal, whether for tipping or for housing development near an existing tip, should be assessed on its merits with account taken of all relevant circumstances including adjacent land uses. Because of this reservation, the 183 m recommendation was not included in the 'code of practice' appended to a Department of the Environment circular acquainting local authorities with the recommendations of the working party in 1971.[10] The Secretary of State for the Environment commended:

to all concerned the Working Party's recommended code of practice for disposal of solid wastes by controlled tipping. ... Furthermore he hopes that when considering applications for permission to use land for the tipping of refuse, local authorities will have regard to the recommended code of practice, much of which will be appropriate for incorporation in conditions attached to planning consents.[10]

Chapter 8 describes the reaction of one group of residents to the discovery of a tipping face approaching, at places, to within 90 m of their homes.

In contrast, the case of the Barwell tip exemplifies what can be achieved by the imaginative use of a planning agreement in minimizing nuisance. In 1972 a developer lodged an application for planning permission for housing on 7 ha of agricultural land at Barwell in Leicestershire. One of the reasons for refusal of consent was:

The land adjoining the application site to the north is proposed to be used by the Hinckly Urban District Council for the tipping of domestic refuse and it is considered that the erection of dwellings adjoining this land would not be in the interests of general amenity and health of the proposed occupants.[11]

The developer appealed against this decision. The 183 m recommendation was discussed at length at the inquiry, when the developer proposed a scheme to ensure that housing would never be within this distance of active tipping areas.

The Secretary of State, however, dismissed the appeal, against his inspector's recommendation, because:

although accepting that residential development of the appeal site is acceptable in principle, he considers it necessary to comply with the recommendation of the Working Party on Refuse Disposal that new development should not, in general, be allowed to approach nearer than 200 yards [183 m] to an established tip before it is completed.[12]

Following the appeal, Leicestershire County Council, who by this time had become the disposal authority as well as planning authority, had further discussions with the developer. A plan was eventually devised (and incorporated within a planning agreement) which ensured that, by synchronizing the rate and direction of tipping with the construction programme, no occupied dwelling ever lay within 183 m of an active tipping face.

With the implementation of Part I of the Control of Pollution Act, 1974, extensive powers of control (both anticipatory and retrospective) over the disposal of 'controlled' waste were conferred upon the waste disposal authorities.[13] More recently, new regulations have been drafted for a control scheme for toxic wastes, which replace the notification procedure under the Deposit of Poisonous Wastes Act, 1972.[14] In summary, the Control of Pollution Act requires that all waste disposal sites (whether new or established, and including sites for disposal by incineration, pulverization, baling, etc., as well as landfill) must be licensed by the waste disposal authority. A precondition of the grant of a licence is that the site is the subject of a valid planning consent (although a site licence and planning permission may be sought simultaneously). To dispose of controlled waste at an unlicensed site is an offence.

Before issuing a site licence, a waste disposal authority must consult and consider the views of the appropriate water authority, the district council (as the collection authority) in whose area the site lies, and any persons prescribed by the Secretary of State.[15] If the water authority and the disposal authority should disagree over the granting of, or the conditions to be attached to, a licence then either may refer the matter to the Secretary of State and any licence eventually issued must be in accordance with his decision. Thus, consultation with the water authority is a mandatory obligation both of the county disposal authority, when considering a site licence application, and of the county planning authority, before giving planning permission. This consultation procedure is of some importance, for few planning officers possess the background in chemistry or hydrogeology necessary in order scientifically to assess the environmental consequences of waste tipping at a particular site. Most county waste disposal units have been formed as part of the Highways Departments; and while they have not lacked expertise in the engineering aspects of waste disposal, they have tended to rely upon the water authorities for advice on the geological and chemical implications.[16]

A waste disposal authority may reject an application for a waste

disposal licence only when it 'is satisfied that its rejection is necessary for the purpose of preventing pollution of water or danger to the
public'.[17] Of course, a local planning authority may reject an application for planning approval for a waste disposal site for these
reasons, or on the lesser grounds that the proposal might give rise to
nuisance from noise or odour, or that it might generally be to the
detriment of the amenity of the area. Where it subsequently appears
to a disposal authority that either water pollution, danger to public
health, or a serious detriment to amenity could arise as a result of
the continuation of the licensed disposal activities, then it is a 'duty'
of the authority to revoke that licence. Modification and revocation of
a site licence do not entail the payment of compensation. If, however,
the cessation of disposal activities were to be achieved by discontinu-
ing the planning approval for waste disposal, then compensation,
from the local planning authority to the owner of the installation,
would be payable. In most circumstances, such payment would not
be consistent with the 'polluter-pays' principle.

Since the Control of Pollution Act, 1974, confers upon the disposal
authorities specific and anticipatory powers of control over waste
tipping, the Department of the Environment has argued that it is no
longer necessary for local planning authorities to seek equivalent
powers by means of planning conditions:

Use of land for the disposal of waste has for many years been subject to planning control. Although this control remains, and indeed planning permission
is a prerequisite of obtaining a disposal licence, the introduction of the
licensing system represents a major change in the application of planning
legislation to waste disposal facilities. In the absence of specific control,
conditions attached to a planning permission have in the past been used for
purposes of water protection and public health which are now met by the
licensing system ... conditions attached to planning permission should only
have regard to matters relating to the use and appearance of land in the
planning context for waste treatment or disposal purposes, for example
considerations of visual amenity, access, tree planting and preservation,
and landscaping generally; the site licence on the other hand will relate more
to the proper conduct of operations and day-to-day management of the sites
and plant, together with the protection of water, the environment and public
health generally.[18]

Site licence conditions are enforceable only for the duration of the
licence (i.e. while waste is being tipped or otherwise disposed of). No
such restriction applies to planning conditions. Where pollution
control measures need to be applied beyond the expiry of the licence,
then it is suggested that such requirements as 'continued access
to and maintenance of bore-holes, leachate treatment systems, etc.,
... restoration of the site' ... should be incorporated as planning

conditions.[18] In a Department of the Environment publication which gives further advice on the licensing system, it is suggested that planning conditions restricting a site's hours of operation or, in the case of a landfill site, the form of restoration might be appropriate.[19] These are areas where, it is conceded, an overlap of responsibility might be expected and where discussions between authorities should determine the division of responsibility in specific cases.

In determining appeals against six enforcement notices served by Basildon District Council in respect of alleged infractions of conditions of the planning approval of a private waste disposal site at Pitsea, the Secretary of State for the Environment acted in accordance with his published advice.[20] Planning consent for the site in question had been granted in 1972 with some thirteen conditions, most of which regulated the tipping operations, e.g. 'the total tonnage of waste to be transported by road shall not exceed 150,000 cubic yards [115,000 m^3] in any 12 months'. In his decision, the Secretary of State not only upheld the appeals but also discharged eight of the conditions at issue, arguing that the licensing provisions of the 1974 Act now afforded a flexible and enforceable means of controlling this and similar sites.

This decision is in line with the official notification of the results of a detailed government sponsored investigation of toxic waste disposal sites:[21]

The main findings, which are based on detailed investigations at 20 landfill sites in the UK plus considerable smaller-scale work, confirm that an ultra-cautious approach to landfill disposal of hazardous waste is not justified, although some substances are not suitable for landfill and each case has to be treated on its merits.[22]

Planning controls and non-'controlled' wastes

It is very important to recognize that there are large amounts of colliery, mineral, and agricultural wastes which do not fall within the ambit of the Control of Pollution Act.[13] The planning authorities will continue to play an important role in controlling the disposal of these wastes, where planning permission is needed for the activity. Mineral applications, of course, are dealt with by the county (now, under the Minerals Act, 1981, designated as the 'mineral planning authority' with the enhanced powers of control) and the use of planning conditions to control possible pollution remains an important instrument.

The Royal Commission on Environmental Pollution has been much concerned with the spreading of agricultural wastes on land:

'an example of an agricultural practice where planning constraints might be considered desirable on environmental grounds is the application to land of slurry from intensive livestock units.'[23] Whilst the Commission proposed that intensive livestock units should, in general, be subject to controls applicable to industrial rather than to agricultural development (Chapter 5), it argued against bringing agricultural wastes within the scope of Part I of the Control of Pollution Act, 1974, provided changes in the law relating to anticipatory controls were introduced. Similarly, given these proposed arrangements for specifying operational conditions, including the spreading of slurry on land, 'in advance with powers for subsequent enforcement, we would see no case for embodying these conditions in planning consents for new intensive livestock unit developments.'[23] In their absence, however, planning conditions are 'logical and defensible' (Chapter 5) and the extension of the 1974 Act might be necessary. The grant or refusal of planning permission, where it is needed, and the use of planning conditions therefore continue to be accepted methods of controlling this particular form of pollution.

Development plans and waste disposal plans

The allocation of land for waste disposal purposes is a necessary consideration in any strategic planning exercise and reference to solid waste was made in every 'report of survey' of a sample of twenty structure plans.[16] Policies on solid waste disposal were found in most 'written statements'; usually these consisted of presumption against granting planning consent for waste disposal sites in locations where pollution (water pollution in particular) might arise or where nuisance might be occasioned to residents. The policy included in Greater Manchester's approved structure plan was typical:

When considering proposals for new sites for waste disposal or waste treatment plants, the local planning authority will have regard to:
  (i) the need for tipping space or waste treatment plants;
  (ii) visual amenity;
  (iii) the effects (traffic, noise, smells, litter and vermin) on residential areas;
  (iv) public health and safety (geology, proximity to water catchment areas, land forms, proximity to the airport, air pollution);
  (v) resource conservation (agricultural land, sites of biological interest, recreation potential, future uses of the site);
  (vi) other County Council policies;
  (vii) any other relevant matters.[24]

The Secretary of State accepted that this policy provided a reasonable basis for decision-making. In general, most such structure plan policies also appear to have been approved.

The policy contained in the approved West Glamorgan Structure Plan goes somewhat further and indirectly encourages disposal methods other than landfill:

It is the policy of the County Council that there is a presumption against the use of land for tipping and for treatment of waste:
(a)   if re-use or re-cycling of such waste is reasonably practicable; or
(b)   where the nature and location of the site is such that the nature of these operations would seriously affect environmental quality; or
(c)   where the nature and location of the site is not conducive to carrying out these operations acording to sound practice.[25]

Local 'subject' plans have proved suitable for the presentation of policies not only on the exploitation of mineral resources but also on requirements for restoration. County-wide subject plans on minerals have been prepared by, among others, Kent and Warwickshire County Councils; Tyne and Wear has prepared a subject plan covering minerals, waste disposal, and land reclamation. One subject plan prepared by Humberside County Council (see Chapter 5) relates to intensive livestock units and to the risk of water pollution which arises as a result of the spreading on land of large quantities of animal wastes and slurries. Humberside's initiative has been welcomed by the Royal Commission on Environmental Pollution; it also maintained that more guidance on the control of pollution associated with intensive livestock units was required from the appropriate government department (the Ministry of Agriculture, Fisheries and Food):

Agricultural bodies are generally opposed to constraint of the kind envisaged in the Humberside County Council plan; for example the proposed limitations on the siting of units or the spreading of slurry within specified distances of housing.
We are not persuaded by these arguments. We think it should be possible to formulate guidelines embodying reasonably precise criteria which would not bear unduly harshly on farmers and which would go far towards avoiding problems of smell nuisance or water pollution. ...
We are doubtful about the 'flexibility' argument; it may too readily be adduced ... to justify the existing system on the basis of a vague, general principle without considered analysis of the pollution implications.[23]

In keeping with one of the requirements of a Common Market directive on waste disposal,[26] the Control of Pollution Act, 1974, contains a provision under which each waste disposal authority is obliged to survey waste arisings and disposal facilities in its area and to prepare a plan outlining its proposals for the disposal of controlled waste in its area.[27] The Department of the Environment explained that:

The survey will need to be wide ranging. As well as providing a picture of the current situation with regard to waste arisings and the provision of disposal facilities, it will be necessary to take a forward look at trends over the next 10 years or so, in order to assess the need for the provision of new, or the expansion of existing, facilities.[28]

Having completed the survey, the disposal authority must then prepare a plan, which must refer, among other matters, to: 'the sites and equipment which the authority and other persons are providing and during that period proposes itself to provide and expects other persons to provide for disposing of controlled waste'[29]

In view of the strategic nature of the waste disposal survey and plan, and the reference to provision of future sites, it is perhaps surprising that neither the 1974 Act nor any subsidiary instrument or circular refers to the need to take account, in the preparation of the disposal plan, of any relevant structure or local plans. However, consultation with the collection authorities is mandatory[30] and thus, given good inter-departmental communication, a district planning authority should be able to express its views on the land use implications of the waste disposal plan. It has been argued that a subject plan, being ordnance survey based and entailing a full public participation exercise, might represent a more appropriate medium for identifying future disposal sites, especially landfill sites, which have high land-take and generate local hostility.[31]

The relationship between planning and waste disposal authorities

While the division of responsibilities between planning and waste disposal functions outlined by the Department of the Environment[18] was accepted by the majority of authorities,[32,33] there remain a few pockets of resentment among the lower tier authorities over the transfer of waste disposal responsibilities implemented in 1976. There are some examples which suggest that the published advice of central government has perhaps underestimated the potential for conflict between counties and districts.[16,33] Such conflict is implicit in some of Warrington's public statements about the Penketh tip described in Chapter 8.

One district council was prepared to go as far as the High Court in its opposition to the decision of the waste disposal authority over a tip in its area. In 1979 North East Derbyshire District Council[34] applied to the Queen's Bench Division for an order of *certiorari* to quash the grant, by Derbyshire County Council to a private company, of a licence to tip waste (including sewage sludge and some toxic materials) on 9 ha of land unrestored after the extraction of fire clays, shales, and coal. In 1969 planning consent had been granted for mineral extraction from 55 ha, subject to conditions, one of which required that the site eventually be backfilled and restored to its former level. The District Council argued that there was no planning consent for waste tipping on this 9 ha site, and hence the issue of a waste disposal licence was unlawful. The County Council and the company argued that the planning condition requiring backfilling was tantamount to a consent for tipping, since, if there were no tipping (and the original condition did not specify the fill material), the owner would be in default of the planning consent. This was a view with which Lord Chief Justice Widgery concurred.[35]

A more common manifestation of a district's underlying dissatisfaction with the county's role in solid waste disposal was the application of planning conditions which allegedly duplicated the powers of the waste disposal authority following a thorough appraisal and consultation.[33] If, for instance, a planning authority was of the opinion that a proposed site was suitable for waste disposal provided that only inert non-toxic wastes, such as building rubble, were tipped there then they would impose a planning condition to that effect. While such a condition would clearly reduce the pollution potential and the alarm of residents near the tip, it precluded the right of the disposal authority to determine what wastes could be accepted. Such planning conditions were particularly resented by disposal authorities when applied to abandoned clay workings which, since the impermeability of the clay itself forms a natural 'bund' preventing the leaching of pollutants, are (hydrogeologically) suited for toxic waste disposal sites.[16,33] These problems should, in principle, be reduced by the recent transfer of waste disposal determination powers to county planning authorities.

No advice has been published on the status of 'need' in the consideration of waste disposal sites. Under the 1974 Act, the only ground for refusing a site licence is the prevention of 'pollution of water or danger to public health'. While a disposal authority could not withhold a licence on the grounds that another site was unnecessary while surplus capacity existed elsewhere, that might prove to be a legitimate reason for the planning authority to withhold planning consent (especially if a relevant development plan designated adequate areas for waste disposal in other, more appropriate locations). This point could only be tested on an appeal against such a refusal. However, an appeal on this ground alone seems unlikely to arise for most planning committees accept, albeit occasionally reluctantly, that the need for more public and private waste disposal sites is urgent.

The search for more sites can only be intensified when the following section of the 1974 Act is finally implemented (as has been recommended by a House of Lords committee on hazardous waste disposal):[3]

It shall be the duty of each disposal authority to ensure that the arrangements made by the authority and other persons for the disposal of waste are adequate for the purpose of disposing of all controlled waste which becomes situated in its area after this section comes into force and all controlled waste which is likely to become so situated.[36]

The reference to 'all controlled waste' in the above means that a waste disposal authority's duty in respect of industrial waste will be equivalent to that conferred upon it in regard to domestic refuse. Little interpretation of this section has been offered, and exactly what shall constitute 'adequate' and legitimate 'arrangements' has not been formally defined. This section does not rule out the current practice of 'exporting' waste from one county to another; however it is anticipated that the onus of arranging for the export of waste will fall upon the disposal authority at the point of origin and not upon the industrialist; and by implication, it is the authority who must bear the cost of transporting waste to its final destination. In addition, this section does not imply that the waste disposal authority should itself operate sites and plant with a sufficient capacity to handle all industrial (and domestic) waste arising within the county; rather it suggests that the authority must ensure that land for sufficient sites is available irrespective of whether those sites are operated by public or private enterprise. In this regard, the co-operation of the county planning committees will be essential.

The implementation of this section of the 1974 Act could add to those areas of potential conflict between district and county authorities—especially where one district council considers that it is being asked to receive an unequal share of the county's wastes.[37] While landfill remains the favoured disposal option for the bulk of industrial wastes, the participation of planning officers of the lower-tier authorities in the selection of new sites by consultation, despite the involvement of county planning officers, will continue to be politically expedient as well as serving as an additional environmental safeguard.

REFERENCES AND NOTES

[1] *Digest of Environmental Pollution Statistics, 1,* Department of the Environment, HMSO, London, 1978.
[2] The area of land actively employed for winning minerals was 49,000 ha in 1974, with a further 45,000 ha covered by permission for working.
[3] House of Lords, *Hazardous Waste Disposal,* Select Committee on Science and Technology, Session 1980-81, 1st Report, HMSO, London, 1981.
[4] 'Survey of Derelict and Despoiled Land, 1974', Department of the Environment, London, 1976.
[5] Local Government Planning and Land Act, 1980, s. 86.

[6] Town and Country Planning Act, 1971, s. 26 and town and Country Planning General Development Order. 1977 (SI 1977, No. 289) Art. 8(1)(b).

[7] Town and Country Planning General Development Order, 1977, Arts. 15(1)(f) and (i).

[8] R. Levitt, *Implementing Public Policy*, Croom Helm, London; 1980.

[9] *Report of the Working Party on Refuse Disposal*, Department of the Environment, HMSO, London, 1971. The Department of the Environment has asked that the following footnote be included: 'The Department of the Environment, while accepting the general tenor of the recommendations contained in the Report of the Working Party on Refuse Disposal considers that the controls over waste disposal introduced subsequent to that Report have partly superseded those recommendations.'

[10] 'Report of the Working Party on Refuse Disposal', Department of the Environment, Circular 26/71, HMSO, London, 1971.

[11] 'Planning Files', Application 72/6076/OS/276C/72, Leicestershire County Council, Leicester, 1972- .

[12] 'Decision Letter on Appeal Relating to Land at Barwell', APP/1214/A/73/6380, Department of the Environment, London, 1975.

[13] Section 30(1) of the 1974 Act defines controlled waste as 'household, industrial and commercial waste'. Mineral waste, agricultural waste, sewage sludge and ash from power stations do not constitute controlled waste and their disposal on land does not require a site licence.

[14] Control of Pollution (Special Wastes) Regulations, 1980 (S.I. 1980, No. 1709) made under the provisions of the Control of Pollution Act, 1974, s. 17. The introduction of some form of scheme is required under a European Economic Community directive ('Council Directive on Toxic and Dangerous Waste', 78/319/EEC, *Official Journal of the European Communities*, 21, L84/43, 31.3.1978) which also gives a list of substances which are especially dangerous to health or to the environment. The directive does not prescribe the quantities or concentrations at which special control is required; in this regard, discretion is left to member states.

[15] Where a site is operated by the waste disposal authority, controls are specified, not in a site licence, but in a resolution of that authority (s. 11 of the 1974 Act).

[16] Questionnaire returns, quoted in C. E. Miller, C. Wood, and J. McLoughlin, 'Land Use Planning and Pollution Control', Report to the Social Science Research Council, Pollution Research Unit, University of Manchester, 1980.

[17] Control of Pollution Act, 1974, s. 5(3).

[18] 'Control of Pollution Act, 1974 - Part I (Waste on Land) Disposal Licences', Department of the Environment, Circular 55/76, HMSO, London, 1976.

[19] 'Licensing of Waste Disposal Sites', *Waste Management Paper 4*, Department of the Environment, HMSO, London, 1976.

[20] Anon, 'Magnitude of Modern Problems of Waste Disposal', *Local Government Review*, 143, (1979) 575-7.

[21] *Hazardous Wastes in Landfill Sites*, Final Report on the Co-operative Programme of Research on the Behaviour of Hazardous Wastes in Landfill Sites, Dept. of the Environment, HMSO, London, 1978.

[22] 'Control of Pollution Act 1974, Part I - Waste on Land', Department of the Environment, Circular 29/78, HMSO, London, 1978.

[23] Royal Commission on Environmental Pollution, *Seventh Report. Agriculture and Pollution*, Cmnd. 7644, HMSO, London, 1979.

[24] 'Structure Plan: Written Statement', Greater Manchester County Council, Manchester, 1979.

[25] 'Structure Plan: Written Statement', West Glamorgan County Council, Manchester, 1979.

[26] 'Council Directive on Waste', 75/442/EEC, *Official Journal of the European Communities*, 18, L194/39, 25.7.1975.

[27] Control of Pollution Act, 1974, s. 2.

[28] 'Waste Disposal Surveys', *Waste Management Paper 2,* Department of the Environment, HMSO, London, 1976.

[29] Control of Pollution Act, 1974, s. 2(2)(f).

[30] Control of Pollution Act, 1974, s. 2(3)(a)(ii).

[31] Planning Officer, Cheshire County Council, 'Personal Communication', 1980.

[32] See for example, the Lancashire Waste Disposal Authority, described in C. E. Miller *et al.,* op. cit., vol. III.

[33] C. E. Miller *et al.,* op. cit., vol. IV.

[34] This district embraces the area of the former Clay Cross UDC, best known for its refusal to comply with certain provisions of the Housing Finance Act 1972. More recently, the concern of members of the North East Derbyshire District Council has led to an inquiry into the dumping, in an open case coal mine at Morton, of equipment contaminated by dioxin as a result of an explosion in 1968 at the Coalite Group works at Bolsover (*The Guardian,* 1 Oct. 1981).

[35] Regina v. Derbyshire County Council ex parte North East Derbyshire District Council (1977) 77 LGR 389.

[36] Control of Pollution Act, 1974, s. 1.

[37] This consideration does not apply to Welsh authorities.

8

THE WASTE DISPOSAL SITE

Gatewarth Farm Tip occupies some 70 ha of flat, low-lying land on the north bank of the River Mersey at Penketh, approximately three kilometres from the centre of Warrington, now in the county of Cheshire. The whole of this site is bounded to the north by the disused St Helens Canal. Phases 1 and 2 (see Fig. 8.1) are bounded by the Sankey Brook, on the opposite bank of which lies a sewage disposal works. Phase 3, separated from the remainder of the site by Whittle Brook, is bounded to the west by a third water course, Penketh Brook. The channel of the River Mersey forms the other boundary of this part of the site (Fig. 8.1).

Immediately to the north of the canal, and running parallel with it, is a double-track railway line. Adjacent to Phases 1 and 2 lie industrial premises; however, across the canal from Phase 3, there is now an area (Penketh Hall Estate) of new owner-occupied housing. Many of these houses are within 200 m of the tipping area; some are within 90 m (Plate 4).

The planning applications

In April 1966, Warrington Rural District Council (RDC) received an application from a local building firm for planning permission to build housing on 10 ha of land at Penketh Hall Farm, designated as an open space in the approved development plan.[1] The application was duly advertised as a departure from this plan and the views of various interested bodies were sought. Penketh Parish Council had no objection to the proposal. The Mersey and Weaver River Authority did not disapprove of the development provided certain measures relating to the drainage of the area were carried out. However, the development was opposed by the Ministry of Agriculture, Fisheries and Food because of the loss of good quality agricultural land.

Lancashire County Council, the local planning authority at that time, recommended that planning permission be withheld in order to adhere to the designation of the land in the development plan. During exchanges between the Rural District and the County over the ensuing months, Warrington was to declare its desire to see the application upheld. In April 1967, the county planning officers conceded and recommended approval subject to a number of conditions.[1]

Nineteen days before the decision to grant planning permission for what was later to become known as the Penketh Hall Estate, a plan-

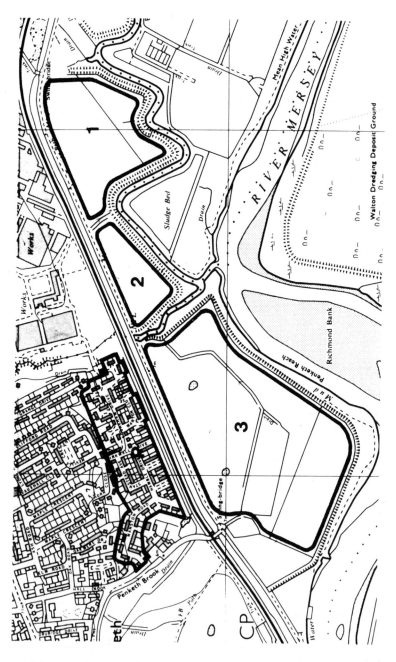

Fig. 8.1   Penketh, Warrington: Gatewarth Farm tip and Penketh Hall Estate

P: Penketh Hall Estate, 1, 2, 3: Gatewarth Farm tip phases, 1 : 10,000
Crown copyright reserved

ning application was received by Warrington RDC from Warrington County Borough Council, the adjacent local authority, which sought permission to tip solid waste on some 60 ha of agricultural land which lay outside the Borough's boundary.[2] The site, designated white land in the development plan, had been acquired by the County Borough.

Warrington RDC urged the County Planning Officer of Lancashire to recommend that planning permission be refused on account of the problems of access to the proposed waste disposal site. However, after protracted discussions between the Rural District, the County Borough, and the County, planning permission was granted for the change of use in January 1968. Ten planning conditions were imposed, one of which required that, each day, the tip face should be sealed with 30 cm of soil or similar material.

However, these conditions were felt by the applicants to be unduly onerous. Following discussions between officers of Warrington County Borough and Lancashire, agreement was reached on the procedures by which the tipping operations should be conducted and the site restored to agricultural use. A second planning application was submitted by the County Borough in April 1968; in November 1968, this application was approved with the imposition of ten planning conditions embodying the agreed procedure on tipping and restoration.[3]

The planning conditions relating to pollution control were:

1. [a scheme and programme should be provided, including details of:]
   (b) A phasing scheme providing for tipping to commence at the north-easterly end of the site, proceeding in a south-westerly direction and for not more than 5 acres [2 ha] of agricultural use at any one time.
   The scheme and programme shall, after approval by the Local Planning Authority, be carried out only in accordance with the proposal submitted to and approved by the Local Planning Authority. The provisions of the approved scheme and programme relating to the restoration of land to the level of adjoining land and to agricultural use shall be carried out.
4. Refuse exposed to the air shall be covered each day with at least 9 inches [23 cm] of earth or other suitable material capable of forming an effective seal, providing that a surface not exceeding 600 sq. yd [500 m²] may be left uncovered during daily tipping operations.
5. At least 12 inches [30 cm] of top soil shall be spread over the completed surfaces of the tip as the development proceeds and the soiled areas shall be sown with grass within one year of soiling.
6. Sufficient screens or other suitable apparatus shall be provided so as to ensure that no paper or other refuse is blown by the wind away from the place of deposit.
7. All reasonable precautions shall be taken to prevent the outbreak of fire and the breeding of flies and vermin in the deposit.
10. Adequate precautions shall be taken to prevent any material entering the watercourse affected by the proposal.[3]

Condition 4 should be compared with its (only marginally more stringent) predecessor; condition 1(b) was imposed as a result of consultation with the Ministry of Agriculture, Fisheries and Food.

During the period of consideration of the superseded application for the tip, an application for approval of reserved matters on the housing development was submitted.[4] Received in November 1967, it was approved by Warrington RDC, following discussions with the County in January 1968. The first houses were occupied in 1969.

The application for approval of reserved matters relating to the second tipping consent was submitted in April 1970.[5] In the consideration of this application a letter, dated May 1970, from Lancashire's Divisional Planning Officer to the Engineer and Surveyor of Warrington RDC, made reference to the adjacent housing development:

At 54ft [16.5m] the tip would stand some 30 ft [9 m] above the canal bank and I do not feel this could be adequately screened from Penketh Hall Estate. ... I should like to receive some written confirmation that conditions 5 and 6 will be complied with, and in the case of 6 (screen fences), the type and location of these, especially near the Penketh Hall Estate.[5]

The details were approved in August 1970, and the County Borough immediately began tipping on the first phase.

The residents of Penketh Hall Estate were later to argue that only negligence or incompetence could explain a decision which resulted in the juxtaposition of a housing estate and a waste disposal site. Indeed, the planning files contain no other reference to a consideration of the housing in the determination of the applications relating to tipping and no reference to a consideration of the converse is apparent. This might suggest that planning permission for the housing was given in ignorance of the proximity of the tip, except that the letter quoted above does not suggest that a planning error had been discovered, rather that some care needed to be taken to safeguard visual amenity.

Moreover, it is unlikely that the juxtaposition arose unknowingly through some failure of communication between the Rural District and the County as numerous exchanges between the two authorities are indicated by the files. Further, it is the considered opinion of one of the senior officers concerned that it was impossible for permission to be given for the tip in ignorance of the permission for housing on the adjacent land.[6]

The waste disposal licence

On local government reorganization in April 1974, the Borough of Warrington was created by the amalgamation of Warrington County

Borough with Warrington RDC and other local authorities spanning the River Mersey. It was the most populous district of the county of Cheshire. As a result of the coming into force of Part I of the Control of Pollution Act, 1974, responsibility for waste disposal at Gatewarth was transferred to Cheshire County Council. However, for twelve months, Warrington Borough Environmental Health Department exercised control over operations at the tip as agents of the County Council. By the end of 1976, tipping had been completed on Phase 1, although the area had not been restored in the manner required by the terms of the planning consent.

In March 1976, Cheshire prepared an application[7] for a waste disposal resolution for Gatewarth. Since the site was owned and operated by the County, Cheshire, as the waste disposal authority, was in effect seeking its own permission to use Gatewarth as a waste disposal site. It followed its normal practice of employing the same consultation and other procedures as apply to any other operator of a waste disposal site. In the absence of any objection from the North West Water Authority, approval of this application was granted by the Highways Subcommittee in March 1977. In accordance with the Control of Pollution Act, 1974, a resolution was passed listing the conditions to be observed in the operation of the tip.

The first of three parts of the site licence application records that Gatewarth Tip had at that time an estimated remaining capacity of $2,500,000 \text{ m}^3$; that the final use of the site was 'yet to be determined'; and that tipping would be permitted for a total period of 44 hours per week. The second part of the application listed the estimated daily maximum of *general* wastes at 440 tonnes. The application also stated, in relation to *difficult* wastes, that the estimated maximum of 400 tonnes per day of radioactive waste (from the demolition of buildings) would apply only between May 1976 and January 1977. There would be an anticipated maximum of 20 tonnes of asbestos tipped per day.

The residents' reaction

With the first phase of tipping completed, earth-moving and filling operations began on Phase 2. The concern of some of the residents in the houses opposite the furthest parts of the tip gradually increased as the tip-face slowly advanced in a south-westerly direction. The prospect of a waste tip within, in many cases, 200 m of their homes was one of which they had not been forewarned when purchasing their houses some years before.

At first, anxious individuals entered into correspondence with Warrington Borough Council. Invariably, they were informed that all waste disposal, Gatewarth Tip included, was now the responsibility of the County Council. Later, the local residents organized themselves into an action committee, under the aegis of the existing Penketh Residents' Association.

Early in 1977, a petition calling for the cessation of waste disposal activities at Gatewarth was organized by the action group. In addition, the residents sought the support of the local Labour MP. In March 1977, the MP forwarded the petition to Warrington Borough Council. In reply, the Borough Secretary informed the action group of the transfer of responsibility for the tip to the County Council. This letter continued by intimating that Warrington's Planning and Estates Officer was, at that time, discussing 'certain elements of the planning permission' with the County Council. Later in March a meeting was convened which provided the residents with another opportunity to express their concerns and to table their demands regarding the tip opposite their homes. It was attended by the MP, a representative of the County Council, Warrington Borough councillors, and members of the Penketh Residents' Association.

These concerns were reiterated in a letter, dated March 1977, from the MP to the Chief Executive of the Cheshire County Council.[8] The latter's reply outlined the planning history of the tip and the adjacent housing, described the wastes (180,000 tonnes) tipped at Gatewarth during the previous twelve months and responded to the anxieties of the local residents concerning the tipping of radioactive materials and of asbestos.

Radioactive waste arose from the demolition of a building belonging to a company which had used radioactive materials. The disposal was conducted in accordance with the provisions of the Radioactive Substances Act, 1960; the site had been given a certificate of authorization (for this particular waste) following an inspection by the Radiochemical Inspectorate of the Department of the Environment. This body had indicated that the average level of radioactivity of the material permitted to be tipped at Gatewarth was no more than the natural background activity in Aberdeen (a city containing many buildings constructed of thorium-bearing granite).[8]

As for asbestos, this was in the form of a scrap from a Cheshire company manufacturing asbestos/cement pipes—a material not considered by the Asbestos Research Council to pose a dust hazard. In addition, the Health and Safety Executive had monitored the tipping of this material at the site and had expressed their satisfaction with the procedures adopted.[8]

In June 1977, a second petition, prepared by the Penketh Residents' Association and bearing nearly 3,000 signatures, was forwarded to Cheshire County Council. Copies were also sent to Warrington Borough Council and to the North West Water Authority. The petition called for the cessation of tipping at Gatewarth on account of the threat it posed to the amenity of the area, and to the health of the neighbouring residents; in addition, the petition alleged certain breaches of the conditions both of planning permission and of the site licence.[8]

In reply, Cheshire's Chief Executive informed the Association that the petition had been reported to the Waste Disposal Panel of the Highways Subcommittee. This letter continued with a report that 'neither the North West Water Authority, the Health and Safety Executive nor any other public agency consulted' had any objection to the manner in which the tip was operated. The Chief Executive then rebutted each of the numerous allegations made in the Association's petition.[8]

The amended Phase 3 scheme

Once the County Council assumed full responsibility for the Gate-warth Tip, it began (in June 1975) to re-examine the operational scheme originally proposed by the former Warrington County Borough. This scheme was considered by the County officers to be both impractical and environmentally unsatisfactory; accordingly a revised scheme was prepared. Among the principal amendments was a proposal that a substantial earth embankment on the south bank of the canal should be formed so that the tip-face would not be visible from the houses in the Penketh Hall Estate. In addition, only inert waste ('non-putrescible, not biodegradable and not giving off fumes, vapours, gases or noxious liquids')[9] would be tipped within 200 yds [183 m] of the housing. The access road, and hence the attendant noise and dust generated by the waste-bearing lorries, would be diverted to the southern boundary of the third phase.

Before implementing this revision of the details of the original planning consent, the County Council was obliged to perform the technicality of granting itself planning permission for the proposed change. Before doing so, it was required to consider the views of the district planning authority in whose area the development in question lay, i.e. Warrington Borough Council. Planning clearance for the revised scheme was submitted in April 1977, and a number of discussions between the County and the District ensued.

In July 1977, Warrington's Borough Secretary wrote to the Penketh Residents' Association, briefly summarizing the planning history of the waste disposal site and the housing estate. He stated that the Borough Council could not comment on the 'kinds of waste material deposited in the tip' since these were not limited by the original planning consent. He did however concede that: 'there was a certain degree of non-compliance with the conditions attached to that permission, although a certain amount of retrospective tree planting has recently been carried out.'[8] These matters were, at that time, the subject of discussion between the Borough and County Councils. He went on to intimate that the Association would be ill-advised to entertain any hope that the Subcommittee would ultimately give anything other than a favourable comment on a scheme which could only be an improvement on the original. If they were so minded, the County Council could always revert to the previous scheme of tipping on Phase 3.

The North West Water Authority was to prove no more sympathetic to the aims of the Penketh Residents' Association. In June, the Authority's support for the cessation of tipping at Gatewarth on the grounds of the pollution of the Mersey and the various brooks which traversed the site had been sought. In July, the Water authority replied that it did not accept that the threat of water pollution was sufficient to warrant the cessation of tipping:

Taking into account the nature of the wastes permitted to be deposited, the nature of the site, the nature and extent of the underlying strata and the use of the watercourses which you consider to be at risk the Authority is of the opinion that the risk of pollution is not unacceptable.[8]

The planning clearance was eventually discussed at the Warrington Borough Planning Subcommittee meeting in August 1977. A spokesman for the Penketh Residents' Association, together with the solicitor retained by the Association, presented the residents' case in opposition to further tipping. Earlier, the Association had distributed a summary of its views to each member of the Subcommittee. This document began by remarking on the disappointing response of the various authorities which had received the earlier petition. The principal objections of the Association were summarized as: inadequate consideration of the implications of the tip when permission was given; breaches of conditions; proximity of the tip to schools and houses (in some case within 100 m); intrusiveness of the earth embankment; and nuisance from noise, dust, birds, and vermin.

These points were reiterated at the meeting. In addition, the Association's representatives argued that the revised scheme, in fact, entailed no major difference from the original and that there was no guarantee that the environmental safeguards relating to the proposed scheme would be enforced with any greater rigour than before. Furthermore, noise, not only from vehicles on the site but also from flocks of birds attracted by the wastes deposited there, was becoming intolerable to many inhabitants (and particularly shift workers) of the nearest road.

However, the main thrust of the residents' case was that the juxtaposition of two such obviously conflicting land uses as housing and waste disposal by infill could have been allowed only by oversight. The building, since 1970, of three primary schools within 400 m of the proposed Phase 3 had only compounded the error. The need to curtail tipping was self-evident; accordingly, the Subcommittee was urged to withhold its endorsement for the proposed scheme, at least until a public inquiry could be convened. Finally, it was reported that the MP had assured the Residents' Association that he would press for such an inquiry if its objectives could not be achieved otherwise.

The Planning and Estates Officer's report[10] to this meeting outlined the background to earlier discussions between officers of the Borough and both County officers and representatives of the residents. It also related the attempts to resolve what was generally recognized to be a less than satisfactory situation. As a result of the representations of the local residents, the revised scheme of tipping had been expedited (but not modified). By diverting the access road, and creating a substantial earth embankment, the worst aspects of tipping could be mitigated. In connection with condition 5, the report continued:

The tip has, in fact, been covered with a mixture of ash, clay and soil and the trees which have been planted along the edge of the tip, which is in a deplorable state, have been planted as a token gesture by the county. These should have been planted before tipping began. They will probably have to be replaced later.[10]

The reply of the County Planner to the Borough's enquiries concerning this failure to comply with condition 5 explained that adequate cover material had not been available following Cheshire's assumption of responsibility for the site. However, finance had been allocated for reinstatement of the tip and the County Council had affirmed that it had every intention of satisfying the condition in question.

The officer's report also stated that 'no objections have been received'.[10] In view of their petitions and calls for the tip's closure, this statement was later viewed by the Penketh Residents' Association with astonishment (although, presumably, the report was referring to the absence of formal objections made in connection with the statutory publication of notices).

The members of the Warrington Planning Subcommittee finally accepted their Officer's recommendations and raised no objection to the proposals provided that the various conditions were adhered to. The Subcommittee further resolved that:

The Chairman of the Sub-Committee, together with the Borough Secretary and the Planning and Estates Officer ... be authorized to attend the meeting of the County Planning Sub-Committee when the above application is considered and an invitation be extended to the County Councillor for Penketh and Cuerdley and also the Borough Councillors for that ward to attend the meeting.[11]

The Penketh Residents' Association requested that they, too, should be allowed to be represented at the forthcoming meeting of the County Planning Subcommittee when the revised scheme for tipping at Gatewarth was to be considered. However, the County Secretary explained that it was not 'the practice of the County Council to receive personal representatives from either interested parties in such cases.' The points raised by the residents would be brought to the attention of the Subcommittee when it met in December 1977.[8]

The County Secretary accepted that 'some [planning] conditions had not been complied with at the time the management of the site was taken over by the County Council in 1975.' However, since then, every effort had been made to secure compliance. On the subject of alleged breaches of the site licence conditions, which amounted to 'an extremely important matter', the Association was asked to supply details. In addition, evidence to support the allegation of the tipping of dangerous substances (in default of the Deposit of Poisonous Waste Act, 1972) would be welcomed by the County.

Before this meeting took place, Warrington's Policy and Resources Committee, chaired by the leader of the Conservative Council (a member representing Penketh) discussed the Gatewarth issue, and particularly the comments made about the amount of notifiable waste being deposited at the tip. They resolved that: 'the attention of the County Council be drawn to the comments made about the amount of notifiable waste being deposited at Gatewarth.' They also raised the question of the transfer of refuse disposal and licensing responsibilities from the County to the District.[12] The members of this committee were therefore taking a more forthright stance than those of the Planning Subcommittee.

Despite deliberations about the residents' allegations, however, when the County Planning Subcommittee finally met in December 1977, with a deputation from the Borough Council present, it was resolved 'that planning clearance be granted for the revised method of tipping.'

Although the cessation of tipping was the residents' principal aim, they had also hoped to secure a closer adherence to the conditions of the planning permission and the waste disposal licence. While Cheshire accepted that condition 5 relating to restoration could not be said to have been observed, it stood by its stated intention to honour the terms of this condition. The County did not hesitate to admit that condition 1(b) had not been observed. Indeed, the officers were at a loss to see how it could have been. If the site were to be divided into 5 acre (2 ha) plots, as specified, and tipping on one plot forbidden until the preceding plot had been restored to agriculture, then tipping would proceed at such a slow pace as to be totally impracticable.

The Association's solicitor took advice from counsel, who pointed out that Warrington Borough Council could take enforcement action against the County Council in respect of the violations of the planning conditions. The leader of Warrington Borough Council (the Penketh representative) has emphasized that the Borough would indeed have taken enforcement action if convincing evidence of violation of the planning conditions had been provided. Such evidence, with the exception of condition 1(b), did not, in his opinion, materialize.[13] Since the Borough had chosen not to enforce this condition, then, counsel suggested, it should be rescinded.

The planning conditions attached to the original permission had proved to be of relatively little value in limiting the environmental effects of the tip though restoration, at least, could be attained as a consequence of their imposition. The relative importance of the primary planning power (the initial decision to proceed with the tip) in comparison to the secondary planning power (to impose conditions) is thus emphasized. Planning conditions can normally only mitigate, not eliminate, environmental impacts. When these are impractical (as condition 1(b) proved to be) or flouted (as was condition 5) or subject to dispute as to adherence (as were some of the other conditions) their effectiveness as environmental safeguards is nullified.

Despite the somewhat nebulous definition of the proper roles of planning and waste disposal licence conditions (Chapter 7), there is little evidence here of conflict or confusion between the District and the County over the proper use of their respective powers. The District councillors were, perhaps, rather more sympathetic to the residents' case (perhaps as a result of their greater proximity) but this did not result in real dispute with the County. Some concern over the Planning Subcommittee's handling of the issue may be evidenced by the discussion of the matter by the more powerful Policy and Resources Committee.

On counsel's advice, a study of the environmental health and safety implications of the tip was commissioned by the Association in 1978. The independent waste disposal consultant reported that the residents' interests would be best served by ensuring that the local planning authority rigorously enforced the planning conditions on site restoration and tree planting in order that visual disamenity be reduced to a minimum. He advised that the environmental conditions around the tip did not justify any other course of action.[8]

The role of the Member of Parliament

The resolution of the Warrington Planning Subcommittee, in so far as it sought adherence to the planning conditions rather than a cessation of tipping, fell far short of the demands of the residents. A letter of August 1977, from the Penketh Residents' Association to their MP, revealed that the Association had by this time given up hope of persuading either the Borough or the County Council to accede to their wishes. Accordingly, they asked the MP to fulfil his earlier promise to call upon the Secretary of State for the Environment to convene a public inquiry into the question of the future of tipping at Gatewarth.

In addition, the Penketh Residents' Association explained that: 'the Sub-Committee apparently failed entirely to appreciate that the location of the tip is and will be in direct violation of the Department of the Environment's rule governing the distance which must exist between such sites and houses.'[8] The residents were claiming that they were merely requiring that the County Council should adhere to a 'rule' of the Department of the Environment which was contained in a report of a working party on refuse disposal.[14] It is evident from the discussion of the relevant section of the report in Chapter 7 that the 'rule' is, in reality, a general recommendation. The following description of Gatewarth Tip given in the Department of the Environment survey of waste disposal sites (prepared one year after the working party's report was published) lends further weight to the inference that the 183 m separation is a recommendation and not a hard and fast rule:

Houses are 200 yards [183 m] from the current tip area but screened completely by factory buildings. Houses will be 100 yards [91 m] from the nearest point of the second main area but landscaping in advance of tipping will screen the filling operations.[15]

In arguing their case for the partial withdrawal, failing the total cessation, of tipping operations the residents cited a precedent in which the 183 m recommendation proved to be an important consideration in the Secretary of State's decision to dismiss an appeal against the refusal of Leicestershire County Council to grant planning permission for housing adjacent to a waste disposal site (see Chapter 7).

However, had Cheshire County Council observed this recommendation and retreated to the 183 m limit, then some 4 ha would have been lost for tipping—this was reported to be equivalent to a loss of 300,000 m^3 or about one year's tipping.[9] In addition, Cheshire maintained that, because of the topography of the site, leaving this land would, according to the North West Water Authority, result in the creation of a malodorous bog.

Nevertheless, the refusal of the County to abide by the recommendation was seen by the Residents' Association as further evidence of its indifference to the interests of the local residents. They could see no difference in principle between the Leicestershire case and the Gatewarth Tip. Moreover, the County's concession that only 'inert' waste shall be tipped within 183 m was dismissed as an empty gesture.

The Assocation's counsel argued that no satisfactory reason had been offered for not observing this recommendation on Phase 3. A prohibition on tipping within 183 m of housing could have been imposed as a planning condition on the original consent, either by a modification order before tipping commenced, or by a discontinuance order once tipping had started. If Warrington Borough Council chose to serve neither form of order, then, counsel submitted, it was possible for the Association to make a formal complaint to the Secretary of State for the Environment calling upon him to use his default powers under the Town and Country Planning Act, 1971. In either case, a public inquiry would be involved.

Following informal discussion in the House of Commons with a Parliamentary Under-Secretary of State at the Department of the Environment, the MP wrote to this Minister in November 1977 outlining the substance of his constituents' complaints regarding Gatewarth and requesting him to meet a deputation. In reply to this letter, another Under-Secretary of State explained that waste disposal was 'very much a local matter over which an elected authority has full control' and that the Secretary of State would not therefore intervene in this case.

The Under-Secretary went on to explain that the working party's comments on the advisability of a 183 m barrier between a waste disposal site and housing amounted to a recommendation and that this buffer strip was certainly not a statutory requirement. The only way to curtail tipping at Gatewarth, he commented, would be for the local planning authority to seek a discontinuance order, which would require confirmation by the Secretary of State. While the possibility of such an order being sought existed, the request from the MP's constituents for an interview with the Under-Secretary could not be granted. For, in the event of the Secretary of State giving a decision over an order, this decision could be challenged in the High Court if prior discussions had taken place between representatives of the Secretary of State and any of the parties concerned.

In a letter of January 1978, the MP replied that these observations, although well intentioned, offered little comfort to his constituents:

What is also important is the fact that you have outlined a Catch 22 situation that the residents are caught in. The County Council give themselves planning permission for a tip as the Planning Authority and as the Refuse Disposal Authority issue themselves with a site licence, and then proceed to ignore their own laid down conditions in both the planning permission and the site licence.

When residents become aggravated at the wilful ignoring of the laid down procedures and turn to the Authorities to protest, who do they find to turn to. The very Authority who are ignoring the conditions which they themselves laid down.[8]

In his reply the Minister corrected the apparent misapprehension of the MP by explaining that it was Warrington Borough Council who could, if they so wished, enforce any planning condition on the tip or initiate a discontinuance order. The Under-Secretary then elaborated his superior's reasons for not intervening in this case:

On the more general question of our intervention you will be aware that in planning matters, successive governments have taken the view that local authorities should be free to carry out their responsibilities with the minimum of interference from central government since they are ultimately answerable to their electors for the way they carry out their duties. This means that the Secretary of State intervenes in planning decisions only in very exceptional circumstances and where issues of national or regional significance are involved.[8]

In addition to his approaches to the Secretary of State, the MP had, in January 1978, written to the County Council suggesting a meeting between Cheshire and representatives of the residents to inspect the tip and for an exchange of views on the problems. In February 1978, four members of the Penketh Residents' Association, together with the MP, met four County councillors at Gatewarth Farm Tip. The residents' representatives were anxious to point out the general visual disamenity of the site—the earthmound, the absence of screening trees, and the failure to restore the completed Phase 1. The members were apparently disturbed by the seeming absence both of wheel-washing equipment and of spraying equipment for the damping of tipped asbestos.[8]

On leaving the site, the party encountered a 'peaceful demonstration of 150 residents', after which a meeting was held at Warrington Town Hall. The four councillors were joined by four County officers; additional members of the Penketh Residents' Association and the MP were also present. The Vice-Chairman of the Residents' Association began by listing the various alleged violations of the planning and site licence conditions. He continued by remarking that residents would seek compensation under the Land Compensation Act,

1973, if Phase 3 were to go ahead. Finally he insisted that if the County Council would not abandon tipping then they should at least refuse to tip within 183 m of housing. These and other objectives of the Association were restated by their solicitor.

When asked categorically whether they would consider abandoning tipping at Gatewarth, the councillors' reported reply was that this land had been allocated for that purpose and that no viable alternative sites or disposal methods were available.[8]

This lack of viable alternatives is a crucial issue. Tipping (landfill) is a cheap method of refuse disposal[14] and the County were naturally reluctant to abandon or even curtail a site with many years' life, whether or not real alternatives existed. In effect, the ratepayers of Penketh Hall Estate were being asked to bear the environmental costs incurred by refuse disposal at Gatewarth so that Cheshire's ratepayers could benefit from cheap disposal: the few (who would happily have paid more) were subsidizing the many.

A report of this site inspection and meeting was submitted by Cheshire's Director of Highways and Transportation to the Highways Subcommittee in March. He also stated that, at a meeting of the Waste Disposal Panel held in January, with members of Warrington Borough Council present, it had been decided that allegations that dangerous substances were being illicitly tipped at Gatewarth had no foundation. The Director's report was accepted and the Subcommittee resolved:

That tipping be continued at the site, but that the effect of the scheme of operations on the residential properties be kept under review and a further report be made in due course;

That the County Valuer be asked to investigate that possibility of obtaining rights to plant an evergreen tree screen on the land between the railway and the housing estate. Subject to these rights being obtained the work to be proceeded as quickly as possible.[16]

At a meeting of the Penketh Parish Council held in March 1978, representatives of the Residents' Association once again raised the subject of Gatewarth Farm Tip. The members of the Parish Council who were also Borough councillors (including the Chairman) asked that evidence of any breaches of the planning and site licence conditions should be brought to the attention of Warrington Borough Council, so that enforcement action could be considered. As a result, a letter[8] listing alleged violations was prepared by the action group and submitted to the Borough. Eight of the ten planning conditions had been, it was claimed, either ignored or violated at various times. Of the alleged contraventions, those of most direct environmental significance were that inadequate precautions had been taken to prevent the breeding of flies and vermin, to prevent the windblown dispersal of paper, and to ensure that no refuse was allowed to reach the watercourses. In addition, various departures from the reserved matters were cited; as was the failure to adhere to the 183 m advice of the Department of the Environment.

When, by the end of April, this letter had not resulted in Warrington Borough Council's serving an enforcement notice on the County Council with respect to alleged breaches of the planning conditions, the action group was moved to write once again to the members of the Borough Council. They deplored the council's inaction and feared lest this could provoke the residents to depart from their hitherto observed course of orderly and responsible protest.[8]

Earlier, in March 1978, the action group had written to the MP, requesting that he submit their case to the Ombudsman. In his letter of May, the MP replied that he had given the matter of Gatewarth Farm tip considerable thought and that he had reached the following conclusions:

(a) That Cheshire County Council intend to carry on tipping.
(b) That Cheshire have no intention of honouring the 200 yards [183 m] recommendation of the Working Party on Refuse Disposal.
(c) That Warrington Borough Council have no intention of taking any proceedings against the County Council in relation to any aspect of the tip.
(d) That there is a gap in the proceedings which inhibits the Secretary of State from intervening in refuse disposal operations.
(e) That discussions (?) [*sic*] have gone on long enough and that this issue must be brought to a conclusion.
(f) That the only avenue open to the residents is the Local Ombudsman.[8]

Accordingly, the MP enclosed a booklet which gave advice on the procedure to be adopted when making representations to the Ombudsman. It is notable that, throughout, the MP (a long-serving and well-respected Labour politician) fought much harder for the residents than did their councillors. This may be attributed to the MP's personality, or to party politics (both Warrington and Cheshire were Conservative-controlled) but a more likely reason is his lack of direct executive involvement. He was able to witness the environmental costs of tipping and to seek redress without having to worry about the financial costs or administrative difficulties of alternative disposal methods or locations.

In the event, the Penketh Residents' Associations chose not to present their case to the Local Government Ombudsman. The residents argued that, even if his report were eventually to prove favourable to their cause, his lack of executive power to direct local authorities would mean that their objectives would be little furthered.

If such a recourse were ever to be taken, then it could perhaps truly be said that the Association had pursued all the available avenues of political protest and lobbying. At one time or another, it had made representations to the Parish Council, the Borough Council, and the County Council; it had elicited the support of the local Member of Parliament who, on their behalf, had lobbied the Secretary of State. Finally, it had made its protests known to the North West Water Authority.

In so far as Cheshire Council had no intention of abandoning tipping on the remaining phase of Gatewarth, this campaign of protest and lobbying must be considered, in the action group's terms, a failure. However, it has been suggested that the residents' campaign was, in fact, successful. The revised scheme of tipping, the introduction of which was brought forward as a result of the residents' campaign, represented a considerable improvement on that originally proposed. Perhaps more importantly, the attention already drawn to Gatewarth by the residents' protests was such as to ensure that tipping on Phase 3 would be carried out with the strictest observation of environmental controls (not least, in order to minimize the risk of further controversy).[9]

Other remedies

The Association's counsel pointed out that certain default powers are conferred upon the Secretary of State for the Environment by the Control of Pollution Act, 1974, as well as by the planning legislation. In the event of a waste disposal authority's failure to perform its statutory duties, such as failure to observe the conditions of its resolutions (as was alleged to have occurred at Gatewarth) then the Secretary of State may issue an order specifying the measures to be taken in order to perform those duties. The exercise of these default powers by the Secretary of State (as under the Town and Country Planning Act, 1971) may be accompanied or preceded by a local inquiry. It may have been to such proceedings that the MP was referring when he promised a public inquiry, though these powers are rarely invoked.

The Department of the Environment had already commented on the merits of intervention by the Secretary of State in the Gatewarth case. Although, as the Association's counsel explained, the reasons advanced by the Secretary of State for not intervening in this case did not negate his reserve role, it was nevertheless evident that the Association would need a clear and compelling demonstration of the environmental hazards posed by Gatewarth Tip before his formal intervention would be forthcoming. It was for this reason that counsel had advised the Association to commission an independent waste disposal consultant to make a study of the environmental, health, and safety implications of the tip.

It is now clear that the residents were unlikely to secure redress of their grievances either through planning legislation or through Part I of the Control of Pollution Act. The comments of the solid waste consultant notwithstanding, it could well be that the Public Health Act, 1936, might have afforded a less procedurally involved source of remedy.

Indeed, if, as the Association has argued, residents were subjected to considerable nuisance due to flies, vermin, and odours emanating from the tip then they had prima-facie grounds for taking action, initially in the Magistrates' Court, against the County Council. However, Warrington Environmental Health Department officers have stated that they have never had any evidence of actionable nuisance. By the same token, if, as has been claimed, the vehicles (lorries and bulldozer) on the tip caused noise nuisance, then the occupiers of the house adjacent to the tip, might have considered summary proceedings under Part III of the Control of Pollution Act against the tip operators (to whom, however, the defence of 'best practicable means' would have been available).

While the possibility of these forms of action in nuisance (including the common law action of private nuisance) remained open to the house occupants, it is unlikely that the courts would have countenanced claims under the Land Compensation Act, 1973.

Cheshire's structure plan policy relating to waste disposal, duly approved by the Secretary of State for the Environment, is that:

Sites for controlled tipping will normally be approved only if they satisfy all the following criteria:
(a) they are large enough to ensure efficient management;
(b) they are closely related to the transportation networks;
(c) they offer prospects of environmental improvement after tipping is completed, or alternatively, make the land more suitable for beneficial use than before;
(d) they pose no threat to surface or underground water supplies, and;
(e) they are not detrimental to the environment of nearby areas.[17]

Gatewarth Farm Tip would presumably not be acceptable under the criteria set down for this policy since, even if an improvement of the previous environment would have occurred once tipping was completed, the site *was* detrimental to the environment of the residents of Penketh Hall Estate. However, any tip is, to some extent, detrimental to nearby areas and this is presumably why the policy contains the expression 'normally': adherence to the structure plan alone will therefore not ensure that incidents similar to those described will never recur.

None of the officers or councillors approached in this study had denied that Gatewarth was, by current standards, a planning error (they differ from the residents only in the extent to which they believe that that error might have reasonably been rectified). In addition, they have argued that the possibility of such an error occurring today has been effectively eradicated, not only by improved procedures of intra- and inter-authority consultation but also by a greater awareness of the environmental implications of planning decisions.

Two of the three phases at Gateworth had been reclaimed to such a reasonable standard at the time of writing that the majority of residents have been impressed. They now accept that the County has been acting in good faith and have relaxed their opposition. One or two residents, however, remain opposed to the tip in principle. The final use of the tip has not yet been decided, despite the reference to agriculture in condition 1(b) of the original planning permission. A crop of hay has, however, been grown on part of Phase 1.

The residents' concern is now directed against the Merseyside and North Wales Electricity Board who are proposing to erect a 400 kV national grid line across the tip to serve Warrington. It must be arguable whether the Board would have sought to locate the very large pylons necessary to carry this voltage at Gatewarth Farm if the land had not already been despoiled by tipping.

REFERENCES AND NOTES

[1] 'Planning Files', Appplication 11/4/4227, Warrington Borough Council, Warrington, 1966- .

[2] 'Planning Files', Application 11/4/3588, Warrington Borough Council, Warrington, 1967- .

[3] 'Planning Files', Application 11/4/5017, Warrington Borough Council, Warrington, 1968- .

[4] 'Planning Files', Application 11/4/4817, Warrington Borough Council, Warrington, 1967- .

[5] 'Planning Files', Application 11/4/5931, Warrington Borough Council, Warrington, 1970- .

[6] Planning Officer, Warrington Borough Council, 'Personal Communication', 1980.

[7] 'Site Licence Application', 60500, Cheshire County Council, Chester, 1976.

[8] 'Files', Penketh Residents' Association, Warrington, 1976- .

[9] Waste Disposal Officer, Cheshire County Council, 'Personal Communication', 1979.

[10] 'Planning and Estates Officer's Report to Planning Sub-Committee', 10 August, Planning Files, Warrington Borough Council, Warrington, 1977.

[11] 'Minutes of Planning Sub-Committee', 10 Aug., Warrington Borough Council, Warrington, 1977.

[12] 'Minutes of Policy and Resources Committee', Warrington Borough Council, Warrington, 1977.

[13] Council Leader, Warrington Borough Council, 'Personal Communication', 1979.

[14] *Report of the Working Party on Refuse Disposal,* Department of the Environment, HMSO, London, 1971.

[15] 'Review of Sites for Waste Disposal', Unpublished document, Department of the Environment, London, 1973.

[16] 'Minutes of the Highways Sub-Committee', 20 Mar., Cheshire County Council, Chester, 1978.

[17] 'Structure Plan: Written Statement of Policies and Proposals', Cheshire County Council, Chester, 1979.

9

PLANNING AND NOISE

The prevention and minimization of noise, perhaps more than any other form of environmental pollution control, is widely recognized as a legitimate and appropriate objective of land use planning. Planning powers have afforded effective means of imposing control over noise sources and over sensitive development in areas where noise nuisance prevails. Collaboration between planning and environmental health officers over planning matters with acoustic implications is now a routine procedure in the vast majority of local authorities, as is the use of planning refusal and planning conditions.[1] In addition, noise is unique among the various forms of pollution in that a central government circular has been devoted solely and specifically to offering advice on the role which planning can play in its control.[2]

The Noise Abatement Act, 1960, brought noise within the statutory nuisance provisions of the Public Health Act, 1936. The 1960 Act was repealed by the Control of Pollution Act, 1974, but the latter contained equivalent powers over noise nuisance: 'Where a local authority is satisfied that noise amounting to a nuisance exists, or is likely to occur or recur ... [it] shall serve a notice ... requiring the abatement of the nuisance.'[3]

The serving of an abatement notice is mandatory and not at the discretion of the local authority once it is satisfied that a nuisance exists or might exist. Although this would appear to offer an effective remedy against noise nuisance, it is a sufficient defence, in summary proceedings in the Magistrates' Court for contravening the terms of a notice, to prove that the 'best practicable means' were used to prevent noise arising from buisness or trade activities.[4] A local authority may choose to seek a more effective remedy by taking proceedings in the High Court where this defence will not apply; however, the authority will still be required to demonstrate that the noise in question substantially disturbs the enjoyment of land or premises.

For these reasons, the existence of statutory controls over noise nuisance (as well as the right to take action in private or public nuisance) has not made redundant the application of planning powers to ensure anticipatory control. It might be argued that the duty to serve an abatement notice[3] when nuisance is thought 'likely to occur' is an anticipatory power and one which therefore could be duplicated by planning conditions. However, for this power to be applicable, nothing less than nuisance must be suspected; planning intervention can be justified at a noise level far below that which could occasion nuisance. By forbidding significant additions to ambient noise levels, planning powers can be employed to preserve a satisfactory noise climate. Further, they can also be utilized to prevent, or determine the nature of, sensitive development in areas experiencing high noise levels.

It must not be assumed that all sources of noise or vibration can be effectively regulated by the application of planning powers. No planning authority can ensure neighbourly consideration among the inhabitants of its area; yet one of the largest single categories of complaints to environmental health departments concerns noise from domestic sources (see Table 9.1).[6]

Planning controls and industrial development

The Department of the Environment's circular on planning and noise has been a seminal influence in the development of planning authorities' awareness of their responsibilities in regard to noise, and in particular, of the need to separate noise sources and noise sensitive land uses.[2] Perhaps this can best be exemplified by the planning conditions attached to permissions to build a steel works in Manchester. Before the circular was issued the planning conditions did not refer to noise. When a second permission was sought, following a change in ownership of the site, and after the appearance of the circular, onerous conditions were negotiated leading to much lower noise emissions than would have resulted from the initial consent.[7]

In the context of industrial noise, the circular states that there should be a strong presumption against allowing, even within towns, development which would increase noise levels in existing residential areas above 75 dB(A) CNL [corrected noise level][8] by day and 65 dB (A) by night.[2] Where a proposed industrial development is known to be a noise source, permission should be given only for immediately anticipated needs and must, according to the circular, incorporate requirements on sound insulation. Moreover, the circular argues that while quantitative conditions limiting boundary noise levels are appropriate:

when there appears to be no other way of ensuring that noise does not build up to unacceptable levels, conditions directed to the physical characteristics of the development, the type and intensity of activity to be carried on there, and hours of operation are preferable.[2]

The circular takes pains to emphasize that any quoted figure should be seen as a guideline and not as a rigid standard. It calls for a

TABLE 9.1

Trends in complaints received by environmental health department, England and Wales, 1971-80 (number per million persons)

Type of Source	1971	1972	1973	1974	1975	1976	1977	1978	1979	1980
Industrial premises	132	135	168	179	192	182	186	220 }	461	464
Commercial premises	75	75	94	133	137	149	139	195 }		
Road works, construction, and demolition	36	46	43	39	56	46	55	73	68	63
Domestic premises	80	90	91	149	165	175	335	420	586	712
All sources	323	346	396	500	550	552	716	908	1115	1239
Noise in streets		22	18	33	48	33	22	29	32	31
Percentage of total population covered by local authorities which provided statistics	72	71	52	76	78	90	95	87	85	89

Note: It is not known whether the overall increase in complaints is due to real increases in noise levels or to greater public awareness of noise, perhaps partly as a result of the implementation of the Control of Pollution Act, 1974.

Source: Reference 5.

TABLE 9.2
Planning conditions in the Welwyn Hatfield case

Conditions imposed by local planning authority	Recommendations of Inspector	Conditions imposed by Secretary of State
5. No work shall be carried out either on the land or within the buildings on Sundays or Bank Holidays, and work shall only take place between the hours of 8.00 a.m. and 6.00 p.m. Mondays to Fridays at 8.00 a.m. and 1.30 p.m. on Saturdays.	5. ... the appeal be dismissed and the condition be confirmed subject to an amendment to exclude incidental work such as that of security patrols and office cleaning.	5. No work shall be carried out either on the land or within the buildings on Sundays or Bank Holidays, and work shall only take place between the the hours of 8.00 a.m. and 1.30 p.m. Saturdays, with the exception of security patrols and office cleaning.
6. Upon the completion of the proposed development the noise generated on the site shall not exceed the following levels measured on the L_{50} scale on the	6. ... the appeal be allowed insofar as the condition be discharged and the following condition substituted: 'Noise from operations conducted	6. Noise from operations conducted on the appeal site shall not exceed L_{50} 46 dB(A) as measured on the western site boundary during the permitted hours.

following points on the western
boundary of the site
Point A   48 dB(A)
Point B   43 dB(A)
Point C   46 dB(A)
Point D   50 dB(A)

7. In addition to the requirements of condition 6 above the
details of the buildings ... shall
include details of the soundproofing
of the buildings to a level to be
agreed with the Local Planning
Authority.

on the appeal site shall not exceed
L_{50} 50 dB(A) as measured on the
western site boundary between the
hours of 8 a.m. and 6 p.m. Mondays to
Fridays; 8 a.m. and 1.30 p.m.
Saturdays and L_{10} 50 dB(A) at any
other time.'

7. ... the appeal be allowed insofar
as the condition be discharged and
the following condition substituted:
'The warehouses hereby permitted shall
be so constructed as to provide sound
attenuation of not less than ... dB(A)
against the internally generated noise
(the dB value inserted shall be that
averaged over the frequency range 100
to 3150 Hz).'

7. [the original condition 7 was deleted]

Source: Reference 10

pragmatic attitude to the planning control of noise. The extent to which the Department of the Environment itself observes an *ad hoc* approach and judges each issue on its individual merits may be inferred from ministerial decisions over planning applications with noise implications.

Four planning conditions, three of which concerned noise control measures, on planning consent for three warehouses at Welham Green in Hertfordshire were the subject of an appeal to the Secretary of State.[9] The noise conditions originally sought by the local planning authority (Welwyn Hatfield District Council), the conditions recommended by the Inspector in his report of the inquiry, and the conditions finally imposed by the Minister were all drawn up with heed paid to the advice of the circular. A comparison of these three sets of conditions is given in Table 9.2. The decision letter of May 1979 contained a number of technical points relating to the details of the boundary noise levels.[10] The Minister held, contrary to his inspector's recommendation, that a condition requiring internal sound-proofing was superfluous given the imposition of a stringent condition on noise levels at the site boundary. Nevertheless, the conditions finally imposed were hardly less demanding than those originally sought.

In the Penwith case, planning conditions similar to those described above were again the subject of an appeal under the 1971 Act. On this occasion, the local planning authority, dissatisfied with the Secretary of State's reason for replacing the original conditions by others considered to be less stringent, applied to the High Court to have the Minister's decision quashed.[11] This action led to a judgment which is of relevance not merely to the planning control of noise, but to the use of planning conditions in general.[12]

Planning approval was granted for an extension to a plastics factory in Penwith, Cornwall, which although intended for packing and ancillary operations, would allow the existing building to be more intensively used. Conditions were imposed on this approval relating not just to the extension, but to the site as a whole; these conditions were the subject of the appeal. In his report the inspector suggested that the Secretary of State might wish to take legal advice on the legitimacy of such conditions. However, condition 4a (Table 9.3), he averred, was not open to objection 'since the overall noise level must take account of the effects of extending the factory'. Condition 3 was considered unnecessarily restrictive in terms of permitted hours. Condition 4b, dealing with air pollution control, was held to be wrong in principle, in that it required expensive works to control gaseous emissions which might never arise; instead, the Inspector recommended a condition requiring an additional, specific planning consent should such processes ever be carried out.

TABLE 9.3

Planning conditions in the Penwith case

Conditions imposed by local planning authority	Recommendations of Inspector	Conditions imposed by Secretary of State
3. No machinery shall be operated in either the existing factory or the extension between the hours of 6 p.m. and 8 a.m. on weekdays or between the hours of 1 p.m. on Saturdays to 8 a.m. on Mondays or on statutory holidays.	3. No machinery shall be operated on the site between the hours of 2200 and 0700 on weekdays or between the hours of 1300 on Saturdays and 0700 on Mondays or on statutory holidays.	3. No machinery shall be operated in the extension between 1300 hours on Saturdays and 0700 hours for the remainder of the week or at any time on statutory holidays.
4a. Noise emanating from operations conducted in the existing factory and the extension hereby permitted shall not exceed 50 dB(A) as measured at the boundaries of the premises ... between the hours of 8 a.m. to 6 p.m. on Mondays to Fridays and 8 a.m. to 1 p.m. on Saturdays.	4a. No objection to this condition.	4a. Noise emanating from operations conducted in the extension hereby permitted shall not exceed 50 dB(A) as measured at the boundaries of the site.
4b. Before the extension hereby permitted is brought into use work shall have been completed in accordance with a scheme to be approved by the Local Planning Authority to ensure that adequate steps have been taken to prevent the emission of dust, grit, fumes or noxious gases from both the existing factory and the extension.	4b. Proposed substitution by condition designed to ensure that no process leading to the emission of dust, grit, fumes or noxious gases should take place without previous specific planning permission.	4b. Notwithstanding the provisions of the Town and Country Planning (Use Classes) Order, 1972, no process leading to the emission of dust, grit, fumes or noxious gases shall take place in the extension without specific planning permission.

Source: Reference 12

On the general validity of the planning authority's conditions, the Secretary of State held that conditions imposed 'for the purpose of remedying existing defects or improving what was on the site already', were *ultra vires*. Accordingly, conditions referring only to the extension were imposed by the Minister.

In its submission to the High Court, the planning authority held that the 1971 Act empowered the granting of consent for the extension, subject to a condition relating to the site as a whole.[13] Counsel for the planning authority cited the judgment in the Pyx Granite case: a planning condition must be reasonably related to the approved development.[14] The judge accepted this argument. During the local inquiry, the planning authority's contention that an intensification of the use of the existing building (and hence increased noise) would result from the operations in the proposed extension had not been contradicted. Thus, it could not be argued that conditions relating to the site as a whole were not reasonably related to the development permitted. In consequence, the planning authority had not been acting *ultra vires*. The Minister's decision was quashed, allowing the local planning authority's conditions to be reconsidered.

It would be erroneous to conclude from the above account of the Penwith case that the Secretary of State's action indicates some shift in attitude away from the planning and noise circular, or that it reveals any inconsistency with earlier planning decisions (such as that in the Welwyn Hatfield case) involving noise. It must be remembered that the Penwith case concerned the Minister's misconstruction of the law as it relates to planning conditions. The principle that planning conditions intended to reduce the risk of noise nuisance, either by boundary limits or by restricted hours of operation, may be applied to industrial buildings, is not compromised by the Minister's decision in this case. Rather, the High Court ruling offers yet another affirmation of a planning authority's right to apply conditions (which may relate to pollution control) on the use of any land in the developer's control, provided they are reasonably related to the development for which planning approval is given.

The guidelines contained in the circular on planning and noise were observed when, after protracted discussions between Bolton Metropolitan Borough and the developers of a works for the manufacture of lead batteries, limits were agreed on the maximum permissible noise levels at the site boundary. These limits, which eventually formed part of a planning agreement, were stringent enough (especially at a night-time L_{10} level of 45 dB(A)) to ensure that the low ambient noise levels would not be significantly exceeded once the works were in operation (Chapter 10).

Kirklees Metropolitan Borough Council imposed a planning condition specifying boundary noise levels on a consent for development at a chemical formulation plant (although, in this instance the night-time L_{10} limit of 55 dB(A) was less demanding than that required by Bolton). However, Kirklees imposed an additional condition which sought to minimize nuisance to nearby residents by preventing lorries entering or leaving the works during night hours (Chapter 6). It is apparent that these two examples of planning control over industrial development are by no means unusual, conditions normally being applied after collaboration between planning and environmental health departments.[1.15]

'Planning controls' and other noise sources

Many new non-industrial sources of noise do not constitute 'development' and consequently do not require planning permission. A working party of the Noise Advisory Council considered the role of planning powers in controlling noise from sports stadia, entertainment establishments, and other public places.[16] The working party's report pointed out that most football grounds pre-date planning legislation and have thus escaped planning controls; also it argues that intensification of use (and hence, increases in noise emissions) by, for instance, two matches per week instead of one would not amount to a material change of use.[17] Many noise-intensive motor sports (e.g. scrambling, stock car racing) constitute permitted development; but the report maintains that the withdrawal of permitted development rights would offer inadequate control over temporary, but nevertheless noisy, activities such as pop festivals and fun fairs.

Noise and nuisance from such traditional urban activities as street trading, hawking and organ grinding remain the subject of archaic statutes and by-laws, and whilst planning consent might be refused for a new public house, dance hall or other licensed premises in an inappropriate location, restricting opening hours by planning conditions, in an effort to reduce noise nuisance, could be considered as a duplication of powers under the licensing laws.

Aircraft and motor vehicles account for a significant proportion of the total number of complaints concerning noise.[6] Legislation, such as the Motor Vehicles (Construction and Use) Regulations, 1973,[18] exists which enable direct control over mobile noise sources. Nevertheless, noise and vibration from road traffic and aircraft constitute further areas where planning control is of secondary importance, though control over noise-sensitive development in the vicinity of these sources is possible.

The construction of trunk roads and the building or extension of airports will, in most instances, require the sanction of, or be undertaken by, a central government department. Ministerial approval of such capital projects automatically confers planning consent. When a local highway authority (the county council) resolves, under the Highways Act, 1959, to build a new highway, planning consent is deemed to be implicit in that authority's resolution. In addition, a highway authority has the power, under the General Development Order, 1977, to issue directions to a local planning authority restricting the grant of planning consent for any development which might lead to a 'material increase in the volume of traffic' on any classified road.[19]

Although the lower-tier authorities do not normally enjoy direct powers of planning control over roads the statutes require that the district councils should be consulted before they are given approval, whereupon the environmental health departments may make representations concerning any deterioration in the noise climate which might result from major highway proposals. The need for consultation between planning, highway, and environmental health departments has become more marked with the advent of powers, conferred upon local authorities by the Heavy Commercial Vehicles (Control and Regulations) Act, 1973, to specify certain routes for heavy lorries in the interests of amenity (which might be impaired by exhaust fumes as well as by noise).

The need for careful consideration of the noise implications of development by public bodies has perhaps become more apparent as a result of the Land Compensation Act, 1973. Under this Act, claims for compensation may be made against a public authority by any owner (or lessee) of land, the value of which depreciates as a result of noise (and of vibration, smell, smoke, or fumes) emanating from any public works. This act applies only to those public works which enjoy immunity from action in nuisance (e.g. a highway authority cannot be held liable for nuisance caused by the users of any of its roads) and such immunity is conferred upon airports by the provisions of the Civil Aviation Act, 1949. The duty to pay compensation ensures that public works are undertaken with due regard to their effects on the locality.[20] In the case of highways, claims may be made for the cost of sound insulation, for dwellings and buildings used for residential purposes, where the L_{10} noise level is greater than 68 dB(A).[21]

Under the Civil Aviation Act, 1971, the Secretary of State for the Environment may designate any 'aerodrome' and specify requirements on noise limitation procedures to be observed there by airline operators. Four airports owned by the British Airports Authority have been so designated; in the remaining regional airports, the

Minister has allowed the local authorities to impose their own controls over aircraft noise. The circular on planning and noise advises that: 'It is not considered appropriate to impose conditions purporting to control the movements of or noise emitted by aircraft in flight, since planning is concerned only with development of land.'[2] The circular concedes that, where a planning authority does have jurisdiction over development involving aircraft (e.g., when land is taken out of agricultural use and acquired by a flying-club), then conditions limiting the number of movements per day or restricting take-off and landing to daylight hours may be applied.

While such noise-intensive sources as airports and motorways lie outside the normal framework of development control, land use planning in its widest sense is central to the lengthy studies and the inquiries which now precede any ministerial decision on the routing of a motorway. Examination of the evidence submitted to the Roskill Commission on the Third London Airport attests to the importance of noise in the deliberations which led the majority to recommend Cublington in Buckinghamshire as the preferred site for another airport.[22] However, Professor Buchanan's minority recommendation of a remote site at Foulness was accepted by the government, who subsequently took no action when it became apparent that a third airport was not then needed. (Crucially, need had not been considered by the Commission, as it was not included in its terms of reference.)

Planning controls and noise-sensitive development

While formal planning powers are of limited application in respect of noise from non-industrial sources, the right, if not the duty, of planning authorities to intervene in the regulation of sensitive land uses in the vicinity of any noise source is well established. Such regulation may consist of requiring developers of housing to provide double glazing and other noise insulation. Alternatively, sound attenuation can be achieved by demanding such measures as fencing or earthworks between housing and adjacent highways. Where existing noise levels are such that nuisance is inevitable then the sanction of planning refusal should, according to the circular on planning and noise, be employed:

There should be a strong presumption against permitting residential development in areas which are or are expected to become subject to excessive noise. ... Where it is proposed to grant permission for residential development in areas of high noise level planning conditions should be imposed to ensure that as far as practicable the effects of noise are mitigated and that, in any event, the internal sound levels in the dwelling should conform to the criteria recommended.[2]

Pursuing this theme, the circular gives advice on the location and design of housing so as to reduce exposure to noise. The use of housing to form noise barriers is advocated and the possibility of using local authorities' powers to acquire land to ensure that the appropriate layout or noise conditions can be employed, is mooted.[2]

The circular suggests levels of noise which might justify the refusal of planning consent: for instance, where road traffic generates noise levels in excess of 70 dB(A), no residential or similarly vulnerable development should be permitted. In areas where annoyance from aircraft exceeds 50 NNI (noise and number index)[8] it is recommended that consent for housing should be withheld; planning conditions designed to mitigate nuisance (e.g. requiring double glazing) are thought appropriate in areas prone to 40-50 NNI. Similar recommendations relating to development close to industrial noise sources are made.[2]

In 1978 Bolton Metropolitan Borough Council refused planning consent for the building of four bungalows on a site considered likely to suffer noise nuisance from nearby industrial premises. The developers appealed and, in their evidence, they argued that, under existing legislation (by implication, the Control of Pollution Act, 1974) the local authority possessed adequate powers to control noise nuisance from the adjacent factory. The planning authority cited the planning and noise circular in support of their decision to forbid housing on the appeal site.[2] The factory, which was situated on land with a long-established right of use for general industry, had been the cause of occasional complaints to occupants of housing some 50 m away. The appeal site, being as near as 15 m, was clearly unsuited for additional housing. The appeal was dismissed.[23]

The Secretary of State has generally been ready to uphold refusals of planning permission on the grounds that new noise-sensitive development, particularly housing, should not be permitted in areas where noise levels were unacceptably high.[24] The advice in the circular on planning and noise[2] has therefore been supported by the Minister on appeal, though examples of new dwellings being constructed, with or without adequate design and insulation, in very noisy areas are quite common.[7]

Development plans and noise abatement zones

The circular on planning and noise states that: 'Noise will often be a factor in the evaluation of alternatives, both in considering the major issues in structure plans and in working out more detailed proposals in local plans.' A general presumption against allowing noise sources in residential areas or permitting sensitive development in areas already subject to noise has formed the basis of policies in a number of development plans. Many structure plans contain policies relating to noise, but this form of pollution is less well represented in structure plan policies than any of the other types.[1] Merseyside County Council, for example, did not include any noise policies in its structure plan.[25]

Greater Manchester's draft structure plan contained four policies relating to noise: one mentioned the standard of 68d B(A) L_{10} (18 hr) for external ambient levels affecting residential development near to motorways; one dealt with other major roads; one with noisy development (Chapter 10); and one with the types of development to be permitted within certain noise contours around Manchester Airport.[26] The first three policies were all deleted as being 'too detailed or ... otherwise not of structural importance' by the Secretary of State for the Environment. There had been very little opposition to these policies and they were only cursorily mentioned at the Examination in Public. The last policy was presumably spared because it is identical to one in the approved Cheshire Structure Plan.[27] It is, perhaps, ironical that these policies were deleted, despite the advice in the planning and noise circular since, as explained in Chapter 10, Greater Manchester had deliberately eschewed the use of quantitative air pollution policies to avoid Cheshire's fate. Several other approved structure plans, including Cheshire's, contain broadly similar noise policies.

Several district councils have included noise policies in local plans, although (as with structure plans) the number of plans containing such policies is smaller than that containing policies designed to control the effects of other types of pollution. A policy included in Islington's Borough Plan refers to quantitative standards for road and rail transport noise: there is a presumption against residential development in areas subject to more than 68 dB(A) (18 hr) from traffic noise, or more than 65 dB(A) (24 hr) in the case of railway noise, unless measures are taken to reduce the impact of noise.[29]

It must be remembered that noise is a localized phenomenon; the physical characteristics of the locality of a source of noise are the principal determinants of sound attenuation, and hence the range within which nuisance might be occasioned. This reason has been advanced by some planning and environmental health officers in support of their contention that strategic policies on noise are inappropriate and that noise control is best formulated by an *ad hoc* examination of individual planning applications.[15] This perhaps explains why a relatively small number of development plans contain noise control policies.

Of the many new forms of noise control contained in Part III of the Control of Pollution Act, 1974, it is the power of local authorities to establish 'noise abatement zones' which is most closely related to land use planning. In summary: the establishment of a noise abatement zone enables a local authority to maintain a satisfactory noise climate, within a designated area, by preventing gradual additions to the ambient noise level, each of which would not in itself constitute a nuisance. Initially, the local authority specifies maximu n levels from classes of fixed noise sources within a given locality; the classes of installation and the locality are designated in an order confirmed by the Secretary of State. Measurements of noise levels emitted from any premises so designated are taken by the authority and recorded in a register; exceeding the registered level without the consent of the authority constitutes an offence. Subsequently, where it appears to the authority that noise emitted from any premises within a zone is 'unacceptable', then a notice may be served specifying a lower level and measures by which that level might be achieved.

The noise abatement zone procedure has an obvious advantage over planning intervention: it applies to established as well as to new development. In addition, it offers a remedy to one notorious shortcoming in planning control: within a zone it would be an offence to allow noise levels to exceed the registered figure as a result of either a change or an intensification of use (e.g. the addition of machinery within a building) and certain changes of use (see Chapter 6) may constitute 'permitted development', and may therefore be undertaken without the need to secure planning approval even though it entails a rise in the emitted noise level.

A further advantage is apparent from a Department of the Environment circular in which a list of classes of premises which might be usefully included within a noise abatement order is given:

(iii) places of environment of assembly—theatres, bingo halls, discotheques, stadia;

(iv) agricultural premises—farms, crop-drying establishments, grain storage installations;

(v) transport installations—railway stations, bus garages, wharves, locomotives and aircraft repair shops, container bases;

(vi) public utility installations—waterworks, power stations, transformer sub-stations, gas works and coal mines.[30]

This list includes classes of premises which, by virtue of being either 'permitted development' or premises of 'statutory undertakers', would normally escape control by local planning authorities. Finally, it must be stated that the enforcement of noise abatement powers, by action in the Magistrates' Court, is generally held to be more effective than that of planning controls, with the lengthy delays associated with appeals in the event of a contested enforcement notice.

The circular goes on to advise:

Where planning permission for extensive new residential development is sought, particularly if areas of mixed residential and industrial properties will result, consideration should be given to the need for a noise abatement zone in that area.[30]

Despite the apparent superiority of the noise abatement zone procedure, however, environmental health officers, no less than planning officers, remain convinced of the valuable role of planning in controlling fixed sources of noise.[15]

The programme of noise measurements involved in designating an area as a noise abatement zone is expensive, and although a single factory could itself constitute a zone, site specific controls (which need not always entail numerical limits) can be imposed as planning conditions or, given the co-operation of the developer, under a planning agreement. Accordingly, few noise abatement zones have been instituted, notwithstanding the successful experience of some local authorities.[31] Most authorities feel, nevertheless, that a judicious application of planning controls, formulated with the assistance of the specialist environmental health officer, can help to minimize the need for resort to any of the powers available under the Control of Pollution Act, 1974.

REFERENCES AND NOTES

[1] Questionnaire returns, quoted in C. E. Miller, C. Wood, and J. McLoughlin, 'Land Use Planning and Pollution Control', Report to the Social Science Research Council, Pollution Research Unit, University of Manchester, 1980, vol. I.

[2] 'Planning and Noise', Circular 10/73, Department of the Environment, HMSO, London, 1973. (This circular is in the process of being revised.)

[3] Control of Pollution Act, 1974, s. 58(1).

[4] It is of interest to note that the Control of Pollution Act, 1974, offers, in s. 72(1) (2), an interpretation of the term 'practicable' identical to that given in s. 34(1) of the Clean Air Act, 1956 (Chapter 2).

[5] *Digest of Environmental Pollution and Water Statistics, 4*, Department of the Environment, HMSO, London, 1982.

[6] Despite the fact that complaints about traffic noise and aircraft noise are not recorded in the table (because they are not controlled by environmental health departments) it is known that traffic is the biggest noise problem. Aircraft noise is also a serious problem and is complained against. (*Digest of Environmental Pollution Statistics, 2*, Department of the Environment, HMSO, London, 1979.)

[7] C. Wood and N. Pendleton, 'Land Use Planning and Pollution Control in Practice', Occasional Paper 4, Department of Town and Country Planning, University of Manchester, 1979.

[8] 'A Guide to Noise Units', Noise Advisory Council, Department of the Environment, London, 1975.

188   *Planning and Pollution*

9 Under the provisions of the Town and Country Planning Act, 1971, s. 36.

10 'Decision Letter on Appeal Relating to Welham Green', APP. 6/332/77, Department of the Environment, London, 1979.

11 Under the provisions of the Town and Country Planning Act, 1971, s. 245.

12 Penwith District Council v. The Secretary of State for the Environment & Anr. (1977) P & CR 269.

13 Town and Country Planning Act, 1971, s. 30 (1)(a).

14 Pyx Granite Co. v. Minister of Housing and Local Government [1958] 1QB 554; [1959] 3 All ER 1.

15 C. E. Miller *et al.*, op. cit., vol. IV.

16 The Noise Advisory Council has ceased to meet as a result of the present (1982) administration's antipathy toward 'quangos'.

17 'Noise in Public Places', Noise Advisory Council, HMSO, London, 1974.

18 Motor Vehicles (Construction and Use) Regulations, 1973 (SI 1973, No. 24).

19 Town and Country Planning General Development Order, 1977 (SI 1977, No. 289), Art. 12.

20 J. McLoughlin, *The Law and Practice Relating to Pollution Control in the United Kingdom,* Graham & Trotman, London, 1976.

21 Noise Insulation Regulations, 1975 (SI 1975, No. 1763).

22 Commission on the Third London Airport, *Report,* HMSO, London, 1970.

23 'Decision Letter on Appeal Relating to Land at Bolton', APP B/07319, Department of the Environment, London, 1979.

24 C. Wood, *Town Planning and Pollution Control,* Manchester University Press, Manchester, 1976.

25 'Structure Plan: Written Statement', Merseyside County Council, Liverpool, 1980.

26 'Structure Plan: Written Statement', Greater Manchester Council, Manchester, 1979. (The 'submitted' plan.)

27 'Decision Letter on Greater Manchester Structure Plan', PNW/5035/483/1, Department of the Environment, Manchester, 1981.

28 'Structure Plan: Written Statement', Cheshire County Council, Chester, 1979.

29 'Islington Development Plan', Islington Borough Council, Islington, 1982 (and accompanying Planning Standard Guidelines).

30 'Control of Pollution Act, 1974: Implementation of Part III—Noise', Circular 2/76, Department of the Environment, HMSO, London, 1976.

31 R. Levitt, *Implementing Public Policy,* Croom Helm, London, 1980.

10

THE LEAD BATTERY WORKS

Lead batteries have been manufactured at Clifton since 1892 and the company concerned, now Chloride Industrial Batteries Ltd, has given work to successive generations of local families. A desire to maintain a tradition which has fostered good industrial relations was one of the reasons why Chloride's management was anxious to find a nearby site for a new factory, which the limitations of space and access at the Clifton Works and a projected increase in production had necessitated.

In 1972 the Department of Industry was approached; it was anxious to encourage new industry in the Merseyside special development area. However, in keeping with its aim of finding a site near its existing works, Chloride then invited the two most adjacent local authorities to suggest locations where industrial development was both desirable and feasible. Two sites were considered but both had drainage problems and both were, in Chloride's opinion, too close to housing areas to be suitable for a lead works.

Chloride's attention then turned to a site at Bank House Farm, Over Hulton, within the administrative area of Bolton County Borough (Plate 5). This was in an area designated 'white land' in the 1957 approved development plan, and was intended to act as a 'buffer' between the built-up areas of Bolton and Salford. However, in February 1973, preliminary informal contacts between Chloride and the County Borough indicated that insuperable opposition to the industrial development of this land was unlikely.

The 14 ha site, some 8 km from the Clifton Works, lies to the south of the A6 (Salford Road), and about 450 m from the end of the continuous ribbon development along this trunk road (Fig. 10.1). Were it not for a dozen or so cottages on either side of Salford Road (the nearest being some 100 m from the wall of the proposed building), the site could be described as truly 'rural' and remote from human habitation. To the south is situated the vast Cutacre Tip. Formerly a colliery spoil tip and now used for waste tipping, it is eventually to be reclaimed by the local authority. To the west, beyond farm land, there are exhausted open-cast mining sites, while to the north is Brackley Colliery, formerly a deep mine, now abandoned; and, beyond that, runs the M61.

The outline planning application

Chloride carried out a survey of the Bank House Farm site, and the

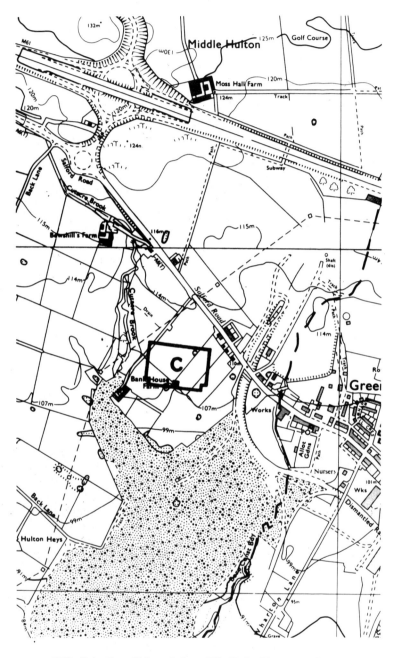

FIG. 10.1   Over Hulton, Bolton: Chloride lead battery works

C: Chloride,   1 : 10,000   Crown copyright reserved

land was found to be suitable for the construction of the proposed factory. In July 1973, the company duly submitted to Bolton County Borough an application for outline planning permission 'for the construction of a factory together with ancillary buildings and offices for the purpose of manufacturing lead/acid storage batteries'.[1]

A document accompanying the planning application revealed that the manufacturing area of the proposed development would cover some 18,000 m^2, with a further 3,600 m^2 for non-manufacturing purposes and 1,000 m^2 for offices. In addition to the main construction, there would be acid tanks, an effluent treatment plant, a water tank, a lead compound, an oxygen plant, and bays for the storage of sludge and scrap. Six hundred hourly paid and 100 salaried staff would be transferred from Clifton, while 200 additional hourly paid operatives would be recruited. The following processes would be involved at the new factory: manufacture of lead oxide from virgin lead; pressure and gravity die-casting of lead-antimony alloys; electrochemical conversion of lead oxide to form active material; assembly operations; sulphuric acid mixing; and battery charging.

In August 1973, Bolton's planning officers embarked upon an extensive series of consultations, both within the Borough and with a variety of external bodies, over this major planning application. Most consultees had no objection to the development provided their interests were protected. The views of the adjacent local authority— Lancashire County Council—were sought as the proposed development, being close to the boundary of the County Borough, could conceivably affect land in their area.

Bolton's Environmental Health Department and the Alkali Inspectorate were involved in the determination of this application from the outset. The proposed factory was unusual in that it would operate both registered and unregistered processes. An oxide mill is a scheduled process and thus 'prior approval' (namely the demonstration that it will operate according to 'best practicable means') is the responsibility of the Alkali Inspectorate. As for the remaining, more numerous, non-scheduled sources of air pollution, prior approval by the local authority is confined (since no combustion process is involved) to the approval of chimney heights under the Clean Air Act, 1956 (Chapter 2). Under existing pollution legislation, there is no power of prior approval relating to noise control measures outside noise abatement zones (Chapter 9). Consequently, apart from powers under the Town and Country Planning Act, 1971, Bolton's right to seek prior approval on the pollution control measures was very limited. It was soon apparent that Bolton intended to exercise these planning powers.

The officers of the Environmental Health Department intimated their intention of carrying out tests to determine the existing levels of lead in the atmosphere near the application site and to consider the land uses, both existing and anticipated over the next twenty years, within 800 m, 1500 m, and 3000 m of the site. In October 1973, the Borough Planning Officer asked the Bolton Medical Officer of Health whether the numbers of dairy farms and food premises within a 300 m radius were greater than elsewhere in the Borough as he was about to refer the application (being a departure from the approved Bolton Town Map) to the Department of the Environment. The Medical Officer of Health provided this information and observed:

Although from the health point of view this factory might be better built in an area where there are no dairy farms and food premises, I do not think that on health grounds the siting of the factory here can be opposed.

The opinion was endorsed by the Medical Officer at the Department of Health and Social Security in London, who, in reply to a letter from Bolton's Medical Officer of Health, wrote in November 1973:

It would appear that no especially vulnerable group of people or processes which might suffer from the factory proximity will be within ¼ mile [400 m]; and the school and farm approaching ½ mile [800 m] distance. In consequence I would feel that we cannot on health grounds oppose the siting of factory. I am sure that it would be wise to monitor the lead deposit and lead in the air in the factory surroundings to ensure that emission falls within the accepted limits.

This attitude of cautious approval was not shared by one neighbouring local authority, Worsley Urban District Council. In response to consultation, Worsley's Engineer and Surveyor wrote, in October, that his committee 'were most concerned that no assurance could be given on the question of atmospheric pollution, and I have been asked to write to you again, most strongly, unless this matter can be satisfactorily resolved.' In reply, the Borough Planning Officer gave an account of the Medical Officer of Health's investigations and promised to continue to keep Worsley informed of the progress of the application.

Fears over possible atmospheric pollution from the proposed factory were not confined to the members of Worsley Urban District Council. A newspaper article reported that '300 angry Over Hulton residents have signed a petition against the plans.' The substance of the protestors' argument was that the chosen site was 'the first open space outside Manchester' and the 'only green space that side of Bolton' and that 'we fear that lead pollution could be a problem with this particular factory.'[2]

In December, the North West Regional Office of the Department of Industry in Manchester issued an Industrial Development Certificate for the new factory. It would appear that Lancashire supported Worsley in their objection to the development on air pollution grounds. However, the County intimated that Worsley's opposition might well be overcome given sufficient assurances. Nevertheless, Lancashire County Council had an additional objection which related to long-term planning strategy on priority for industrial development: other sites were considered preferable.

In December 1973, the Borough Planning Officer wrote to the County Planning Department arguing that their strategic objection did not constitute sufficient grounds for refusing planning permission. He continued by stating that he now understood that if Worsley were satisfied with assurances over pollution, then the County would be also. He also wrote to Worsley giving a provisional list of the planning conditions he intended to advise the Planning Committee to append to any planning consent. If these conditions were found to be satisfactory and if the committee saw fit to grant Chloride outline approval, then Worsley would be consulted again during the consideration of reserved matters. From a letter of February 1974, it would appear that these safeguards did give sufficient assurance to the members of Worsley's Housing and Town Planning Committee; however, they reserved the right to comment on subsequent detailed plans.

The County's concern, however, was not so readily assuaged. In January 1974, the County Planning Officer informed Bolton's Borough Planning Officer that the County still felt 'that the present availability of large, formally approved sites in the area does offer a choice of alternative locations for the project'.

In February 1974, Chloride wrote to Bolton's Industrial Liaison Officer stressing the need for expedition in the determination of this application. However, progress was to be further impeded by the concern of the Department of the Environment who, in a belated reply to Bolton's Borough Solicitor, observed that the Chloride site was within a sketch Green Belt 'accepted as being broadly sound on 28/1/57'. This letter continued: 'the Secretary of State hereby directs your Council not to grant permission on the application without special authorisation.'

In response, Bolton's Borough Planning Officer described the land in question as poor in terms of landscape, being flat, with few trees and dominated by Cutacre Tip, and stated that it was now considered suitable for the use proposed by Chloride. He also took the opportunity of countering Lancashire's strategic objection. Before this matter was resolved, the reorganization of local government supervened.

On 1 April 1974, the County Borough of Bolton and several smaller local authorities were amalgamated to form the Metropolitan Borough of Bolton in the County of Greater Manchester. Worsley became part of neighbouring Salford Borough. Six weeks after reorganization, the Department of the Environment informed the Chief Executive of the new Council that: 'It has been decided, on the information before the Department, that they should not intervene and therefore your Council is hereby authorised to decide the application as they think fit.' No explanation of this change of attitude was provided.

In May 1974, Bolton's Director of Planning informed the Greater Manchester County Planning Officer that he proposed to recommend (to Bolton's Planning Committee) approval subject to conditions, which he listed together with their justification. A week later the Assistant County Planning Officer replied that he felt that the application should have been categorized as a 'county matter'. Indeed, sites at Irlam and Altrincham were urged upon Chloride as possible alternatives by the Greater Manchester County shortly after reorganization. However these sites were not acceptable, principally on account of their distance from Chloride's existing workforce.

In the event, the application remained with Bolton for determination because of the lengthy consideration already given to it by the County Borough prior to reorganization. Almost exactly one year after the receipt of the application, the Planning Committee granted conditional outline planning permission for the Chloride development in August 1974. Nine planning conditions were imposed. Two conditions, one a reserved matter, related to pollution control.

3. No development shall be started until full details of the following reserved matters have been submitted to and approved by the District Planning Authority.
   (e) processes to be carried out; together with the precautions to be taken to avoid any form of pollution or risk of explosion.
4. All emissions shall comply with standards applied to registered lead works by HM Alkali and Clean Air Inspectorate, as set out in Appendix V of the Chief Alkali Inspector's Annual Report 1966.[3]

Condition 4 carried with it the explanation—'so as not to prejudice the possible future development of adjoining land'.

In August, the Secrtary of the Greater Manchester Council informed Bolton that the County Planning Committee had declared that they would have been minded to approve Chloride's application subject to conditions. These conditions consisted of environmental safeguards not dissimilar to those actually applied by Bolton.

Bolton's concern to limit potential pollution, particularly atmospheric emissions of lead dust, from the proposed factory was implicit in the conditions imposed on the outline planning permission. It would appear that these conditions were intended to be taken literally, i.e. stringent safeguards on pollution prevention had to be demonstrated before approval of reserved matters would be granted and the development allowed to proceed. It must be remembered that this planning application from Chloride was being considered only a year or so after the peak of widespread public concern over, and unusually lengthy media coverage of, the question of health hazards from lead in the environment. (Attention had been concentrated on lead levels in the vicinity of a number of large lead works, especially the smelter at Avonmouth).

In a period of high unemployment, industrial developments which generate additional jobs and rate revenue will encounter opposition from few local authorities. In this respect, Bolton was no exception—witness the local authority's reaction to the suggestion, firstly from Lancashire and later Greater Manchester, that the Chloride factory might be better sited elsewhere. Moreover, Bolton's demands for the most stringent and all-encompassing environmental control measures stemmed, not from any wish to be obstructive, but from an awareness of the effect which fears of pollution (and lead pollution in particular) can have on public, and hence political, opinion. In other words, without a convincing demonstration by the developer that all reasonable technical measures had been taken to minimize the risk of pollution, it was conceivable that the weight of local opinion could have made a refusal of planning consent the politically preferable option. Bolton were earnestly seeking to reconcile environmental and economic goals.

Despite assurances from Chloride that their new factory would pose no threat to the health of the public, local opposition to the development remained. Petitions were raised and letters of protest were published in the local press. One prominent protester engaged in lengthy correspondence with Bolton's Planning Department and sought the support of his MP who, at one stage, wrote to the Secretary of State for the Environment suggesting that a public inquiry be held to consider the merits of the application.

In a letter of August 1974, Bolton's Deputy Director of Planning explained to the MP that the Chloride application, being a departure from the approved Town Map for Bolton, had been duly advertised and submitted to the Department of the Environment, who had finally chosen to allow Bolton to decide the matter as they saw fit. He listed the bodies already consulted and stated that no smelting would be involved at the new works. He concluded that a public inquiry could now be convened only in the event of a revocation of outline planning permission, which, he added, was 'very unlikely'. It was partly in anticipation of hostile public opinion, no doubt, that Bolton attempted to secure all possible means to minimize the adverse effects of the proposed factory, from lead emissions, from noise and, to a lesser extent, from visual intrusion. In the event, the public protests against the development and the intervention of the MP were short-lived.

The detailed planning application

A large number of meetings were held to deliberate over the environmental safeguards. One, in July 1974 (shortly before outline planning permission was granted) resulted in the developers undertaking to supply Bolton with data on noise levels emitted by the oxide mills. There was also a report that the Environmental Health Department was engaged in monitoring existing lead levels in the air around the application site and would discuss with Chloride target levels to be aimed for after development. The developers confirmed that no lead smelting would be carried out at the new factory and that details of stack heights, ventilation, and filtration systems would be discussed with Bolton.

A month later the Director of Environmental Health wrote to Chloride, listing those matters on which Bolton required information: these included the processes involved; the atmospheric contaminants; the control procedures; the standards to be applied and the methods of monitoring; and data on noise, water pollution, fire, and explosion at the proposed plant. In September 1974, Chloride replied, affirming that this information would be supplied.

In October 1974, the application for detailed planning consent was received by Bolton Metropolitan Borough Council. A month later, a meeting was held with Chloride, three officers from the Environmental Health Department, two from the Planning Department, and the District Alkali Inspector present. The Inspector explained that his statutory concern was confined to 'scheduled' processes, of which the oxide mill process was the only example anticipated at the new factory; however, he had already intimated that he was prepared to offer advice on the control of emissions from the non-scheduled processes.

At a meeting in March 1975, Chloride explained that the new factory would produce 1,000,000 lead batteries per annum and that it would release an estimated maximum of 20.16 lb. (9.1 kg) of lead to the atmosphere per week. It was further explained that the exhaust gases from the (registrable) oxide mills would be filtered and residual emissions released via a stack in accordance with the requirements of the Alkali Inspectorate. In addition, there would be seventy-six other chimney stacks to serve ventilation systems and non-scheduled processes. At this point, the environmental health officers made what, with hindsight, can be seen as a significant intervention: they declared that the local authority would require regrouping of the stacks and filtration of emissions from *all* stacks discharging lead-bearing emissions. The requirement that the stacks be regrouped was strictly an aesthetic consideration intended to improve the appearance of the factory exterior. The second requirement was more important in so far as it was aimed at minimizing lead discharges from all stacks, not only from the scheduled oxide mills' stack but also from those serving other processes which could give rise to emissions of lead.

These matters were the principal items on the agenda of a further meeting of senior personnel in March 1975. Chloride agreed that all local exhausts would be cleaned using a combination of fabric, electrostatic, and disposable panel filters. Estimated maximum lead discharges would then be 0.027 lb. (12.2 g)/hr from the oxide mills, and 0.06 lb. (27.2 g)/hr from the remaining sources. In addition, the number of stacks would be reduced, from the seventy-eight originally proposed, to eighteen. Of course, these modifications required by the local authority were not inexpensive and Chloride warned that they could not 'guarantee that the increased cost would be acceptable to the company'. (There had been some newspaper speculation[4] that the project might be aborted because of rising costs.)

In April 1975, Bolton's Planning Department began a process of consultations over a revised application (which had been received a month earlier) for approval of detailed plans, no less extensive than that given to the outline permission. Copies of the application were sent for comments to numerous bodies including the Alkali Inspectorate and Wigan Metropolitan Borough Planning Department: the covering letter revealed that the Environmental Health Departments of Bolton and Wigan were in communication over the pollution implications of the development.

Noise from the proposed factory was becoming a very important issue. A survey of existing noise levels on the boundary of the application site had already been carried out by officers of the Environmental Health Department, and Chloride had commissioned consultants to prepare a report on the noise characteristics of the new plant. The results of these two exercises were to become the subject of a series of meetings over the ensuing months. In considering the report on noise prepared by the consultants, the environmental health officers observed, in May, that 'the acceptable increase in noise level above existing noise levels must not exceed 10 dB(A) at night time'. They went on to explain that they were particularly concerned about the noise levels to be experienced at a point on the boundary of the site adjacent to the nearest cottage on Salford Road: they stated that the acceptable night time level at this point should be 40 dB(A). Exceptionally low levels had been measured for a limited period around 3 a.m. (when traffic flows on the A6 road were at their lowest); and it appeared that this period 'influenced the base-line unduly'.

Earlier, in a memorandum of April, the Director of Environmental Health had informed the Development Control Section of the Planning Department of his concern at possible increases in noise levels, resulting from traffic on the service road leading to the proposed works, which could lead to claims, under the Land Compensation Act, 1973, against the local authority from the inhabitants of the nearby cottages. A subsequent internal memorandum of May 1975 to the Environmental Health Department reveals that the Director of Planning had for some time been urged by certain councillors to ensure that informed experts be involved in the consideration of the environmental safeguards in regard to Chloride's new plant. Accordingly, the Director of Planning had contacted the Department of the Environment, who suggested that the Government Laboratory at Warren Spring be approached, together with the Alkali Inspectorate. Warren Spring had subsequently agreed to act as consultants. The reply from the Director of Environmental Health made it clear that this suggestion was considered to be superfluous and added: 'I am consulting both the Alkali Inspectorate and the Air Pollution Control Unit of the DOE and will let you have their observations as soon as possible.'

The consultation with the Alkali Inspectorate took the form of a letter of May 1975 giving details of revised total lead emissions, and chimney heights, and listing the safeguards (envisaged as planning conditions) intended to accompany and detailed permission. Those relevant to pollution control were:

1. The lead emissions from the individual stacks ... shall not exceed the indicated value in lb. per hour and the total lead emission from the factory shall not exceed 8.16 lb. [3.7 kg] per 168 hr week.
2. Lead emission values shall be confirmed by Chloride Industrial Batteries Ltd, sampling each stack continuously for an 8 hour working period at intervals conforming with the requirements of the Environmental Health Department and the Local Authority shall have the right to take such samples as they may consider necessary.
3. All sampling records shall be forwarded to the Environmental Health Department at monthly intervals. A works emission register shall be kept of all sampling results together with the reasons for any abnormally high values and remedial action taken. The register shall be open to inspection by the Local Authority.

4. All local exhaust ventilation from lead processes shall be cleaned before discharge to the external atmosphere and fail-safe systems and/or failure detectors and alarms shall be used wherever practicable. Any failure of the filtration system on the lead oxide mills shall be reported without delay to HM Alkali and Clean Air Inspectorate, the Department of Environmental Health and the Factory Inspectorate.
5. No additional equipment or process likely to give rise to an increase in total lead emission to the external atmosphere shall be installed without prior consent of the Local Authority.
6. Noise. (clause to be inserted later) [sic]
7. All necessary precautions shall be taken to prevent the emission of lead to the external atmosphere from operations carried out at the factory and without prejudice to the generality of the foregoing provision all waste materials leaving the factory which could give rise to lead emissions shall be stored and transported in sealed containers of adequate durability.
8. All vehicles leaving the factory shall be subjected to wheel washing and if necessary body cleansing where there is any likelihood of contamination of the vehicle by lead dust.

The reply from the District Alkali Inspector, dated May 1975, objected to some of these conditions:

1. Your first condition may well prove to be unenforceable in a Court—it makes no allowance for possible mechanical failure beyond the Company's control. In any case under the [Alkali Act] requirements, the minimum standards we are imposing would allow up to 0.6lb. [0.2 kg] per hour of lead from the oxide north chimney (100 lb. [45.4 kg] per week of 168 hours). I would suggest that you re-write to at least confine your limit to the stacks of the unregistered processes and even here relax the limit a little but only to such an extent as would maintain safe levels.
2. & 3. The registered stack (No. 19) will of course be subject to our routine sampling and the Company will also be required to undertake routine sampling of this stack. With regard to the unregistered stacks Nos. 1-18, I would suggest that you redraft to comply with the Control of Pollution Act, 1974.
4. It is part of the agreed [best practicable means] that the Company shall notify both you and us of any failure to registered process and your final sentence is not really necessary.
7. DOE Planning Officers consider that this sort of vague condition is not enforceable and should be omitted apart from the reference to waste.
I have no comment on your remaining conditions.
The above is an expression of personal opinion and is without prejudice to the consideration by the Secretary of State for the Environment of any application or appeal that may come before him. It is of course the prerogative of your Planning Committee to impose such conditions as they require but I would draw your attention to MHLG circular 5/68:[5]
(a) Planning conditions should be precise and enforceable and
(b) Planning conditions should not cut across existing statutory requirements.

Data on lead emissions to the atmosphere and related calculations on the increases in ambient lead concentrations were proposed by Chloride in May 1975, and became the basis for further discussions between the developers and the local authority. Table 10.1 presents some of the figures.

As part of its 'best practicable means' requirements for lead works, the Alkali Inspectorate enforces a 'presumptive limit' on lead emissions to the atmosphere, which (in the case of works of the size of the proposed factory) is defined thus:

Class I Works, i.e. those with a volume of emisson less than 7,000 cubic feet [200 m³] per minute. Each emission to air shall contain not more than 0.05 grain per cubic foot [0.115 g m³] of lead compounds, calculated as lead. Mass rate of emission for the site shall not exceed 0.6lb. [270 g] per hour.[7]

Using Chloride's figure[8] of 500 cu.ft (15 m³) per minute for the throughput of air for oxide mills of the type to be installed at Over Hulton, it can be shown that the Alkali Inspectorate's 'presumptive limit' above is equivalent to requiring a maximum hourly emission rate of 0.21 lb. (95g)/hr for each oxide mill; which, in turn, is equivalent to a maximum weekly emission from this one (scheduled) source of 36 lb. (16.3 kg). These figures are to be compared with Chloride's estimated maxima (from Table 10.1) of 0.0006 lb. (0.26 g)/ hr and 0.1 lb. (45 g)/wk for each oxide mill.

At a meeting later in May, Chloride remarked that it might be unable to satisfy all Bolton's requirements on noise, on account of the enormous expenditure necessary, which it believed could not be justified. Not for the first time, Chloride expressed the need for expedition in consideration of the detailed planning application.

TABLE 10.1

Estimated emissions of lead to the atmosphere from works

Source	Max. rate of lead emission (lb./hr)(g/hr)	Operating hours per (7-day week)	Total weekly lead emission (lb.)(g)
a. (Two) oxide mills' stacks	0.00119 (0.5)	168	0.2 (91)
b. All other stacks	0.075 (34.0)	80	6.0 (2724)
c. Roof mounted extraction fans	0.0245 (11.1)	80	1.96 (890)
Total			8.16 (3705)

Source: Reference 6.

Despite the company's reservations, agreement was reached on permitted noise levels at the Salford Road boundary and at other site boundaries, when Bolton agreed to relax their 40 dB(A) standard by 5 dB(A) at a meeting three days later. The finally agreed figures are listed in Table 10.2. Chloride stated that their noise expert had:

been consulted closely throughout this work and it is his opinion that the measures which it is proposed to implement should result in noise levels which will not exceed those [in Table 10.2]. He considers that these levels are achievable and reasonable.

TABLE 10.2
Estimated maximum site boundary noise levels

Period		Site perimeter bounding the A6 (dB(A) corrected)	Remainder of site perimeter
Night Time:	10.00 p.m. to 7.00 a.m.	45	50-55
Day Time:	7.00 a.m. to 6.00 p.m.		
	Monday to Friday	55	60-65
	Saturday and Sunday	50	55-60
Evenings:	6.00 p.m. to 10.00 p.m.	50	55-60

Source: Reference 1

On 21 May the Environmental Health Department forwarded a copy of the detailed plans and other pertinent documents to the 'Noise, Clean Air and Coastal Protection Unit' of the Department of the Environment in London for its comments. Its reply, dated 29 May, read:

We understand that these proposals would meet the requirements of the Alkali and Clean Air Inspector for the registrable process and comply with his advice in respect of non-registrable works. The Council's provision for the control of noise and effluents also appears satisfactory. It does not therefore seem likely that this project would in any way create a health hazard but you will appreciate that your request for a reply before 30 May has precluded a detailed consideration of the matter.

Interestingly, no comment was made about the potential conflict between the planning conditions suggested and the Alkali Inspectorate's powers.

Late in May, the Director of Environmental Health informed his colleague in the Planning Department of the Alkali Inspectorate's reaction to the proposed planning conditions. He observed:

My own feeling is that the Company have indicated their readiness to meet these conditions by agreement. I am of the opinion therefore that we should continue to seek to achieve the planning requirements I have previously indicated.

This was a reference to an earlier informal mention of the possibility of a planning agreement under the Town and Country Planning Act. The form of such an agreement was quickly outlined by Bolton, in a letter of 3 June 1975, which contained *inter alia* the draft of a clause requiring an individual limit on lead discharges from *each* stack. By 5 June, Chloride had informed the Director of Planning of its readiness to enter into an agreement and this willingness was confirmed in a letter from its Group Legal Advisor, which reiterated the provisional clauses to be included in the agreement. These were incorporated as a condition to be attached to the planning permission:

Before the development hereby approved is commenced an agreement under Section 52 of the Town and Country Planning Act, 1971, shall be entered into with the District Planning Authority:
(a) limiting lead emissions from the factory,
(b) requiring the monitoring of lead emissions,
(c) preventing the introduction of new processes, plant or machinery likely to give rise to an increase in total lead emission,
(d) controlling all other operations which could result in emission of lead to the external atmosphere,
(e) requiring the wheel washing of all vehicles on exit together with body cleansing in certain circumstances,
(f) limiting noise levels, and
(g) concerning certain surface water drainage matters;
    all these matters having been agreed to by the Applicant in a letter dated 9 June 1975.

At a meeting of Bolton Planning Committee on 12 June 1975, the Director of Planning recommended that detailed planning permission be granted subject to the condition that a planning agreement be drawn up. This advice was accepted and consent granted subject to a number of conditions, including that quoted above. A few days later the Director of Enivronmental Health addressing the Environmental Health and Public Control Committee, concluded:

Provided that all the plant is maintained in good condition, it is considered by those officers who have been examining the entire project that the known environmental health hazards have been properly catered for by the planned installations.

The planning agreement

With the formal approval of reserved matters, attention was then turned to the preparation of the planning agreement—a process which was to involve a further round of meetings, correspondence, and discussions between the developers, the local authority, and the pollution control authorities. Following a meeting of the 'environmental working group', which was intended to oversee the final preparation and implementation of environmental control measures at the Chloride works, one of its members, the District Alkali Inspector, was moved to write to the Director of Environmental Health:

1. I refer to discussion of the Working Party on the [Chloride] works meeting on Friday 12 September last, attended on our behalf by the Assistant Alkali Inspector at Manchester.
2. I understand that the letter of agreement between Bolton Corporation and CIBL on which you propose to base planning conditions will call for an overall lead emission from the whole works not exceeding 8.161 lb. [3504 g] per week of 168 hours—this is to include the oxide manufacturing process which will be registered under the Alkali, etc., Works Reg. Acts.
3. This overall emission figure does not agree with presumptive limits agreed for Registered Lead Works, indicating compliance with Section 7(1) of the [Alkali Act] and Section 5(1) of the Health and Safety at Work etc., Act (1974). Such presumptive limits would permit a much higher emission, and provision for dealing with such higher emissions is included in the requirements of Section 9(5) of the Alkali Act. This does not imply that we would expect, under normal conditions, a larger emission than the design figure quoted by the Company which we know from experience of this type of mill to be reasonable.
4. Para. 8 of MHLG circular 5/68[5] emphasises the undesirability of imposing planning conditions which seek to control matters already controlled under statute or common law, as such conditions invite confusion. I suggest that any such conditions as to overall lead emissions which your council might wish to impose should be drafted so as to specifically exclude the registered process or processes, emissions from which will be controllable under existing statutory requirements, and a matter for the Alkali Inspectorate's sole control.

In his reply, dated October 1975, the Director of Environmental Health explained the background to Bolton's desire to secure the most stringent environmental safeguards:

It is clearly recognised that the oxide manufacturing process is registrable under the Alkali Act and the prime control rests with the Alkali Inspectorate. Indeed, the proposed planning agreement emphasises this factor in stating inter alia that 'the Operator shall at all times conform with the standards applied to registered works by HM Alkali and Clean Air Inspectorate and any recommendations that are made by the Government from time to time concerning the prevention of lead pollution of the environment.'

You will remember that initially there was a good deal of opposition by both the public and Council members to the siting of a lead acid battery factory in the district. That opposition has been largely overcome and fears allayed by the informal negotiations carried out by the Company, by several officers of this authority, and by keeping the adjoining authorities of Salford and Wigan fully informed of the position.

Chloride came to us and voluntarily suggested that they wanted to set the highest possible environmental control standards. They produced a lead emission table which, with a 50% tolerance factor, gave a mass emission rate not exceeding 8.16 lb. [3705 g] per 168 hr wk. They have consistently stated that they can in all practical terms meet and monitor this emission standard.

You will appreciate my Council are broadly concerned with overall emissions standard and it was on figures freely negotiated by the Company that the project was recommended to the Planning and Environmental Health and Public Control Committee. ... Clearly my Authority would now be unwilling to re-negotiate lead emission standards with the Company aimed at formally sanctioning, on their part, overall higher emission rates than in practical terms can be achieved.

Considerable discussion took place within the local authority on the precise wording of the planning agreement, in particular, on the clause relating to lead emissions. In addition to the Departments of Planning and Environmental Health, the Chief Legal Officer was actively involved. In the ensuing months there were frequent contacts between Chloride and the Environmental Health Department on the format by which Chloride would present the data resulting from their monitoring of lead emissions, and on the precise form of the planning agreement.

In spite of Bolton's repeated attempts to draw up a planning agreement in a form which would prove acceptable to the Alkali Inspectorate while not detracting from the Borough's insistence on controls over all sources of lead emission, the Inspectorate was obliged to disclaim any responsibility for enforcing, or assisting in the enforcement, of the agreement. A letter of December 1976, from the new District Alkali Inspector, read:

1. With reference to our meeting of November 8, we have now concluded our discussions with Chloride over the 'prior approval' aspects of the Over Hulton works.

2. In this respect, I am pleased to inform you that we have agreed on a limit of emission from the registrable oxide mill equivalent to 0.1 lb. [45 g] of lead/week of 168 hr.[9]

3. My Chief Inspector has asked me to make it clear to all interested parties that any reference to this presumptive limit in any agreement not associated with [the Alkali Act] would not prejudice the statutory responsibilities of the Alkali Inspectorate on scheduled processes including our rights to decide or change anything necessary in the light of experience, and in accordance with our responsibilities for 'best practicable means'.

4. In addition, I have informed the company that our consent refers only to the requirements of [the Alkali Act] and does not bear in any way any

planning or byelaw requirements and is without prejudice to the consideration by the Secretary of State for the Environment of any application or appeal that may come before him.

This letter, and the Inspectorate's antagonism both to the proposed planning conditions and to the planning agreement exemplify its opposition, as a point of principle, to the application of planning powers to matters which come within the jurisdiction of the Alkali Act. (The Inspectorate quoted the Department of the Environment's circular on planning conditions[5] in both cases.) This applies irrespective of whether a planning condition or planning agreement imposes an emission limit which is greater than, less than or, indeed, equal to, the 'presumptive limit'.

By the same token, Bolton's desire to retain some control, by means of a clause in the planning agreement, over the scheduled process was no less a matter of principle. Having exacted stringent limits on the non-scheduled sources, to have then surrendered control over one, albeit lesser, source of lead emission would have been, for Bolton's councillors, an abrogation of their responsibilities to the local public: in short, it would have been inconsistent with their wish to claim, publicly and with full justification, to have secured *total* control over the environmental implications of the development. Here, then, the local authority was determined to exert its planning powers, the only powers of prior approval at its disposal, despite the Alkali Inspectorate's opposition. It was largely this opposition, and Chloride's anxiety to be granted detailed planning permission, which led to the incorporation of the pollution control provisions in a planning agreement rather than as conditions to a planning permission.

However, these issues of principle over exactly who should enforce emission limits on the oxide mill can be seen in their true significance when it is recalled that it was Chloride itself which proposed the (numerical) standard to be enforced. Since Chloride's declared estimate of the maximum (with a 50 per cent tolerance) emission from the oxide mill is two orders of magnitude less than the presumptive limit,[7] it is hardly surprising that the District Alkali Inspector, after exercising his right of discretion to use flexability and to take local and other circumstances into account, subsequently fixed the *actual* presumptive limit to be observed by Chloride with regard to the (one) oxide mill at the operator's own figure of 0.1 lb. (45 g) lead per 168 hour week. However, it must be emphasized that controls on the scheduled process under 'best practicable means' are not confined to limits on emissions but include requirements on handling of raw materials, vehicle washing, etc.[7] With regard to the oxide mill, the controls were thus self-imposed and, in practice, they will, no doubt, be stringently self-enforced.

On 1 March 1977, the planning agreement was finally signed by the Mayor and Director of Administration of the Borough Council of Bolton, and by directors of the Chloride Group Ltd, Electric Power Storage Ltd, and Chloride Industrial Batteries Ltd. The sub-clause relating to noise and air pollution control were:

3. The owner and the Managing Agent hereby covenant and agree with the Council that the said property shall be permanently subject to the following restrictions and provisions regulating its development and use:

    (a) Total lead emissions to the atmosphere from all lead process stacks at the said property (other than stacks serving the oxide mills) shall not exceed seven decimal point nine six pounds [3614 g] per one hundred and sixty-eight hour week being the hours of a full seven day period from Sunday morning to the following Saturday midnight.

    (b) The regrouping of the stacks shall not take place without the consent of the Director of Environmental Health of the Council (hereinafter referred to as 'the Director') but such regrouping of stacks shall not be objected to on environmental health grounds provided the alterations do not result in an increase in lead emissions.

    (c) Lead emissions from each stack at the said property shall be monitored and samples taken by the Managing Agent (the Owner's samples) for an eight-hour working period (or such longer working period if mutually agreed) at intervals to be agreed with the Director and in the case of the oxide mills with Her Majesty's Alkali and Clean Air Inspectorate and to enable lead emission values to be calculated the Council shall be allowed to take samples from the non-registered processes from time to time as it considers necessary (the Councils samples). Records of the Owner's samples shall be kept by the Managing Agent in a lead emissions register.

    (d) The latest available copy of the lead emission sampling records relating to the stacks shall be forwarded to the Director at the end of each calendar month for inspection. The Director shall have the right to inspect all records kept for the purposes of lead control during normal business hours on reasonable notice being given (except in case of emergency) and shall forward to the Owner copies of the records of the Council's samples.

    (e) The lead emission register for the said property shall record the reasons for any abnormally high values discovered on monitoring lead emissions and details of remedial action taken.

    (f) All local exhaust ventilation from the lead processes being carried out in the said property shall be cleaned prior to discharge to the external atmosphere and the cleaning system shall incorporate wherever practical a fail-safe system or failure detectors and an alarm which shall operate if the cleaning system is not functioning properly or at all.

    (g) Any failure to the filtration system on the lead oxide mills shall be reported immediately to the Director, the Alkali Inspector and the Factory Inspector.

    (h) No additional equipment or process likely to give rise to any increase in total lead emissions to the external atmosphere shall be installed or carried out without the prior knowledge and consent of the Council.

(i) The Owner and the Managing Agent shall operate the oxide mills in comformity with the best practicable means requirements of Her Majesty's Alkali and Clean Air Inspectorate which specifies a maximum lead concentration of nought decimal point two pounds [91 g] per one hundred and sixty-eight hour week as described above and shall implement such relevant legislation codes or practice and recommendations as are made by the Government from time to time concerning the minimisation of lead pollution of the environment so that all necessary precautions shall be taken to minimise the emission of lead to the external atmosphere and any surface lead pollution of the environment.

(j) All waste materials which could give rise to lead emission leaving the property or otherwise in the property likely to come into contact with the external atmosphere shall be stored and transported in enclosed containers of adequate durability to prevent effectively lead emission or lead contamination particular care being given to the handling in this context of the residual sludge from the treatment plant referred to in the planning application.

(k) Notification of the waste disposal arrangements shall be given to the Director and disposal shall be in accordance with the Deposit of Poisonous Wastes Act, 1972, and the Control of Pollution Act, 1974, and subsequent amending or replacing legislation and in accordance with any other statutes governing waste disposal or treatment. Prior to any changes in arrangements for disposal notification shall be given to the Director.

(l) Every vehicle prior to leaving the said property shall have its wheels washed to prevent lead contamination and where the body or other parts of the vehicle have come into contact or are likely to come into contact with lead contamination those parts also shall be cleansed save that the requirements of this sub-clause shall not apply to vehicles entering or leaving the factory car park using the sole access as shown more particularly on Drawing ... forming part of the planning application.

(m) The noise emanating from the factory building shall be limited to those levels contained in the report shown in [Table 10(2)] for the periods and locations therein described.

(n) The Director shall be able to enter the said property from time to time on reasonable notice being given (except in case of emergency) to monitor noise levels to ensure conformity with the levels referred to in the Table [10(2)] or at any time to enter the said property for the purpose of monitoring noise levels where there has been a complaint concerning noise.

Postscript

In July 1977 an enquiry was received by Bolton's Environmental Health Department from the London Borough of Ealing who, faced with a planning application for a lead works, was anxious to have the advice of a local authority with a proven record of success in the handling of developments of this nature.

Chloride (and the Environmental Health Department) were confident that any increase in lead concentrations in the atmosphere near the new works would prove to be barely, if at all, measurable. Indeed, monitoring stations 100 m from the site have yielded mean lead concentrations of 0.35 μg/m^3 compared with preconstruction levels of 0.38 μg/m^3. Readings are higher ·close to the boundary but these results are, not unnaturally, regarded with considerable satisfaction by those involved. Noise levels are within the agreed limits, the necessary attenuation being achieved by insulating the main building and constructing a large bund along Salford Road.

It will be observed that the spirit of co-operation and compliance which Chloride adopted in discussions with the local authority was very marked. Where disputes did arise, they were usually about points of fine detail rather than of principle and were readily and amicably resolved, thought not always without added expenditure by the developer. Indeed, the local authority's concern for the local environment was no greater than that of the developers themselves.

Chloride was determined that the new works should be above suspicion and the most advanced factory of its kind in Europe, if not the world. There may well have been an element of 'environmental public relations' involved (one of the figures within the company who was prominent in determining that standards served as President of the Institute of Industrial Hygiene during part of the period concerned) but this appears, nevertheless, to have been a case where the 'polluter-pays' principle was adhered to. Many observers believe that Chloride paid too high a price to satisfy this principle; that their controls were unnecessarily stringent, especially since they were to some extent self-imposed. They even link the environmental control expenditure involved to the company's subsequent financial difficulties, but there is no evidence to justify this.

While there can be no doubt that the controversy of the lead issue was significant in the way in which Bolton approached Chloride's application, this is not to suggest that Bolton's actions were no more than a political strategem. On the contrary, the local authority's persistence in requiring a high degree of filtration of all lead-bearing emissions and in setting very low night-time noise levels, requiring considerable expenditure on filtration equipment and sound-proofing measures, reveals a genuine concern that the new factory should have a minimal environmental impact. Similarly, the lengthy and extensive consultation procedure, involving a wide variety of bodies (including the neighbouring authorities), underlines the desire of

Bolton's councillors and officers to ensure that all the environmental aspects of the works were fully considered in advance (and seen to have been so). The accountability of Bolton's elected representatives was thus an important element: their vigorous attempts to achieve environmental safeguards forestalled any widespread public opposition to the development.

The officers of Bolton Metropolitan Borough demonstrated considerable initiative in controlling pollution from the works. This emanated largely from the environmental health officers, but their proposals were supported and complemented by the activities of the Planning Department. The confidence of the officers in their ability to mitigate the anticipated environmental impact of lead battery manufacture (which stemmed from their professional interests, expertise, and experience) was illustrated both by their rejection of the idea of consultancy advice and by their refusal to be restrained by the protestations of the Alkali Inspectorate. They did, nevertheless, consult widely and attempted to incorporate the responses obtained in the conditions they imposed upon Chloride.

It is significant that Bolton chose to impose their environmental controls as standards: in the first place by the use of emission limits on lead, with the avowed aim of attempting to make any increase in concentrations barely discernible; and in the second place by the use of ambient noise standards to minimize increases in noise levels. The standards were, of course, applicable only to this development but they imply the need for monitoring and an eschewal of more traditional *ad hoc* measures of control.

The Greater Manchester Structure Plan policies on air pollution were drawn up to be as stringent as possible, to be rigorously land use based and to allow for the possibility of exceptional circumstances. The fate of Cheshire County Council's air quality targets (Chapter 3) was very much in the mind of the Greater Manchester planners and the policies were carefully phrased so as to obviate anticipated objection by the Department of the Environment. In the event, there was virtually no dissension from them and they survived unscathed, being approved by the Secretary of State for the Environment in 1981.

Had the Greater Manchester Structure Plan been in force, Bolton could have drawn substantial support for their actions from the policy on toxic elements:

The local planning authority in seeking to keep the concentrations of potentially toxic elements as low as practicable, in their exercise of development control powers, will exercise careful control over the location of any development in relation to both its air pollution potential and, where appropriate, the character of adjoining development.[10,11]

In their assessment of whether the development was likely to be acceptable, the Bolton officers assumed very low emission levels. They then ensured their control over these levels by granting permission conditionally and by entering into a planning agreement. The Council thus went substantially beyond the stated provisions of the Structure Plan policy, which specifies only control over location. Nevertheless, Bolton operated very much in the spirit of this policy. The noise policy most relevant to this case in the submitted structure plan was: 'Development which is likely to produce major noise annoyance affecting wide or sensitive areas (e.g. residential areas) will not normally be permitted.'[12]This was deleted by the Secretary of State but it would have done little more than encourage the Bolton officers in their approach to the Chloride development. They were again acting within its spirit in managing to negotiate very stringent standards. Once more, however, their emphasis was upon the acceptability of the development in the location selected, provided noise emissions were low enough, rather than on control over location alone.

Despite the successful outcome in this case, it is perhaps necessary to conclude that a local authority's formal powers to control developments of this kind (i.e. involving heavy metals) are not commensurate with the pollution risks involved. In order to ensure truly effective 'prior approval', the local authority felt obliged to use, not pollution control legislation, but development control powers under the Town and Country Planning Act, 1971. Had the developers been less compliant, had they considered the conditions relating to pollution to be unreasonable or impracticable, had they believed their imposition to be an abuse of statutory planning powers, then Bolton's only means of forestalling what they held to be a pollution hazard would have been to refuse planning permission. Such an action, with the consequent loss both of rate revenue and of employment opportunities, would obviously have been taken with reluctance.

In this context, it should be noted, however, that had the developer objected to the planning agreement, either wholly or in part, then the local planning authority would have imposed identical requirements in the form of planning conditions. If, in turn, the developers had objected to planning conditions and appealed to the Secretary of State for the Environment, considerable time would have elapsed between the lodging of the appeal and the ministerial decision. The notional cost, in terms of lost production, incurred by the appeal might well then have exceeded the expenditure necessary to comply with the council's original demands.

Indeed, Chloride has suggested that the prospect of delays and hindrance (by way of appeals and protracted discussions) to their expansion proposals could have led to a decision to locate the new factory abroad, notwithstanding its local allegiance. It appears, then, that Bolton was successful in achieving and reconciling both its economic and its environmental goals. The Chloride factory, providing numerous jobs, has been constructed to such high environmental standards that the Alkali Inspectorate have arranged visits to demonstrate to both industrialists and pollution controllers just what can be achieved in a lead battery works.

REFERENCES AND NOTES

[1] This and other information about planning and environmental health decisions was supplied from the files of Bolton Planning and Environmental Health Departments.

[2] *Farnworth Journal*, 7 Nov. 1973.

[3] *103rd Annual Report on Alkali, etc., Works 1966*, Ministry of Housing and Local Government, HMSO, London, 1967.

[4] *Bolton Evening News*, 29 Jan. 1975.

[5] 'The use of conditions in planning permissions', Circular 5/68, Ministry of Housing and Local Government, HMSO, London.

[6] 'Consultation document on in-plant and out-plant environmental dust control for the proposed CIBL factory at Over Hulton', Chloride Industrial Batteries Ltd, Swinton, 1975.

[7] *111th Annual Report on Alkali, etc., Works 1974*, Department of the Environment, HMSO, London, 1975.

[8] Occupational Hygienist, Chloride, 'Personal Communication', 1979.

[9] This figure assumes the installation of one oxide mill. Discussions between Chloride and the local authority, and the resulting agreement, were predicated upon the assumption that two such mills would ultimately be installed (hence the 0.2 lbs. (91 g) in clause 3(i) of the planning agreement).

[10] 'Structure Plan: Written Statement', Greater Manchester council, Manchester, 1981. (The 'approved' plan.)

[11] The following passage formed part of the submitted structure plan but, because the regulations that govern the form and control of structure plans changed between submission and approval, this and similar material was excluded from the approved version:

Recent research, including monitoring being undertaken in the Manchester area, has highlighted the concentrations of heavy metals and other elements in the urban atmosphere and there is a continuing controversy over the appropriate standards of control which should be operated. Whilst on the basis of current (1977) criteria there is no significant short term danger from elements found in air-borne dust in the conurbation, not much is known about the long term effects of small concentrations. Therefore, it is considered to be common prudence to keep the concentrations of potentially toxic elements as low as is practicable.[12]

[12] 'Structure Plan: Written Statement', Greater Manchester Council, Manchester, 1979. (The 'submitted' plan.)

11
CONCLUSIONS

The preceding chapters have pointed to a number of areas where changes in the law or in the practice of land use planning might enable more effective controls over pollution to be applied. But in appraising the various cases, the essentially political character of many planning decisions requires that attention should be focused, not merely on the legal and administrative aspects of individual decisions, but on the extent to which the planning process allows environmental protection to be considered among the relevant issues. Even where decision-makers give due weight to environmental arguments, their decision will incur opposition from some aggrieved interest group; but such dissatisfaction, if shared by a sufficient proportion of the relevant electorate, can assist in the installation of an alternative administration with different policies and priorities.

Of course, it is rare for planning decisions on individual developments to be crucial issues at local (far less, parliamentary) elections. However, an administration's attitude to the environment in its overall planning policies might be seen as significant to part of that growing and influential body of voters with no fixed allegiance to any political party. For example, it would be unwise to neglect the political weight of the environmental lobby opposed to the expansion of the nuclear power programme. Thus, the strength of local opposition contributed to the Atomic Energy Authority's decision to withdraw planning applications for test drilling in a number of areas as part of a search for geologically suitable locations for the subterranean disposal of highly active nuclear wastes.

Yet a recognition of the place of the land use planning system within the democratic processes of local and central government does not obviate the need for a re-examination of the legislation and the administrative procedures involved. Even though a planning authority may act unquestionably *intra vires*, decisions may be taken or policies devised in ignorance of many of the implications, with inadequate technical advice, or with some interested parties being denied an opportunity to state their cases. Moreover, where a certain degree of pollution is accepted, the costs of the resulting damage may be distributed in a socially unjust manner. The importance of a review of these procedures goes beyond a concern for the environment; for if the planning system is perceived to be inherently unfair or biased towards one particular interest, a belief in the illegitimacy of the overall political structure can be fostered.

Legislative changes

Before advocating amendments in planning legislation to ensure more effective safeguards over the environment, it must be remembered that this is but one of many objectives of land use planning. Moreover, it must be emphasized that land uses which become sources of pollution constitute only a small fraction of the total of applications considered by local planning authorities. In turn, ensuring that new sensitive development is not juxtaposed with established pollution sources does not require additional powers; rather it requires a conscious political will to resist the temptation to 'in fill' with public housing[1] or factory units those areas of land which fail to attract other uses.

Of more urgent need than amendments in legislation is a tightening of the procedures by which potential pollution problems are identified prior to the decision whether or not to grant planning permission. While there has been a general improvement in the liaison between planning and environmental health departments and other control bodies, the need for consideration of all the implications of schemes which place industrial and residential development in proximity cannot be overstated. This is particularly true in view of recent government advice which suggests that such proposals should be accepted wherever they assist the growth of small-scale, job-creating enterprises, especially within the inner city.[2] Consideration of the effects of pollution sources in neighbouring areas is now a routine procedure in the great majority of local authorities, and the risk of a recurrence of planning errors (as exemplified by the Elton expansion scheme, the Penketh Tip, or the St Helens acid plant) is thereby reduced. However, the effects of central government expenditure cuts on skilled manpower in both the planning and environmental health departments of local authorities combined with repeated exhortations[2] to increase the speed with which planning decisions are taken tend to militate against adequate assessment of every potential pollution problem.

It could be argued that planning intervention is not justified in circumstances where additional pollution can be regulated by other agencies of pollution control. However, this view presumes the applicability of other powers and the readiness of the appropriate agency to enforce them with a vigour which the planning authority would consider commensurate with the degree of pollution involved. Where anticipatory control over a given form of pollution proved inadequate, the pollution control authorities may, in fact, welcome intervention by the use of planning powers. This is particularly true in the case of the water authorities, and is likely to continue to be so whilst Part II of the Control of Pollution Act, 1974, remains largely unimplemented. And while curbs on public expenditure continue and investment in sewerage and sewage treatment is limited, there will still be a need for planning authorities to delay development in areas where the overloading of inadequate disposal facilities can result in additional pollution of watercourses (Chapter 5).

Public anxiety over the disposal, on landfill sites, of toxic wastes has occasioned calls for more effective controls over solid waste disposal. The recently introduced regulations over special wastes were drafted so as to minimize the risk of particularly toxic materials being disposed of, whether by oversight or by design, at unlicensed sites or at sites suitable only for relatively inert wastes.[3] It is questionable whether a determined enforcement of these latest regulations together with those over other controlled wastes will be sufficient to assuage the (all too often, justified) fears of those who reside in the vicinity of landfill sites. The most effective contribution which planning authorities can make is to provide an additional safeguard against the licensing of environmentally unacceptable sites. They continue to provide the only anticipatory powers for ensuring the appropriate disposal of 'non-controlled' wastes (Chapter 7).

Attempts to use planning powers to control air pollution from scheduled processes have been motivated, not so much by limitations in the powers of the Alkali Inspectorate, but by planning authorities' belief in the inadequacy of the interpretation and enforcement of those powers. That planning powers can be effective in this context is amply demonstrated by the Secretary of State's repeated opposition to attempts by planning authorities to control emissions from any works registered under the Alkali, etc., Works Regulation Act, 1906. Chapter 10 bears witness to the effectiveness of planning agreements, given the willing co-operation of the developer, in regulating emissions. Planning conditions, of course, provide the only currently available means of anticipatory control over non-registered, non-combustion processes (Chapter 2).

Perhaps of most concern to the more environmentally conscious planning authorities is not the control of intermittent and localized nuisances, but a desire to secure, over the longer term, a gradual reduction in the ambient concentrations of pollutants such as sulphur dioxide and suspended particulates. While it is recognized that such reductions will result primarily from the smoke control programmes of the environmental health departments and from the effects of national legislation in reducing the sulphur content of fuel oil and diesel oil, some planning authorities wish to maintain a strategic role in regard to atmospheric quality. Permitting additional sources of pollution in areas where target values of air quality are exceeded serves to delay the achievement of that target. Cheshire County Council sought to include, within its structure plan, policies which supported the refusal of planning consent for any development whose atmospheric emissions would cause the guidelines to be exceeded. These policies failed to receive the endorsement of the Secretary of State; but it was never suggested that Chesire was actually *ultra vires* (Chapter 3). The acceptance of such policies requires no change in legislation but rather a shift in the attitudes of central government.

In contrast, the planning control of noise has hitherto enjoyed the approval of central government (Chapter 9). Whether this will continue, given the greater powers conferred upon environmental health departments by the Control of Pollution Act, 1974, remains to be seen.[4] It might be defensible to call for more effective controls over mobile sources of noise, but there seems to be little justification from the case studies for increased regulation of noise emissions from industrial and commercial premises. Moreover, noise is one form of pollution where a genuine consensus of views would appear to exist between planning and pollution control officers on their respective roles; the co-operation between departments, in controlling noise from new development, described in Chapter 10 is by no means unique.[5,6]

Overall, existing best practice in the application of planning powers to control pollution appears to be adequate. To bring the practice of the remaining planning authorities up to that standard requires not so much major legislative change but a shift in attitudes and procedures in some authorities. Such a change could undoubtedly be fostered by issuing advice, in the form of central government circulars on the proper use of planning powers in the control of pollution. The seminal influence of the circular on planning and noise[7] (Chapter 9), now out of date, and the confusion about the precise scope of planning powers existing in both planning and environmental health departments[5,6] provide adequate justification for the revision and extension of this advice.

There is a case for amending the General Development Order[8] to make more consultation with the pollution control authorities mandatory. For example, Department of the Environment circulars have repeatedly stressed the need to consult the Alkali Inspectorate where planning approvals for new registered works are sought.[9] As the Royal Commission on Environmental Pollution has argued (p. 20) this could be made a statutory requirement; the Elton case suggests that consultation over major sensitive development in the proximity of existing registered works should similarly become mandatory.

Planning intervention, of course, is possible only when 'development' is contemplated and the case studies indicate the need for a clearer interpretation of this term. Chapter 6 offers clear evidence of the need for a less inclusive definition of Class IV (or 'general industrial building') of the Use Classes Order.[10] Within this all-embracing category, no planning consent is needed when an environmentally innocuous use of a building or land is superseded by one which pollutes neighbouring areas. The Linthwaite case also suggests a need for removing from the definition of 'permitted development' (in the General Development Order)[8] those anomalies under which a planning authority is denied the power of approval of development which can enable a more intensive use of existing plant and buildings and thereby increases the associated threat to the environment.[11] Perhaps the most important legislative change, however, might be the introduction of environmental impact assessment in the UK.

Environmental impact assessment

The primary purpose of what has come to be known as 'environmental impact assessment' is to enable a decision relating to a project to be made in the full awareness of its potential effect, both direct and indirect, on the environment. A draft directive of the Commission of the European Communities has been issued which defines the ends to be achieved but leaves the individual Member States free to determine the means they must use to do so.[12] It seems likely that environmental impact assessment, as proposed, could be integrated into the existing UK planning system by means of minor changes to statutory instruments.

The draft directive lists, in Annex 1, several types of public and private sector development which 'shall be made subject to an assessment'. These include oil refineries, motorways, etc. There are then numerous projects in Annex 2 (including reservoirs, oil extraction, etc., and modifications to the listed types of development) which are to be made subject to an assessment 'whenever their characteristics so require'. Finally, unlisted projects are to be subject to an assessment where they are 'likely to have a significant affect on the environment having regard in particular to the environmental sensitivity of the site'. There are provisions for exemptions from assessment where particular circumstances apply.[12]

Where a proposed project requires an assessment under the draft directive, the developer must prepare the following information:

1. a description of the proposed project and, where applicable, of the reasonable alternatives for the site and design of the project (including a forecast, by type and quantity, of the expected liquid, solid and gaseous emissions, and of the radiation, noise, vibration and odours resulting from the operation of the development);
2. a description of the environment likely to be significantly affected (including, in particular, water, air, solid, climate, flora and fauna);
3. an assessment of the important effects of the proposed project on the environment (including those resulting from the emission of wastes, from pollutants and from nuisance, as well as the secondary effects linked to the elimination of these);
4. a description of the measures envisaged to eliminate, reduce or compensate adverse effects on the environment;
5. a description of the relationship of the proposed project with existing environmental and land use plans and standards for the area likely to be affected (obviously including any air quality and ambient noise standards);
6. a justification for choosing the proposed project from the other alternatives;
7. a non-technical summary of the above items.[13]

The planning authority has to make this information publicly available and arrange consultations with the relevant authorities before making its own 'assessment of the likely significant effects of the proposed project' and reaching its decision whether to grant permission (with or without conditions) or to refuse it. Finally, there are provisions for monitoring the impacts of the development, once in operation, on the environment.[12]

Even if the Department of the Environment were to use the discretion allowed by the directive to institute an environmental impact assessment involving the absolute minimum change to existing planning procedures in the UK, this would have an important effect on the consideration of major developments. Further, the probability is that, in practice, there might be an unofficial extension of a mandatory environmental impact assessment system to other, non-mandatory projects.[14]

The sulphuric acid works at St Helens would have been an Annex 1 project and subject to an environmental impact assessment under the proposed arrangements. It seems likely that the decision to grant planning permission might well not have been made, because the pollution consequences should have been foreseen with at least a reasonable degree of accuracy as much more information would have been forthcoming. The Chloride works would also have required an assessment though the outcome would probably have been the same, the decision being based upon broadly similar information to that eventually provided. Had the environmental impact assessment procedure been in force at the time, UKF's refusal to monitor its emissions might well not have been countenanced, as checks on conditions are required by the directive.

The Penketh tip and the Elton housing (both Annex 2 projects) would have been subject to environmental impact assessment, had they met whatever minimum size criteria are adopted by the Department of the Environment. It seems likely that, in the light of information about the environmental consequences of the tip, permission might have been refused, a larger buffer between it and housing might have been agreed, construction of the housing might have been postponed, or more stringent conditions might have been placed upon the operation of the tip. Had an environmental impact assessment been carried out on the housing at Elton, the description of the environment and review of existing plans and standards should have revealed the potentially adverse effects of the development of air pollution arising from the oil refinery and, perhaps, caused the project to be abandoned. The Linthwaite chemical formulation plant (an Annex 2 project) might well have been subject to an assessment, depending on the criteria adopted in the UK, since a 'modification project' includes substantial changes in the use of buildings, installations or facilities. While the outcome may have been the same, the conditions imposed would have been enforceable immediately. The directive, in fact, offers a means of partially overcoming the problems of permitted changes and intensification of use.[15] It would thus extend, as well as reinforce, existing UK planning powers for controlling pollution problems.

While it is at present possible for a planning authority to ask a developer for a comprehensive statement of the pollution implications of a proposed development, the onus of preparing an environmental impact assessment falls upon the developer. The provision of more information, the necessity for increased consultation, and the compulsion *actually* to examine environmental impacts in detail seem certain to increase consideration of the environment in decisions currently taken within the planning system. Decisions may not be changed, and economic factors may still outweigh environmental factors, but the ramifications of the decision should become more explicit. The temptation for local authorities to impose conditions to attempt to overcome these ramifications will, of course, be substantial.

The 'polluter-pays' principle

Although the implementation of an environmental impact assessment procedure could serve to minimize the risk of planning decisions being taken in ignorance of environmental consequences, there will obviously continue to be a need for the application of planning powers to control pollution. Planning refusal will still afford an ultimate sanction against those developments assessed to have unacceptable impacts and the use of planning conditions may increase as attempts are made to derive some compromise between economic and environmental demands. But land use planning, like any other pollution control system, must be judged not simply in terms of its efficiency in reducing or preventing waste discharge, but also by its ability to enable those whose quality of life is impaired by pollution to receive some form of compensation. However, the preceding chapters have yielded little evidence of land use planning being inherently compatible with the 'polluter-pays' principle (see Chapter 1).

Had St Helens Borough Council been successful in their attempts to use a discontinuance order to remove the sulphuric acid plant which had proved a source of pollution, then the mandatory payment of compensation to the owners of the plant would have entailed a complete reversal of this principle (Chapter 4). This would not have been so had the closure been achieved by action in statutory nuisance. Moreover, it is possible that had the local pressure group been less anxious to persuade the planning authority to seek nothing less than the plant's closure they might have been better advised to direct their efforts to taking civil action (in private nuisance or perhaps under common law)[16] to secure financial compensation for those residents who had suffered the effects of fugitive clouds of sulphur dioxide.

When planning approval for the acid plant was originally sought, the planning authority imposed conditions specifying maximum permissible rates of discharge of sulphur oxides, in the mistaken belief that observance of these conditions could remove the threat of nuisance to local residents. Little thought appears to have been given to the possibility of the occurrence of abnormal conditions under which these limits could be exceeded or to any schemes for compensating those third parties who might suffer the consequences of such excessive discharges. Yet, had the authority been so minded, it is unlikely that planning powers would enable any such scheme to be enforced.

In theory, an authority might grant planning consent only if a developer were prepared to enter into a planning agreement, one clause of which specified a scale of compensation according to the degree and form of harm suffered as a result of pollution arising from the development in question. For example, the length of time during which boundary noise levels exceeded a predetermined figure could form the basis for calculating payment to residents within a certain distance of a factory where noise, especially at night-time, was inevitable. But, in practice, defining exactly who would be entitled to compensation and establishing the techniques by which pollution damage could be measured and translated into monetary values would pose intractable problems for those drafting such an agreement.[17]

If a planning authority, having failed to persuade a developer to enter a planning agreement, attempted to use planning conditions to establish a scheme of compensation for third parties, there can be little doubt that they would incur the opposition of the Secretary of State. Furthermore, the judiciary would almost certainly consider such conditions to be *ultra vires,* being less than 'reasonably related' to the use of the land in question.

If planning powers (both retrospective and anticipatory) fail to embrace the 'polluter-pays' principle, this must be seen as a major shortcoming of the planning control of pollution. However, it must be recognized that, with but few exceptions, this shortcoming is common to other systems of statutory pollution control. The traditional 'best practicable means' approach, as enshrined in the Alkali, etc., Works Regulation Act, 1906, ensures that emissions are reduced below the level which could endanger health and further reductions to limit nuisance are imposed only if they can be shown to be practicable. But no provision is made for compensation for those who bear the effects of nuisance from these emissions, for which arrestment cannot be justified by whatever criterion of practicability is adopted.

Under the Control of Pollution Act, 1974, the Secretary of State may, by order, permit a regional water authority to demand payment for the discharge of trade or sewage effluent to the sewers.[18] However, in general, the statutory powers of both the planning and pollution control authorities only partially satisfy the principle: they can require the polluter to pay the cost of pollution control plant but they cannot demand that he meet (or in economic terms, 'internalize') the environmental costs of the residual pollution which that equipment fails to arrest.

Civil action to secure monetary compensation is available to those individuals who suffer pollution damage which entails an infringement of some 'right' in the legal sense of this term. In the main, these common law rights have been associated with the ownership or occupation of land, and this source of redress has tended to be limited to the more affluent sections of society. With the growth in the pollution of 'common property resources' such as the atmosphere, where damage is not confined to a small number of individuals in a well-defined locality, public authorities were created and given statutory powers to control pollution on behalf of the public at large. Notwithstanding, it is the common law actions which remain the more effective means of securing financial redress for pollution damage. (There is statutory provision for compensation for loss of property values attributable to smells, smoke, fumes, and noise from public works for which action in nuisance does not apply.)[19]

Since the residents living close to Gateworth Farm Tip chose not to seek monetary compensation under the Land Compensation Act, 1973, they lobbied the local planning authority to use its (in fact, very limited) powers of intervention to require, failing the cessation of tipping on Gateworth Farm, a stricter observance of planning conditions originally intended to minimize nuisance to adjacent areas (Chapter 8). Given the circumstances of this case, it is arguable that the most equitable outcome might have been temporary reductions in the rateable values of the houses nearest unrestored tipping areas. Such a solution would be consistent with the 'polluter-pays' principle if the community which bore the marginally greater rate burden, following the reduced contribution from those suffering the pollution, coincided with the community whose wastes constituted the bulk of the polluting matter tipped on the site in question.

By today's standards the Penketh case must be reckoned as an unfortunate planning decision, not perhaps on the scale of the St Helens acid plant or the Elton village expansion, but nevertheless another demonstration of the need to ensure an adequate separation of incompatible land uses and of the value of some form of environmental impact assessment wherever a potential major conflict is anticipated. Once a planning error has been committed, attempts at minimizing pollution and nuisance are seldom effective or practicable and success in obtaining redress for actual pollution damage suffered can rarely be assured.

Planning, pollution, and social justice

An activity which generates benefits for certain individuals whilst entailing detriment to the quality of life of others must, in the absence of some form of compensation, be considered socially unjust.[20] Where the 'polluter-pays' principle applies, then such injustice is minimized. The inability of land use planning to enforce an adherence to this principle requires that planning authorities should adopt some other criterion by which to judge those instances in which pollution of third parties is recognized as being inevitable. Cost-benefit analysis has been used in the past to assist decision-making in large-scale and environmentally sensitive issues. Irrespective of the technical difficulties in ascribing monetary values to nuisance or loss of amenity, even where benefits are seen to exceed costs, social inequities can remain. For example, the total benefits which can be attributed to the sale and use of the product of the St Helens sulphuric acid plant would almost certainly outweigh the costs, expressed in money terms, borne by the victims of the occasional excessive discharges. Yet the original error in allowing the plant to be sited in a manifestly inappropriate location constitutes a palpable injustice. By the same token, the undoubted environmental benefits gained nationally from the combustion of smokeless fuel, rather than unprocessed coal, does not alone justify allowing processing to continue in an area where the resulting localized air pollution concentration evokes images of a Dickensian 'Coketown' (Chapter 2).

A planning authority must consider the social and spatial distributions of costs and benefits as well as the difference between estimates of their respective totals. The Linthwaite case (Chapter 6) affords an illustration. The profits from the operations accrued to a small number of shareholders and little was reinvested in the Kirklees area; benefits from the use of the plant's products were distributed nationally and internationally but the small number of jobs created was filled by local men. Again, actual damage resulting from airborne defoliants from the plant was confined to a narrow area but the plant threatened severe pollution of the River Colne and the destruction of fisheries could have diminished the recreational opportunities of a wider population. Increased awareness of distributional factors (which could be revealed by an adequate environmental impact assessment) might direct a planning authority to a decision contrary to that indicated by a simple comparison of aggregated costs and benefits.

When faced with proposals which involve such dissimilar distributions, a planning authority cannot make a practice of simply rejecting those which leave the local population, to which it is directly answerable, with a net detriment and no means of compensation. To do so invites appeal to the Secretary of State who, while not indifferent to local opinion, is obliged to take account of wider regional and national interests. Yet, despite the elevation of a planning decision to the central level of government, the question of social justice and pollution must still be addressed. In this regard the evidence of recent decisions suggests that the concept of 'need' can play a crucial role: typically, any residual nuisance or loss of amenity which may defeat the stringent control measures to be applied is defended by reference to the greater and more widespread disbenefits which would result if the development in question were to be refused, delayed, or sited elsewhere.

It should not be assumed that ministerial assessment of need always concurs with that of the applicant. For example, the Secretary of State for Energy, after consulting the Secretary of State for Wales, decided not to grant permission for an open-cast coal site in Clwyd because he felt the need for open-cast coal was insufficient to outweigh the adverse environmental impacts.[21] Recently the North West Water Authority and British Nuclear Fuels Ltd were involved in a protracted local inquiry concerned primarily with applications, under the Water Resources Act of 1963 and 1971, to abstract water from Ennerdale Water and Wastwater in the Lake District National Park. A determination to allow nothing to diminish the unique natural beauty of this unspoilt area of the national park was the primary motivation for the Secretary of State's decision to accept the inspector's recommendations and to reject the proposals of both applicants. In reaching this decision, the Secretary of State cast doubt on the water authority's forecasts of demand: these 'did not reflect the results of pursuing water conservation policies'.[22]

In general, a demonstration of the superfluity inherent in developers' proposals has become a standard item in the arguments presented by environmentalists at public inquiries. Chapter 3 offers a by no means rare example of a local pressure group questioning the industrialist's prediction of the demand which constitutes the development's *raison d'être*. In turn, a detailed list of the severe and widespread economic effects of the closure of their sulphuric acid plant formed a significant part of Leathers' case at the inquiry into the proposed discontinuance order (Chapter 4) and is equally typical.

A number of recent planning inquiries concerned with large-scale development have become no less than forums for the public examination and criticism of national policy on transport, energy, water management, etc.[23] Like the earlier Roskill Commission, an inquiry into an application by the British Airports Authority to develop Stansted into London's third airport has entailed consideration not only of alternative sites but also of the need for another airport at all given the current pessimistic forecasts of air traffic demand. Similarly the inquiry into the plan to exploit coal deposits under the Vale of Belvoir, as well as being a classic amenity versus economy confrontation, involved fundamental questions of energy policy and the Secretary of State's decision to refuse permission reflected the lack of urgent need for the fuel. In a wider context, energy policy was also an issue at the Windscale inquiry; yet far more attention was paid to such matters as the risk from routine and accidental releases of radio-activity to the environment, the proliferation of nuclear weapons, and the threat posed by terrorists. Indeed, the report of this inquiry devoted less than 10% per cent of its pages to 'conventional planning issues' (a term which is taken to include 'noise and nuisance, water supplies, sewerage and sewage treatment' as well as the general suitability of the site and the visual impact of the proposed plants).[24]

This tacit acceptance by central government of discussion of need in planning inquiries is a relatively recent phenomenon, and one which must be attributed in part to the pressure of public opinion (especially in connection with inquiries over the routeing of new motorways). However, there is no explicit indication in the Town and Country Planning Act, 1971, or related legislation that need may be a 'material consideration' which justifies refusing a planning application; in the past, Secretaries of State have taken advantage of this fact when up-holding appeals against planning refusals on grounds of inadequate need. If a liberal definition of what constitutes a legitimate planning issue is now accepted in the case of major investments by nationalized industries and statutory undertakers, equity demands that a similar attitude should prevail in the case of developments of purely local significance, especially those which pose a threat of pollution. When a planning authority decides whether a polluting development is, on balance, acceptable, it should not be required to exclude consideration of the need for that development in terms of the degree and the distri-bution of the disbenefits which would result from its rejection; nor should it be denied the right to take account of alternative and less polluting means of meeting that need.

Of course, it is possible to cite arguments against allowing 'need' to become a legitimate matter for consideration in planning decisions. It is a normative and subjective concept and an individual's percep-tion of what is socially beneficial cannot be entirely divorced from his self-interests. Attitudes towards the need for technological products, the manufacture of which entails pollution, are inevitably influenced by more general values and beliefs concerning industrial society itself.[25] In so far as need is reflected by economic demand, it can be argued that market forces alone reveal a need for a good or service. Requiring an entrepreneur to justify any development designed to meet that demand by reference to some criterion of need could be seen as an encroachment upon his commercial freedom.[26]

Despite these objections, however, one system of pollution control can be identified which does require a demonstration of need: it forms the first of three principles recommended as a basis for radiological protection, by the International Commission on Radiological Protection (ICRP):

1. no practice shall be adopted unless its introduction produces a positive net benefit;
2. all exposures shall be kept as low as reasonably achievable, economic and social factors being taken into account; and
3. the dose equivalent to individuals shall not exceed the limits recommended for the appropriate circumstances by the Commission.[27]

These principles apply to the protection of the public at large as well as to employees within the nuclear power industry or other industries where ionizing radiation is present. The ICRP is a group of internationally recognized experts independent of national governments; its recommendations are almost invariably adopted by the industrialized nations. In the United Kingdom, the National Radiological Protection Board has advised the central government that the ICRP recommendations provide a satisfactory basis for controlling the exposure of persons to ionizing radiation in workplaces and in the general environment.[28] Similar advice was given to the Health and Safety Commission during the consultations associated with a draft of a directive of the Council of the European Communities which requires the adoption, by 1983, of a system of radiological protection along the lines of the latest ICRP proposals.[29]

Exactly how the first principle will be implemented remains to be seen; interpretation of the term 'positive net benefit' could prove to be problematic. In the case of exposures associated with any stage of the nuclear fuel cycle, it cannot entirely avoid the value judgments to which both sides are prone in the debate between nuclear and fossil fuelled energy options. The Secretary of State for the Environment cannot remain totally aloof from this debate, for it is he who must authorize discharges of radioactive waste to the atmospheric, terrestrial, and marine environments, and any such authorization must take account of 'positive net benefit' which would be forgone if the practice from which the discharges arise were discontinued.[30]

The 'as low as reasonably achievable' requirement of the ICRP's second principle is readily comparable with the 'best practicable means' approach of the Alkali, etc., Works Regulation Act, 1906, and other statutes; and its acceptance by central government is therefore unsurprising. However, in the International Commission on Radiological Protection's recommendations, this criterion of reasonable achievability coexists with a quantitative environmental quality standard;[31] a similar combination of controls over inactive pollutants (smoke and sulphur dioxide) was vigorously opposed by the Department of the Environment and the Alkali Inspectorate when proposed by Cheshire County Council. Despite the advent of air quality guidelines under European legislation the Department of the Environment's circular on clean air[9] explains that the directive specifically states that they do not imply an automatic prohibition on pollution sources in areas where the guidelines are exceeded (p. 52). However, the Department of the Environment has accepted the recommendation of the Royal Commission on Environmental Pollution which called for the specification, in the certificate of authorization for each major nuclear installation, a limit (to be derived from the ICRP's limit on dose uptake by the public) on the atmospheric discharge of radioactivity.[32] Hitherto, liquid effluents and buried wastes have been subject to enforceable quantitative limits but gaseous emissions have been regulated solely by the 'best practicable means' criterion.

Central government has therefore endorsed a system of regulating radioactive pollution which includes quantitative standards of environmental quality and demonstrations of 'net benefit', yet equivalent controls have not been readily accepted in the case of inactive pollutants. This equivocal approach cannot be defended simply in terms of differences in the biological effects of radioactivity and other forms of pollution. (The proponents of an expanded nuclear power programme often emphasize the greater health risks associated with the emissions from coal-fired power stations compared with those from equivalent nuclear plants.)[33] The 'as low as reasonably achievable' principle rests on the argument that, in the absence of convincing evidence of a threshold in the dose-cancer risk relationship, all exposures however small should be minimized; but knowledge of the effects of, for instance, lead compounds is similarly incomplete. In addition, there are reasons (e.g. metallic corrosion, damage to vegetation and buildings), quite apart from the benefits to public health, in favour of continued efforts to reduce emissions of oxide of sulphur, carbon, and nitrogen.

Pollution is concerned with the relationship between individuals and the environment; the essential injustice of pollution is not just a matter of half-lives. While the clear weight of public concern may explain the introduction of gradually more stringent controls over ionizing radiation and active wastes, it cannot alone justify their denial to those whose duty it is to regulate the less feared, but not necessarily less toxic, non-radioactive pollutants. Allowing planning authorities to consider any polluting development in terms of the needs which it is intended, directly or indirectly, to satisfy could help to redress this imbalance. Existing planning procedures often include such consideration informally. Once again, what is advocated does not require a change in legislation; rather it calls for a further change in the attitudes of the Department of the Environment. Permitting need to become an accepted 'material consideration' in planning decisions does not prejudice the power of the Secretary of State to revise any refusal of consent, but the written justification for his decision to uphold the appeal should identify why he believes the authority's reasons for considering ·a development to be superfluous are erroneous.

This proposed devolution to local government of consideration of need in planning decisions does not overcome the problem of subjectivity; it simply transfers its resolution to the elected representatives of those who bear the environmental costs. This might tend to counter what may be seen as a *de facto* 'right to pollute' which has arisen because of restraints upon the publication of information concerning polluting wastes, limitations of the common law in curtailing nuisance and pollution and in compensating third parties, traditional reliance by the pollution control authorities upon extra-legal pressure to deter polluters, and restrictions upon the powers of private individuals to enforce many of the pollution control statutes.[34] Provided that the terms of the appropriate authorization (the licence issued by the waste disposal authority, a water authority's consent to discharge, the Alkali Inspectorate's presumptive limit) are observed, then whether the discharge, notwithstanding its legality, should occur at all is rarely questioned. Some planning authorities have sought to question this 'right to pollute'; on the whole, they have not been encouraged by central government.

With radioactive wastes, the regulatory system (especially the 'net benefit' criterion) is such that a 'right to pollute' cannot be said to exist, or at very least, it is more than outweighed by a constant pressure for reduction and for demonstrations that effects upon the population are barely detectable. Undoubtedly, a rigorous enforcement of the Control of Pollution Act, 1974, with its emphasis on a wider public availability of information relating to pollution, will assist the gradual demise of this assumed privilege. Yet, in minimizing the juxtaposition of incompatible land uses and in imposing conditions, planning authorities can continue to play a crucial role by preventing or limiting the occurrence of those forms of pollution which cannot be effectively controlled retrospectively. But equity must be considered as well as efficiency. If the procedures of land use planning have not ensured that the social costs of unavoidable pollution are distributed in a just manner in the past, this is a weakness common to other agencies of pollution regulation, of which few, if any, can compare with planning authorities in the extent to which the decision-makers are directly answerable to those who may suffer the effects of pollution. The instances of pollution, and its control, described in the case studies bear witness to the need to maintain and strengthen the role of local planning authorities within a vigilant and responsible local democracy.

REFERENCES AND NOTES

[1] C. M. Wood, and N. Pendleton, 'Land Use Planning and Pollution Control in Practice', Occasional Paper 4, Department of Town and Country Planning, University of Manchester, 1979.

[2] 'Development Control - Policy and Practice', Circular 22/80, Department of the Environment, HMSO, London, 1980.

[3] Control of Pollution (Special Waste) Regulations, 1980 (SI 1980, No. 1709).

[4] It is known that the government is considering replacing its circular on planning and noise (Chapter 9), which contains very positive advice on the control of noise by the use of planning powers.[5]

[5] C. E. Miller, C. Wood, and J. McLoughlin, 'Land Use Planning and Pollution Control', Report to the Social Science Research Council, Pollution Research Unit, University of Manchester, 1980, vol. IV.

[6] C. E. Miller, et al., op. cit., vol. I.

[7] 'Planning and Noise', Circular 10/73, Department of the Environment, HMSO, London, 1973.

[8] Town and Country Planning General Development Order, 1977 (SI 1977, No. 289).

[9] 'Clean Air', Circular 11/81, Department of the Environment, HMSO, London, 1981.

[10] Town and Country Planning (Use Classes) Order, 1972 (SI 1972, No. 1385).

[11] Another case of intensification is provided by an example in Stockport, where a one-man dairy business in a residential area was taken over and was soon used as a major distribution depot, with sixteen vehicles commencing work at 4 a.m. An enforcement notice was served, and while the inspector agreed the intensification of use amounted to a 'material change of use', the Secretary of State disagreed.[5]

[12] *Environmental Assessment of Projects,* Select Committee on the European Communities, 11th Report, House of Lords, Session 1980-1, HMSO, London 1980.

[13] This summary is not verbatim, but reflects the scope of the Annex 3 of the directive as far as it relates to pollution.

[14] Many local planning authorities have sought 'voluntary' environmental impact assessments and over fifty such assessments have already been carried out, often on the basis of the 'Aberdeen' manual: B. D. Clark, K. Chapman, R. Bisset, P. Wathern, and M. Barrett, *A Manual for the Assessment of Major Development Proposals,* Department of the Environment, HMSO, London, 1981.

[15] Extensions of use, together with changes of use, are subsumed within the definition of a 'modification project' and modifications to Annex 1 projects are included in the list of Annex 2 projects which may be subject to environmental impact assessment.[12]

[16] Perhaps by action under the rule in Rylands v. Fletcher (1866) LR 1 Ex 268.

[17] Nevertheless, this hypothetical use of planning agreements is arguably less questionable than 'planning bargaining' under which a developer 'negotiates' a planning consent by agreeing to include a number of community benefits or services or by paying the planning authority a sum of money to finance municipal projects having little connection with the development site. (D. Heap, and A. J. Ward, 'Planning Bargaining - The Pros and the Cons: or How Much Can the System Stand?' *Journal of Planning & Environmental Law,* [1980], 631-7).

[18] Control of Pollution Act, 1974, s. 52.

[19] Land Compensation Act, 1973.

[20] This assertion is consistent with Rawls' celebrated 'difference principle'. (J. Rawls, *A Theory of Justice,* Harvard University Press, Cambridge, Mass., 1971).

[21] Following the inquiry, held under the Opencast Coal Act, 1958, the national annual opencast coal production target was exceeded and environmental factors were

accordingly given more weight than the inspector had assigned to them. (Secretary of State for Energy, 'Decision Letter in respect of NCB application for authorization to work coal by opencast methods at Pont Einion', May, Welsh Office, Cardiff, 1981.)

[22] 'Decision Letter of Ennerdale Water and Wastwater: Provision of Additional Water Resources', 22 Dec., Department of the Environment, London, 1981.

[23] D. W. Pearce, *et al.*, *Decision Making for Energy Futures*, Macmillan, London, 1979.

[24] The Hon. Mr Justice Parker, *The Windscale Inquiry: Report* Department of the Environment, HMSO, London, 1978.

[25] S. Cotgrove, and A. Duff, 'Environmentalism, middle class radicalism and politics', *Sociological Review*, NS 28 (1980), 333-51.

[26] D. W. Pearce, 'Public Goods, Public Bads, Public Inquiries: A Normative Economic Approach to the "Big Inquiry"', Discussion Paper 80-03, University of Aberdeen, 1980.

[27] 'Recommendations of the International Commission on Radiological Protection', *Annals of the ICRP* 1, (1977), 3. (Originally published in ICRP Publication 26.)

[28] National Radiological Protection Board, 'Recommendations of the ICRP (ICRP Publication 26): Statement by the NRPB on their Acceptability for Application in the UK', ASP 1, HMSO, London, 1977.

[29] National Radiological Protection Board, 'Advice to the Health and Safety Commission from the NRPB on the Acceptability of the Dose Limits Contained within the Draft Euratom Directive (Document 5020/78)' ASP 3, HMSO, London, 1979.

[30] Radioactive Substance Act, 1980, s. 6. This power is exercised jointly with the Minister of Agriculture, Fisheries and Food in the case of discharges from sites licensed under the Nuclear Installations Act, 1965.

[31] The ICRP recommended annual limit on effective dose (5 mSv) to members of the public may be likened to an environmental quality objective, for it entails limits on permitted *concentrations* of activity in the environment (the atmosphere in particular, but also on land in the case of the dose received from the ingestion of contaminated foodstuffs). In the actual implementation of radiological protection controls over radioactive waste, the certificate of authorization under the Radioactive Substances Act, 1960, contain *emission* limits on various radioisotopes. However, these limits are set by reference to models of the various mechanisms or pathways by which the activity can be taken up by man; and their numerical values are chosen so as to ensure that the ICRP limit on dose is not exceeded.

[32] Royal Commission on Environmental Pollution, *Sixth Report, Nuclear Power and the Environment*, Cmnd. 6618, HMSO, London, 1976.

[33] See for instance Sir J. Hill, 'Risk v. Benefit', *Atom*, 293, (1981), 64-8.

[34] Enforcement of the Water Act, 1945, may be undertaken by members of the public only with the consent of the Attorney-General; in the case of the Water Resources Act, 1963, the consent of the Director of Public Prosecutions is required.

INDEX

Health and Social Security, Department of 119, 192
Humberside County Structure Plan 102-3

Ince Marshes 37, 42, 45-8, 59
infraction letter 20, 71
intensification (of land use) 4, 123, 136 180, 186, 217, 219
International Commission on Radiological Protection 225

Kirklees Metropolitan Borough Council 113-36

Lake District National Park 223
Land Compensation Act, 1973 167, 182, 198, 221
lead 189-211, 226
Leathers Chemical Co. Ltd. 65-90
Local Government Act, 1972 3, 81
Local Government, Planning and Land Act, 1980 140
local plans 6, 30-3, 101-5, 147

Member of Parliament 70, 72, 121, 158, 164-9, 195-6
Mersey, River 31, 35, 42, 53, 103, 153, 160
Merseyside County Structure Plan 88, 97, 103, 185
minerals 138, 145-7
Ministry of Agriculture, Fisheries and Food 29, 38, 58, 103, 141, 147, 153
modification order 165

National Coal Board 4, 24, 138
National Radiological Protection Board 225
National Water Council 108
need 8, 149, 222-7
nitrates 51, 100
noise 39, 117, 170, 173-87, 196-208, 215
Noise Abatement Act, 1960 173
noise abatement zone 2, 186-7
Noise Advisory Council 181
North West Water Authority 94, 104, 106, 157, 165, 169, 223
nuisance 24, 28, 39, 54, 78, 118, 182, 221
private 1, 9
public 2, 9
statutory 9, 12, 25, 86, 173, 219

odour 25-6, 29, 39, 119, 138, 144
oleum 62, 71, 78, 86
Ombudsman (Local Government Commissioner) 168

permitted development 4, 43, 130, 133, 138, 181, 186-7, 218
planning:
agreement 2, 9, 27, 96, 142, 202-7
appeal 6, 11, 37, 178, 184
condition 2-11, 22-30, 43-54, 66-74, 97-136, 143-69, 174-87, 194-210
inquiry 7, 37, 47-54, 71-4, 78-83, 129-33, 165, 178
refusal 3, 5, 94-9, 121, 125-7, 183, 219
'polluter-pays' principle 13, 25, 54, 85, 136, 144, 208, 219-21
presumptive limit 19, 72, 200-5
prill 51
Public Health Act, 1936 13, 25-6, 28, 95, 170, 173
(Drainage of Trade Premises), 1937 95, 116
(Recurring Nuisances), 1969 133
Pyx Granite Co. 10, 180

radioactivity 1, 58, 158, 224-7
radiation 1, 225-7
Radiochemical Inspectorate (Department of the Environment) 158
regional water authority 93-108, 116, 123, 143
retrospective power 11, 28, 117, 220
revocation order 46-7, 195
right 1, 13, 95, 220, 227
riparian owner 1, 94
river authority 107
Rivers (Prevention of Pollution) Act, 1951 98, 116
Roskill Commission 183, 223
Royal Commission on Environmental Pollution 6, 21, 29, 32, 50, 58, 83, 100, 145-6, 216, 226

Secretary of State for the Environment 6, 19-30, 42-59, 74-86, 99-105, 142-8, 164-71, 178-87, 193, 214, 220-7
sewage disposal 94-9, 106-7, 138, 214
sewerage 94-9, 106, 214
Shell Chemicals 37, 39